A Pasty-Faced Nothing

MIKE MUNRO

A Pasty-Faced Nothing

RANDOM HOUSE AUSTRALIA

Random House Australia Pty Ltd
20 Alfred Street, Milsons Point, NSW 2061
http://www.randomhouse.com.au

Sydney New York Toronto
London Auckland Johannesburg

First published by Random House Australia 2003

National Library of Australia
Cataloguing-in-Publication Entry

Munro, Mike.
A pasty-faced nothing.

ISBN 1 74051 211 1.

1. Munro, Mike. 2. Television personalities –
Australia – Biography. I Title.

791.45092

Cover photo by Scott Cameron
Cover design by Darian Causby/Highway 51
Typeset by Midland Typesetters, Maryborough, Victoria
Printed and bound by Griffin Press, Netley, South Australia

10 9 8 7 6 5 4 3 2 1

To my best friend, Lea, our pride and joy,
Sean and Amy, and
my courageous Mum, Beryl.

ACKNOWLEDGEMENTS

I was so heartened by the many friends and family who supported me, helped me with research and who have read work in progress. Particular thanks go to Maree Munro, Vera Nock, Bernice Fogarty, Gerri Sutton, John Hartigan, Col Allan, Deirdre Macken, Adrian Lane-Mullins, Mark Day, Jo-Ann Brown, Trish Lake and the Cleary family. From Random House, Jane Palfreyman, Vanessa Mickan and Lydia Papandrea.

FOREWORD

This book may not win a Pulitzer Prize but it will warm your heart. It is ultimately about success; about determination, humility and love. Mike Munro writes the way he talks – with passion and a twinkle in his eye.

He takes us on an extraordinary journey. At first the newborn son of a Sydney wag and his doting wife, to separation and a struggle for survival, and then the black years of his mother's alcoholism and his battle to save her from herself. He tells of his abuse by his mother and her battle with the bottle. How she sacrifices much of her life to start a new one so that her only child might succeed. Schoolboy, altarboy, badboy – Munro's teenage life is revealed with humour and honesty.

He presages his media career by working in a pub – excellent training for the rigors of newsroom culture. He is fortunate to land a job at the *Daily Mirror* when it was at its peak, staffed by some of the most talented and lunatic journalists Sydney witnessed, and the skills that had allowed him to survive a dysfunctional and lonely early life found a perfect home. Several qualities distinguish the successful newspaper reporter from those who would not make it – courage, imagination and the ability to quickly win the confidence of others – and Munro had them in spades. I know this because I worked in the same newsroom.

As his budding career flourishes so does his personal life. A beautiful and charming wife, the love of his life. And children who would never want for love or care.

But it was in television that Munro was to become a star and in this book we are taken behind the scenes; inside the Nine Network's engine room of stardom. It is both candid and fascinating.

In his early years at Channel Nine, Munro established his television persona – energetic, hungry and credible. And then *60 Minutes*, travelling the world with stars, crooks and the Pope.

Finally, as reporter and then host of *A Current Affair*, he becomes a household face and name.

Mike Munro's story is inspirational. He had many excuses to fail but chose not to use them. This book is a wonderfully personal account of winning at life.

Col Allan
Editor-In-Chief
New York Post
New York, New York
October 2003

PROLOGUE

I remember the first time it happened. It was early evening and she was singing and laughing and repeating the same line of a song over and over again. I can't remember the words but it was a happy song. She was not only singing and laughing but hiccupping. She'd sing half a line and hiccup and we'd both laugh, hilariously laugh. She was a vibrant, attractive woman with raven hair, beautiful teeth and a wonderful smile. She had a very good figure – full-busted and thin-waisted – and a lovely, round, open, welcoming face.

I was only four. I was sitting on the floor with my arm resting on the sofa, on which she lay stretched out. I looked up at her, saying over and over, 'Do it again Mummy, do it again.' So of course she would sing and hiccup again. Such an innocent, fun start to what was going to become 28 years of suffering that would only end in death.

I have even earlier memories. I'm not sure whether they are of actual beatings by my father on my Mum, or whether they were instilled in my mind over the years by Mum telling me them over and over again. She pretended to despise my father so much, but of course she didn't – I believe she loved him, loved him until the day she died. Though they were separated for almost three decades, until Mum died, they were never divorced. Dad had a number of relationships over the years, but my mother never went out with another man all her life, devoting her modest, sad existence to her son.

I'm not sure why she left Dad. Maybe it was the beatings. Maybe it was the womanising. Maybe it was the gambling. Or maybe it was because he couldn't provide her with the high-flying lifestyle she so desperately wanted. They were both frustrated socialites who spent all their money on today. In their early years they were like characters straight out of *Guys and Dolls* – they'd spend what they had on clothing, restaurants and parties, while living in a tiny two-bedroom apartment in Cronulla in Sydney's south. And that's where I remember the first beating in the bedroom. Mum was collapsed on the bed as my father beat her and I remember screaming 'Stop Daddy, stop.' But he didn't; he just pushed me aside and I fell backwards. I was three years old.

1

My Mum was born Beryl Jean Stannard on the 3rd of December 1926 in the Sydney suburb of Balmain. Eva, her mother, was a hard woman who showed very little affection towards her baby daughter. Alfred, her father, was generous and gentle, always willing to lend a hand or money to anyone in need. Because of Alf's easy-going ways Eva was the dominant partner in the marriage.

When the Great Depression hit, Alf, like so many other Australians, lost his job, which had been driving private buses in and around Balmain. The couple had always rented, their only luxury beautiful antique furniture. When Alf lost his job, they also lost all their antiques, and were forced to give up their rented home. My Mum was only six at the time and my grandmother, Eva, was pregnant with her second child. They moved in with Eva's mother for a while but it didn't last long as they had never got on. Eva and Alf packed up again and moved in with Alf's family. Alf's younger sister, Vera, was only eight years older than Mum and became not only Mum's best friend but also her surrogate mother. The two were inseparable.

Despite being virtually destitute, Eva refused to give up her dancing, so poor old Alf would do any work he could get.

'He'd even sell some beer bottles or whatever to get Eva enough money to go to her dances,' Vera remembered later. 'He didn't go to the dances but he knew she loved them so much. He was very soft and I think he knew she had several men friends at these dances.'

The marriage was obviously doomed but lasted until Mum was 11 years old. Alf came home one day to find all their furniture gone. The house was empty and Eva had disappeared with my mother. She had left their second child, Billy, who was only five years old, with her mother. Eva had left Alf no explanation.

It turned out that Eva had run off to the New South Wales southern highlands, taking a job as a live-in help for a man in Moss Vale. She and my mother remained there for two years, then Eva returned to Sydney and promptly left Mum, now 13 years of age, with the same grandmother who Billy had been left with. Because the two children spent long periods living separately, they were anything but close. The idea of family had never been instilled in either of them. My Mum lived with her grandmother, whom she didn't get on with, during the week, and her best mate and aunt, Vera, on the weekends.

'She couldn't wait to come over and stay with us on weekends,' Vera said. 'I think it was because of our close relationship and because I was a little older than her and I took her everywhere with me. We had so much fun together during our teens and 20s that we just became closer and closer.'

The very day she turned 18 Mum moved out of her grandmother's home and into Vera's. It was the beginning of probably the only time in her life when she was truly happy.

'From then on I reared her,' Vera said. 'Beryl was very mature for her age, having been through so many bad times, and I was probably a little immature so we were perfect for each other.'

Mum was 20 when she first met Raymond Michael Munro, my father. Born in 1925, and the youngest of Elsie and Henry Munro's five children, he had grown up in Camperdown in Sydney. Although he was named and baptised as Raymond Michael, all his life he was called Mick.

Monica Crowley, one of four girls who lived next to the Munros, told me what they were like: 'They were always an immaculately dressed and well-behaved family. I can't remember exactly what Henry did for a living but I know he worked very hard because he was always gone well before we left for school and arrived home after dark every day.'

She said the Munro household next door was a 'busy' one and always 'colourful'. She remembers the family playing cricket out the front of the house in the street, and the two youngest boys practising their race calling in the back yard.

'Even when Mick was 12 and 14 years old he was already a wheeler and dealer of a kid,' she said. As well as being 'pleasing to the eye' Mick was always an entertaining practical joker and had 'loads of sparkling personality'.

'He was always making us laugh. I remember my father would bring home watermelons and all the Munros and us four girls would sit around eating mountains of watermelon. But Mick wasn't content with sitting too long so he'd tie the watermelon skins around his feet and use them as skis to skate on, making us all laugh.'

Monica says Mick was particularly kind to the younger children and would often take them to Shirley Temple movies at the old Regent cinema next to Sydney Town Hall. She remembers him carving doll faces out of chokos from a nearby vine for the little ones or carving out pieces of timber with his penknife and 'sending them down the gutter on rainy days as we all ran alongside them'.

'He made time for the little kids whereas many of the older children didn't bother. He was often very kind, but because he was the youngest and so spoilt he probably never matured. I guess as he grew up he stayed that Peter Pan character,' she said. 'To us Mick seemed to be able to do anything because he had learned it all from his older brothers and sisters. We knew he was a cheeky villain and a charmer but you couldn't help but like him.'

Of his mother, Elsie, Monica remembers a kind and patient woman who used to help Monica and her sisters dress their dolls. She spoilt Mick, the youngest, absolutely rotten. His brothers and sisters would go off to school every day but Elsie would tell him to 'wait around the corner until they're all gone and come back and spend the day with Mummy'. He barely ever went to school and had his mother protect him whenever teachers inquired where the youngest Munro child was. He grew up being taught by his own mother that it was okay to break the rules. That the rules were meant for some people, but not him.

As a young adult, Mick worked at an electrical parts factory in Leichhardt, where Eva also worked. Tallish, dark and handsome, he had a reputation as a ladies' man. He was strong, of medium build, and had thick, black, wavy hair and brown eyes. He fancied himself as a street fighter, although I bet it was more imagination than ability. He was extremely proud of his large, barrel chest. But it was his charm and personality that always won people over.

'Mick would brag that he could get any girl he wanted,' Vera said. 'He was a personality man with good looks and lived a fast, flashy lifestyle.'

Eva knew her 20-year-old daughter had never been out with a man and, because of all the upheavals in her young life, was an easy target for a wolf like my father. Eva made a bet with Mick that he couldn't get Beryl to agree to go on a date with him. Before he agreed to the bet he demanded that he be able to see what she looked like first. He went to the large removalist company where she was working and stood outside until he caught a glimpse of her. At 20 Mum was a vivacious brunette with big, dark, smiling eyes and almost perfect teeth. She also had a sensational figure. Naturally my father's interest was well and truly heightened.

'Eva bet Mick 10 shillings he could not talk Beryl into going on a date,' Vera said. 'And of course he proved Eva wrong when he swept her off her feet. He would visit her during her lunch hour . . . Two or three times he stood outside her offices before starting up a conversation with her.'

Mum fell for Dad hook, line and sinker but sadly never knew that the relationship started only as a bet made by her own callous mother. Mum told Vera at the time: 'I have at last found somebody who really cares for me.'

In many ways my mother and father were very different, but they both loved a good time. My father was an expert when it came to living for today. If he'd had a win at the racetrack (horses, trots or dogs – he followed them all) he'd blow the lot until he had his next win. During the late 1940s he and my mother were seen at all of Sydney's top establishment restaurants and expensive nightspots like Romano's, Prince's and Valentine's.

'Beryl was a real name-dropper and social climber,' Vera said. 'She didn't know any better because her mother had never been around to teach her much about anything.

'I never trusted Mick. Beryl had changed already.

Mick had taken my husband Henry down for a large sum of money and I confronted Beryl. I pleaded with her not to go out with him any more but she ignored me. It was the first time she had ever ignored something I asked of her.'

My father had even been living under Vera and Henry's roof when he stole from Henry. Vera had just given birth to their first-born when Henry had to go into hospital to have his appendix out. Henry ran a greengrocery stall at Sydney's Paddy's Markets. He was going to be off work for two weeks and made the mistake of asking my father to look after his market stall. With my father living in his home, Henry naturally never dreamed my father would steal from him. But he did. Dad told the wholesalers who delivered to the stall that Henry would pay them once he was discharged from hospital. My father sold as much as he could and pocketed all the money. This went on for the entire fortnight Henry was in hospital and convalescing. When he returned he discovered that there had been no money coming in, and he still owed for the past two weeks' produce. There was a showdown between the two men but because Vera and Henry thought so much of my mother it all blew over – until the next time. That was when Dad tried to big-note himself by bringing home mountains of meat from the local butcher, pretending he had bought the meat himself. No such luck. He had told the butcher that Henry would fix him up later. The hide of the man was breathtaking.

My parents went out for two years and were engaged

for another two years before they married. During the last six months of their engagement my mother converted to Catholicism, my father's religion. My father was by now one of the top salesmen for Dustflow, a company that had the franchise to sell the latest in suction vacuum cleaners. Dustflow even agreed to pay for my parents' wedding reception at Valentine's, in Pitt Street, across the road from their offices.

Once my parents were married they began renting a tiny unit in Catherine Street, Leichhardt, where they paid £1 a week in rent. Mum was extremely happy with her life – as long as my father was winning at the races. Dad was always in and out of jobs. He would earn some money and spend it all at the track, then return to work to get more money so he could do it all again. Several nights a week Mum and Dad would stay with Vera and Henry, despite my father having ripped Henry off. He always managed to get away with such things. Everyone saw him as a lovable rogue and he could either fight or joke his way out of most tight spots.

'They would come over and stay with us so often and it took me a long while to realise why,' Vera said. 'After several years I realised it was because they didn't have any money. Both of them were living on Beryl's work money which Mick often used for his gambling. He never gave her any housekeeping in return. She would come over and wait to see if Mick returned that night with money. If he had won at the races they'd be able to go home and eat. If he had lost they'd stay overnight with us so they could eat something.'

Mum was slowly waking up to what she had married into. She worked for two years after their wedding but then decided enough was enough. She resigned from her job with the removalist company in a desperate bid to make my father take responsibility for her – and the child they were now having. Yet even after I was born in 1953 my father continued spending virtually everything on gambling and giving very little to my mother. She stayed most nights of the week with Vera and Henry, now with a newborn baby, wondering whether or not my father would turn up and take her home. Many times he wouldn't arrive at all; his womanising had begun. He sold Hills Hoist clotheslines, and then got a job selling the latest tape recorders. He broke all sorts of sales records, and was the only salesman at that firm in his mid-20s who had a company car. Had he had any sort of work ethic he could have gone a long way in business. He definitely had the gift of the gab – but that's about all he had. He was a highly valued member of staff but just kept spending every penny he received on gambling.

When I was about 18 months old the three of us had to shoot through because the police were after my father. Plain-clothes detectives came to Vera and Henry's front door.

'They were looking for Mick over a lot of stolen tape recorders,' said Vera. 'They had various trading dockets bearing false names. One of the dockets even had part of my name, and Henry's name, on it. We couldn't believe Mick had implicated us in his scam after all we'd done for him. We were looking at being charged with buying stolen tape recorders. I told the police that Mick had shot through with his wife and child but that I had no idea where they'd gone.'

The three of us had gone underground in Queensland. We were there for almost two years before we returned to Sydney because Mum had found out her father was dying of cancer. I was now three years old. Mum was almost at the end of her tether. The one and only great love of her life had not only proved to be a con man but was giving her very little financially, being constantly disloyal to her with his womanising, and coming and going as he pleased. Years later, when I was 15, my father would brag to me about the day he was forced to flee a woman's bedroom by jumping out the window when her husband arrived home unexpectedly. 'You were playing on the floor at the time with some toys,' he told me.

I was dumbfounded, not only that he actually took his three-year-old son along with him into another woman's bedroom but that he thought that as a teenager I'd be impressed. Far from being impressed I hit him as hard as I could in the stomach. He replied by punching me in the side of the head and knocking me out cold.

When I was four we moved to a house at Brighton-le-Sands. For a brief time I was fairly happy. Mum and Dad took time to sit down with me at night and help me learn. I remember distinctly being taught how to write the figure five. It was a difficult one for me, and they were both patient and understanding.

But there was no daily routine because often Dad would disappear for days on end. Mum couldn't hide her disappointment or, eventually, her temper. They began to argue constantly. At first neither of them held grudges and were able to move on each time – but it got harder and harder to do. When they weren't fighting they would have a laugh with each other or seek out their high-flying friends at one of the top restaurants or at the horse races. I'll always remember Mum's laugh – a broad, infectious laugh. Things became tense and they grew argumentative when Dad had gambled and lost his sizeable wage along with any winnings he'd managed to accumulate, and there was no money for food and other weekly essentials. That's when Mum went off. Like Dad, she wanted the best of both worlds – but at least she could tell the difference, whereas my father never could. They were living for the day and for themselves, rather than setting a plan for the future, working hard and building on it.

I was very insecure because of the constant arguments so most nights I would come into their bedroom and sleep with them. And they would let me, which wasn't too healthy. Rather than persevere and put me back to bed they would let me have my own way. In that sense they weren't strong; they certainly weren't helping me become more independent and secure. But although they may have been weak, they were certainly loving.

I remember the police coming to the front door a lot at Brighton-le-Sands. Dad was always in trouble with the police for petty theft and various cons. He certainly

loved the role of hanging out with questionable characters, who he blew up in his imagination and boasted
about. They were the number one, two, three, four and
five public enemies in the country if you listened to him
– but they were all just petty crims. I remember not long
after I turned four standing next to Mum at the front
door when two uniformed policemen arrived wanting
Dad. Mum told them she hadn't seen him for two or
three days. No, she said, it wasn't unusual for him to be
gone that long without any word.

By the time police were regularly knocking at the
door all the money had run out. Dad had given up his
job as one of the top salesmen in Sydney. I think Mum
had had enough and was probably considering leaving.
It was one thing for my father to gamble away the
weekly wage – it was quite another for him to be committing adultery and having the police knocking at the
door seeking information about stolen goods. Above all
she wanted a decent and honest life.

Another one of the triggers to Mum leaving my
father came one afternoon when he was supposed to
pick me up from pre-school and didn't turn up. I was
four and was absolutely terrified. There I was, still new
to the area, standing outside the school gate having no
idea where to go or what to do. It was winter, too, so
daylight was fading fast. People walked past and asked
me if I was okay and when I said that I was waiting for
my Dad, naturally they just left me there to wait for
him. Eventually, after sunset, someone came along and,
knowing that something was wrong, took me to the

police. They took me home to Mum, who was frantic. Mum didn't have a car — never once drove all her life — so she had had no way to get to me. I think that incident really made her decide to leave him. At 30 Mum packed up and we left.

It was 1957 and it was an extraordinary step for Mum to go out into an intolerant society as the sole parent of a four year old. At that time it must have been such a difficult decision for a strongly Catholic woman to leave her husband and start all over again. But I don't think she realised how lonely or socially difficult it would be as a single parent in the 1950s and 60s. I grew up thinking how different we were to other families — we only knew one other separated woman, who also had a son. In those days the avalanche of divorce was still teetering. Years later Mum would tell me how much she hated going to dinner parties with her friends and always being the odd one out. She would never dare get a divorce because it was forbidden by the Church.

When Mum left Dad she and I went to live with her mother and step-father in a grubby laneway in Leich-hardt, in Sydney's inner west. They had a tiny house, and we were forced to almost live on top of each other. We were there for about three or four months. It felt like three or four years. My grandmother wanted no part of us. And my step-grandfather despised us.

Soon after we had moved to Leichhardt, Christmas rolled around. Dad spent Christmas Eve in his car outside the house and came to the front door on Christmas morning with presents. Mum wouldn't accept them and wouldn't let him in the front door. He begged and pleaded just to be allowed to come into the house and drop them off. My mother would not budge a millimetre. She had utterly turned on him this time and would never go back. As a four year old I not only felt sorry for him having to spend Christmas Eve sleeping in his car but I really wanted *my* presents. But I was not allowed to have them. When my father left them at the front door Mum threw them out onto the street. I remember whispering to my father through a front window asking him how Santa Claus had managed to get his presents into the car when it didn't have a chimney. He told me Santa had left his presents on the roof, which sounded perfectly feasible. All Christmas Day my father waited outside in the laneway while we stayed inside the house. Eventually he gave up and left.

Now I think, isn't it funny: four years of age, that's probably one of your very first exciting Christmases, but mine was just full of arguments, hate and abuse, and having to stay inside with my grandmother and step-grandfather who didn't want us there. This was my first conscious introduction to Christmas. Awful. And while I don't mind Christmas now, all of my childhood Christmases would turn out to be something to dread.

My father came to try to visit a number of times over the next couple of months. Meanwhile, Mum was hatching a plan to disappear with me. She knew that to have any chance of making it on her own she would have to sever all ties with her past life and completely disappear. She had to do it that way, or else risk weakening and caving in to my father's sweet tongue.

Dad's eldest brother, Leo, a very religious man, helped Mum get a job as a housekeeper at Marist Brothers Sacred Heart in Mosman, on Sydney's lower north shore. Mum made him swear that he would never tell Dad where we were.

We moved from the working-class inner west to the middle-class north into two tiny rooms out the back of the brothers' monastery. One room was a lounge room containing one chair. The second room was our bedroom, which contained our only other item of furniture, a double bed I had to share with my mother. There was also a poky bathroom with a toilet and shower. A small courtyard separated us from the monastery kitchen where Mum would spend most of the next eight years of her life cooking breakfast, lunch and dinner for up to 12 Marist brothers, all on her own.

I went straight into the kindergarten at the Sisters of Mercy infants school, which was across the road (named Cardinal Street – can you believe it?) from the Marist Brothers. The nuns lived in a separate convent next door to the brothers. My daily routine was pretty basic. Mum started her day at 5.30am so she could have breakfast served to the brothers by 7.30am. I got myself showered and dressed for school and then helped Mum wash up the breakfast dishes before walking across the road to kindergarten. I'd come 'home' each day to have lunch once the brothers had eaten and then make the 90-second return walk back across Cardinal Street. Most afternoons after kindy I'd play in the grounds of Marist Brothers outside the kitchen window where Mum could see me. I was expected to set the dining room table every night for the brothers and generally help Mum if she needed it. Apart from the three major meals of the day Mum also prepared morning and afternoon teas and did all the cleaning up as well as all the washing, including the linen and towels, for the whole monastery. She worked very hard despite the fact that her only real gains were food, board and my education. She didn't have a hope of saving anything or moving us into our own rented accommodation for a long time.

Most nights we'd have dinner together in the monastery kitchen because it had a small serving table we could sit at. And then we'd walk across to our flat to watch the television the brothers had lent us. Mum loved her movies and the Hollywood stars. For hours she'd tell me who this and that star was and what relationship they'd had with other stars. She knew all the movies they'd been in and who they'd starred alongside. I'm sure she was the closest female equivalent to Bill Collins. She made it all so interesting that I was fascinated by it too.

At first these were good years. They were good because although this was when Mum started drinking, the alcohol hadn't fully taken hold yet. I remember celebrating my fifth birthday sitting in that dark little kitchen, just Mum and me. No one else, just the two of us singing 'Happy Birthday' over my cake. Each of us eventually started to make friends, but friendships didn't really replace having a man to share her life with, so she became desperately lonely. She was working 16 hours a day. And this is when the singing and the hilarity of the hiccupping started.

At first Mum stayed sober most of the day, until she took the six steps across the little courtyard from the kitchen to our flat. Very rarely was Mum required once she and I had washed up, so as soon as we'd finished she would have a drink and escape to an easier-going, more mellow life under the influence. As time passed, those six steps between the kitchen and the flat made it easy for Mum to take a couple of nips before she and I had actually finished washing up from dinner. She'd leave me wiping up and make some excuse to 'shoot over to the flat' to get something. At first the grog must have been a great relief from her loneliness, the long days and having to bring up a young son on her own. She was almost jolly in those first couple of years of drinking.

But by the time I was six she was a fully fledged, gold-plated, 100% alcoholic. After the initial fun and giggling came ugly, spiteful and violent behaviour. I didn't really understand what was happening. All I knew was that as soon as she had a drink her mood turned black and mean. In the early days she drank brandy neat – no ice, no water, nothing. She would ask her friends to buy her a half-bottle of brandy up the road, and none of them picked up the signs. She always drank in the bathroom, secretively, with the door closed, and hid the bottle in the dirty-clothes basket. So as a six year old I would take the bottle out of the basket and pour the brandy down the toilet when she collapsed into bed at night. Now at this stage Mum was earning £10 pounds a week. The only money she had was that 10 quid, and for me to throw out her brandy absolutely infuriated her. And I would do it quite regularly.

The only problem was that every time I poured the brandy down the toilet I would be thrashed. She didn't care how she beat me, or what she beat me with. I became so adept at protecting myself that when the ironing cord came my way I knew what position to hold my arm in so that it wouldn't hurt as much because it would curl around my arm. Once it had curled around my arm I could try to wrench the cord from her hands, particularly if she was heavily drunk. But then she got clever and, rather than hit me just using the cord, she would turn the cord around and beat me using the end with the pronged plug that goes into the electrical socket in the wall. She used belts too, eventually hitting me with the belt-buckle end. I knew every time I touched her booze I would bear the brunt of her wrath but I also knew that, whatever the cost, I had to try and help her 'get better'. The more often I threw the drink out, the more I was bashed, and the more I was bashed the more determined I became to stop her from drinking. I was determined to keep doing it because to my young mind this stuff just made my Mum not my Mum.

One day when she was talking to some brothers in

the kitchen I marched in and said: 'Oh excuse me Brother, Mum needs to go to the toilet.' That was my funny way of saying 'I need to talk to you Mum'. She started on me immediately we were alone, and I hid behind a cheap, metal crucifix. I held it up in front of me, pleading with her not to hurt me again. I remember it like it was yesterday. 'Please, please don't hurt me.' She didn't then, I think because she was sober. But later on that night, as the drink started to take hold, the spitefulness started. She remembered what I'd said and out came the belt and the ironing cord. Well, she absolutely thrashed me black and blue. I got it all night.

I don't think she really knew what she was doing though. She was a very decent and kind-hearted woman who meant well and basically devoted her entire life to me. As misguided as she was I think she certainly wanted the best for both of us, but through the alcohol, she was slowly but surely giving up and throwing away her life. As a six year old I knew somehow that what she was doing to herself and me was not deliberate but I knew that it was bad for her and it was certainly bad for our relationship. Apart from that, I didn't want to get beaten all the time when she was drunk. When she was sober she was fantastic. She was kind and thoughtful and had a great sense of humour. She was also extremely well read. She used to read a tremendous amount when she wasn't drinking, but then once she did drink she turned ugly.

* * *

By the time my father finally found out where we were living – two years after we had disappeared – Mum had instilled in me a great fear that if I went anywhere with him he would take me away and put me in a boys' home. That he would put me in a caged truck and never let me come home to Mum again. From then on, for many years I used to have nightmares about it. I can still see an image from the nightmare now – me screaming for help out the back of a caged truck being driven away from Mum. It's ironic that the only life I knew and wanted was with an alcoholic and I wouldn't have had it any other way.

Once Dad had found where we were living he would occasionally come to visit me, bringing with him a beautiful Labrador called Mister. At the most I saw him twice a year and the first I would know of it was when he spotted me playing in the school grounds or knocked on the doors of nearby houses to ask people to fetch me. I would sit on the footpath outside the school and talk to him for two or three hours, flatly refusing to get in his car because I was afraid of the boys' home. Mum put the fear of God into me about going with him because I was her life and she was not prepared to share me with anyone. And she was using me to hurt him for all the hurt he had caused her. So throughout my early years I got to know my father on a footpath, never any further than 30 metres away from the front door of the monastery.

Mister provided most of the amusement and conver-sation during my father's erratic visits. I hadn't known

Dad for the last two years so by the time he found us at Marist Brothers we had to virtually start all over again. Our conversation was often stilted, which is why we both relied so heavily on good ol' Mister. He was a show dog and my father got him to perform all sorts of tricks and started to show me how to get him to obey. But I was always on guard for any sort of caged truck that might appear.

During those visits on the footpath I at least got to know my father and slowly began to trust him more. Respect was another matter altogether. As Mum constantly reminded me, my father didn't 'pay a penny towards our upkeep'. I suppose that just as I was getting to the age when my father and I could have developed a close relationship I was also realising that he had paid nothing in the way of maintenance. Birthdays and Christmases were forgotten most of the time but there were always the guilty spur-of-the-moment gifts like a Robin Hood or Davy Crockett outfit. The sudden arrival of my father on the footpath or at school during lunchtime became more about 'What surprise will I get this time?' than about being pleased to see my father. He'd obviously just had a win somewhere and had turned up to buy my affection. And as a kid who had nothing it worked a treat. I looked upon him as more of a Santa Claus than a dad. Our relationship was about as deep as a puddle.

Mum tried to stop him from seeing me on the footpath outside the Marist Brothers but their arguments became so loud and embarrassing that she was forced to relent. I would certainly pay for his visits once he left. They left Mum in a foul mood. And once she had a drink her mood become even blacker and I would have to be very careful, otherwise I'd really cop it.

2

I was certainly a wild child – I was cheeky, mischievous and not scared to answer back if challenged by an adult. I was an extremely hyperactive kid who could not sit for too long or be content to read a book for hours on end as I can today. Always being 'on the move' I turned up everywhere in the area and was quite well known. I was an outcast to most adults – 'that housekeeper's brat'.

I think because I was a lonely kid I would go out of my way to seek attention by being the class clown or street jester. The nuns who taught us from kindergarten to year three were particularly strict and loved dishing out canings with the handle of a feather duster either on the palms or the backside, and I got my fair share.

When I was in third class, one morning I sneaked into class one and rearranged Sister Beatrice's entire social studies presentation. She had painstakingly prepared a display of the mammal food chain using models of animals. I moved all the animals out of order. When class started Sister Beatrice was naturally furious that some destructive little smartarse had undone all her hard work and left her embarrassed in front of 25 or so seven year olds. When she asked who had done it I owned up immediately. It was almost like a death wish. But really it was just one of many sad attempts at grabbing attention, even if it did mean four 'cuts' with the handle of the feather duster. At the base of my right index finger I still have the scar to prove Sister Beatrice's marksmanship with the cane. She gave it to me with everything she had. I think the only reason I didn't get expelled was because Mum was the housekeeper across Cardinal Street with the Marist Brothers.

On the other hand, more progressive nuns, like Sister Michael, encouraged my mischievous nature and outgoing personality by playing handball with me and my friends after school or playing chasings with us around the school and church grounds.

On one occasion, after school my friend Mark and I were shooting passing cars with peashooters from behind a hedge. One motorist who was hit saw us duck behind it. He slammed on his brakes and returned to where we were.

'He's coming back,' Mark yelled, 'let's get out of here!'

Before we ran and hid I had the presence of mind to run to the door of our flat and lock Mum inside. I knew she was drunk and sound asleep but if she woke to find an irate motorist complaining about being shot at I'd really cop it from her. And just as well I did because as we peered over the hedge we came face to face with the driver, who demanded to know where our mother was.

'She's not at home, she's at work,' I told him, praying Mum wouldn't hear the yelling and try to open the front door. Fortunately the man drove off and Mum remained in her normal drunken stupor.

Mark was one of three mates I had made who were to become lifelong friends – Mark Harris, Terry Camden and Geoff Geraghty. In fact, we still hold card nights three or four times a year, and Terry ended up marrying my wife's sister Kim and became my brother-in-law! When I was young these three boys were crucial to my survival and extremely influential in my upbringing. They came from solid families with brothers, sisters, and a mother and a father – except Geoff, whose mother had died when he was two. They were good kids and positive influences in my life. In effect they were my family – they didn't know it but they were. I could quite easily have gone off the rails. Going anywhere at 10.00 or 11.00pm would have been no trouble for me because by 8.00 most nights Mum was already in bed drunk, but there was no one for me to run the streets with.

Most parents advised their kids to avoid me but Mum, God love her, would always have my friends stay over at our house, particularly Mark. Mum would have him over, feed him and he'd often stay the night, sleeping on the floor on an old foam mattress. However I think only once in probably 15 years was I ever invited to stay at Mark's house. I remember that night distinctly. It was so exciting. His parents definitely regarded me with suspicion as the drunk's kid, and one of his sisters always called me 'the leech'. It was around this time, what with Mum's alcoholism and society's disdain for us, that I started to develop a hide thicker than an elephant's. It was the only way I knew to survive. To constantly be able to shrug off the next insult, either in class or socially. To always expect the worst because if it didn't happen, it was such a wonderful bonus.

Another very important influence in my life was the Catholic Church. For us four friends, becoming altar boys around the age of 10 or 11 was almost a given. Mark's older brother led the way and was already a 'senior' altar boy by the time we joined. Terry and Geoff didn't last as long as Mark and I did, but if we were short on numbers on big festival days they could always fill in. One of the real bonuses was the fact that the church actually purchased the entire outfit for us. We didn't have to outlay a cent. And just as well too. Mum told me that as much as she would have loved to have bought the outfit it would have taken her far too long to save up for it. So we were fitted out for the custom-made – not off-the-shelf – full-length red robe and white-lace tunic. We were even provided with little black 'jiffies' slippers and wardrobe space in the altar boys' change room, which also doubled as the space where the communion hosts were made and the candles stored.

We were pleased as punch the day we were presented with our outfits. Surely this meant we were certainties to go to heaven. Or at the very worst, spend a few million years in purgatory before getting right of passage to St Peter. Whatever happened we were sure altar boys would never burn in hell.

I was an altar boy four or five days a week with various priests – Father Clements, Bishop Muldoon and Monsignor Cusack, a crusty old thing who ruled the parish like Caesar. I would have to lay out the priests' or the bishop's garments in the vestry and wait while they blessed them and put them on over their black street clothes. Normally there were two or three altar boys for a Mass and once we were all ready and lined up, we solemnly marched out onto the altar to begin the ceremony.

For the first time in my life I felt important. I was in an area where other people weren't allowed to go. I could look back on the entire Mosman congregation and see them looking at me – well, that's what it felt like, even though they were really looking at the priest. But I felt special and it really helped me. I enjoyed the community spirit; and the Good Friday three-hour marathon Stations of the Cross and midnight Mass on Christmas Eve were always exciting and colourful affairs. It was purely a voluntary job, although once a year there was an altar boys' picnic for all the kids serving churches in the immediate district. In those days there were a lot more priests and a lot more churches and a lot more altar boys.

Being an altar boy was a lot of fun, too. Mark and I were complete heretics sometimes. We'd be talking during the most solemn part of the Mass. Mark would say something like, 'Did you see *Combat* last night? Did you see how good it was?' and then we'd realise what he'd said and burst out laughing. The priest would hear us laughing and the congregation would see us talking and then we'd get into trouble when we got off the altar.

Whenever we were hungry we'd gobble up the communion hosts that had not yet been blessed. They might have already been cut out into circles, or were still in squares – either way we'd tuck in and fill our faces full of them, and to this day I can still smell the wafer bread being cooked on an old-fashioned sandwich maker. And I can still smell the wax and the incense, and the vestry where the priest or the bishop used to get dressed for Mass.

It was around the time I became an altar boy that Mum developed a description of me that she was to use for years to come: 'street angel, house devil'. Most of the time she would use it tongue in cheek; sometimes when she had been drinking she would put a bit more feeling into it.

It was only one of a number of derisory names she had for me. But by far her favourite taunt was: 'You'll never amount to anything because you're nothing but a pasty-faced nothing.' Not exactly the way that a doting mother would normally speak to her son. I told myself that it was the alcohol talking, but nevertheless it did play on my mind for years. I think it's one of the reasons I have worked so hard – I was determined to prove to Mum and myself that I could do something with my life, that I really wasn't a nothing. But gee, if I had a dollar for every time Mum called me 'a pasty-faced nothing' I'd never have to work again.

Mum's best friend for almost 30 years was a very kind woman called Bernice Fogarty, the mother of two other boys at the Marist Brothers School. A friendship developed between the two women because they were both well read, opinionated and did what they could for their local church groups. They were always involved together in community projects like fêtes, dances and other fundraisers, and Mum was always pestering Bernice to take her out to do Meals on Wheels for the elderly and the ill. I think that Bernice, like many people in the area, forgave Mum for her drinking because when she was sober she was such a likeable character – a caring Christian and Catholic who attended Mass every week and always made a donation using the church envelope.

'We could never work out in the early years why Beryl would always be so hard and unfair on you,' Bernice told me as an adult. 'On the one hand she would be forever singing your praises and telling us about "Michael doing this, and Michael doing that". She was also fiercely protective of you when it came to other children who had a father and a family around them. She was all too aware how different your lives were to everyone else around you.

'But on the other hand she would be forever critical, even ridicule you to your face, constantly belittling you. I remember on one occasion in our home when she was again boring us about how wonderful Michael was when you suddenly walked into the room. Well, she immediately turned on you, yelling that you hadn't wiped your feet coming into the house and for the next 10 minutes berated you about being a rude and inhospitable guest in someone else's home. She then told you to get out of her sight.'

Bernice said that on this particular occasion she actually tackled Mum about it: 'One minute you're telling all of us how supposedly perfect Michael is and the next you're rubbishing him as soon as he walks into the room.'

Mum simply brushed if off, saying that because I didn't have a father figure around me she had to act as both.

Most of the brothers treated us pretty well. Mum ran an efficient, clean and well-stocked house. They recognised how hard she worked and respected her for it. They were very compassionate and generous in their own way – Mum hardly ever paid school fees, particularly under one kind and generous principal called Brother Coman, a great bloke. Years later I found a beautiful note he had written to Mum in which he thanked her for her contribution to my schooling but was sure to add, 'only when you can afford it'.

Then there were some brothers who were very conscious of the fact that Mum was just a housekeeper. There was one particular brother called Brother Herbert. When I was nine years old he was my fourth-class teacher. He had the class of 30 pupils divided up into academic tiers of A, B, C and D. I was in D. He treated me badly and often humiliated me by calling me 'the housekeeper's kid' in front of the whole class. I developed such low self-esteem that I never really regained my confidence in any classroom, right up to the end of high school. It didn't help that I was very immature and extremely hyperactive – today I'd probably be labelled ADD or ADHD.

I remember coming home one day and I'd never been so excited; I was absolutely over the moon because Brother Herbert had promoted me from D to C! It was such a big moment for me.

I ran straight into the kitchen and said: 'Hey Mum, Mum, guess what? Brother Herbert's promoted me from D to C.'

Mum looked at me – it was 3.30 or 4.00 in the afternoon and by then she might have already had one or two drinks while she was preparing the night's dinner for the brothers – and she said 'Yes, C for cad'. And I was so deflated. I already knew what 'cad' meant because Mum often used the term to describe me. It was just the alcohol talking. It was only ever the alcohol. It was easier for me to blame the alcohol rather than Mum because she was the only living thing I had in the world and I was determined to hold on to her no matter what.

Every night of my life in those early years – and indeed almost every night of my later life – I prayed that my mother would become sober. I prayed to Our Lady that she would help my mother become sober and therefore better. Over the years the Virgin Mary became a second mother to me; I would pray to my surrogate mother to help my real mother. And although Mum never did get sober, I think that's the mystery of faith. I can't really explain it. Other people would argue that Our Lady wasn't helping her so why keep praying, but I just don't think it works that way. I suppose I desperately needed to hold on to anything that gave me a feeling of belonging, and to this day I still regularly pray to Mary.

One of the things that began to emerge about me around 10 or 11 was that I loved to play practical jokes on people. The class clown most likely to fail. I suppose it was a way of seeking the attention I wasn't getting much of at home. I was now cleaning ski boots at a ski hire store every day after school. I was paid the grand sum of 10 shillings a week – about a dollar – for two hours' work each afternoon. That meant I could afford one of those whoopee cushions that make a farting sound when they're sat on. This thing amused me for years, but not those I preyed on. Foremost were the grand dames of Mosman who played bridge at the local library. In those days the library was housed in a magnificent Victorian mansion on Military Road called Boronia House, which still stands today. Terry and I would often go to the library, not to read of course, but to embarrass all the ladies in front of each other. We'd pretend to flick through some book on physics while waiting for the final lady to take her seat with her friends at the bridge table. I think this is where I learned to always keep a straight face. As I grew up, practical jokes and surprises, from whoopee cushions to gorilla masks, would continue to be humorous escapes for me.

Another great distraction from the difficulties at home was Balmoral Beach. It was a paradise, an absolute oasis, and only a 10-minute walk from the school. In those days Balmoral was really only used by locals rather than being a popular spot for people from all over Sydney. It's a beautiful area and should be shared by all Sydneysiders, but in those days it was mainly used by us local kids.

There was the 'slippery rock' we'd sneak away to, looking directly out through the heads to sea. At slippery rock you'd be washed in and out by the tide, and at particularly low tide you'd be sucked down into the outgoing tide and then thrown back along the thick moss covering the rocks. It was a lot of fun, if you knew how to land and you knew the exact location of all the rocks well enough.

And Balmoral was where we started to meet a lot of the local girls in the neighbourhood, although we were at the wrong school. Most of the well-to-do kids attended Riverview, Queenwood, Loreto Convent Kirribilli or North Sydney Boys High School. The real problem was that it was embarrassing running into friends when I was with Mum, who loved the beach. They'd run up to gawk and see what state she was in. Having already had a few drinks before leaving Mum was often at her meanest when we got to Balmoral. I think she probably snuck something in her bag for when she got down there, which meant that once she hit the beach she would read for as long as possible and then just sleep it off on the sand for the rest of the afternoon. She loved the sun. She would sunbake for hours and never really get burnt. She was one of those people who'd go brown naturally, whereas I was someone who went red, then peeled, went red, then peeled, and got freckles, freckles, and more freckles. Mum just went browner and browner as she lay asleep drunk on the beach.

So this was the period when I really started to wander and explore, and gain some sort of independence. I was often lonely because while I had good friends, when they had family functions to go to on weekends I had no one to muck around with. And a lot of the time I didn't have Mum to talk to because she was drunk. Once I was walking along the back wall of the babies rock pool and I was hit by a big wave that crashed over the top of the rock wall. To save myself from falling into the ocean I threw myself onto the wall, and oyster shells cut deeply into my left knee. I went back to Mum, bleeding profusely, but she was so drunk I couldn't wake her up. I didn't know what to do. A lady told me to go to First Aid at the other end of the beach, so I walked way down the other end of Balmoral, to the baths, with blood pouring out of my knee. They patched it up temporarily and told me to tell my mum to take me to a doctor. I knew there was no point in telling her that because she could be just as volatile coming out of a stupor as she could be going into one. It probably needed five or six stitches, and I still have an angry scar there. It reminds me of Mum being too drunk on the beach to do anything.

Although I knew that Mum couldn't really help drinking because she was addicted, as I got older I wasn't going to just sit back and cop all the abuse without answering back. She might lunge at me and hit me with the plug of the ironing cord or her belt buckle, while I'd call her a 'dirty drinker'. As she was in complete denial about her drinking this would send her right off. Sometimes my only form of defence was to retreat into the darkness of the school playground. I would hide in some cubbyhole in the school grounds while Mum tried vainly to find me. By far the driest and most comfy hiding place was the cupboard where the school's sports equipment was stored. I knew where the brothers kept the key, so I could let myself in. It contained footy and cricket gear, a vaulting horse and heaps of soft mats – perfect for sleeping on. Many times I'd sleep there until very early the next morning. Then I'd put the key back in its hiding place and sneak back into our flat for my morning shower. Mum would come in as bright as a button, as friendly as you'd like, to say good morning.

'You're up early,' she'd say, completely forgetting her crazed obsession the night before to get hold of me and beat me.

'Yeah, I just couldn't sleep,' I normally told her.

'Are you okay, nothing wrong is there?' she might ask, showing real and loving concern for me. It was at moments like these I knew beyond any doubt that my mother loved me deeply but had never been taught how to show it, and she had a drinking problem.

We stayed at the monastery for eight years, until finally Mum's drinking became so bad the brothers had to sack her. They'd been very patient, very patient I think. It must have become awfully difficult for them. I do remember them complaining that dinner wasn't ready or that their clothes weren't washed. 'Where is Mrs Munro? Where's Mum? We're trying to find Mummy, where is she?' I'd always know that she had collapsed but pretended I didn't know where she was.

When I was born Mum had been a complete tee-totaller. Dad said he could not get her to have a drink when they were together. She turned to the alcohol for comfort and company after she left him. She had no one and nothing except a child that she adored but couldn't really share her life with. In the space of eight years she had gone from a teetotaller to a chronic drunk. So the brothers had to ask her to leave. I was 12 years old.

3

Mum didn't tell me she was fired; she would never have told me that. If I had put it to her she would have belted me, so it never came up. But I knew there had been those problems about missed meals and unwashed clothes. When I found out we were leaving the safety and security of the Marist Brothers I was scared. The only real life I had was around that school compound.

My mum got a good job straight away, working in a personnel agency. I think the brothers may have helped her find our next residence, not realising what a hellhole it would be. We moved probably a kilometre away to a horrible place in Gerard Street. Of all the places we were to end up living in – and there were about 10 of them over the years – this was by far the worst. We lived there with an old lady who owned it and another old lady who was either a tenant or her lover, I'm not sure. We had two rooms. Our bedroom contained our bed, which I still had to share with my mother, and our wardrobe. The other room had a table and some chairs where we could eat. The two rooms were separated by the old ladies' TV room. These mean old women would not let us watch their television set, and we didn't have one of our own. We shared their bathroom and their kitchen but were not allowed to cook when the women were cooking. It was a miserable place, a terrible hole and we stayed there for about a year. I hated it.

And of course I really missed Marist Brothers. Even though we had only had those two little rooms, we were at least comfortable, and had decent food. I had a play-ground area and felt I belonged. The church was right across the road as well. Not only was there the upheaval of moving, but I had also now reached high school age and had to swap to the Marist Brothers high school at North Sydney. I know the Mosman Marist Brothers again paved an easy path for Mum when it came to paying school fees. But while I was still being taught by brothers, they were not the ones I had lived with and come to know at Mosman. Suddenly I had been thrown into a new school, and an awful world of mean old ladies who didn't want Mum and me. Of course, from their point of view, they'd rented to a raging alcoholic.

Mum was drinking more than ever. It was at Gerard Street that I actually saw her take a drink for the first time. She was a complete closet drinker who never once drank in public. She would never ever drink at a pub; she would always go up and buy a bottle from the bottle shop at the Hotel Mosman and bring it back and drink in private.

I hid under our bed for almost an hour waiting for Mum to come in, close the door and have her first drink of the day. Looking into a mirror behind me, I saw her come in, take the bottle from underneath a pile of clothes on top of the wardrobe and swig from it. She was standing right next to my head. I could almost taste the excitement and fear of finally seeing my mother take a drink. It was a terrible, terrible moment, because then I knew we were both in trouble. I guess until that moment I had clung to the thinnest hope that she wasn't an alcoholic – that her violent outbursts stemmed from some other problem. Deep down I knew they were all due to her drinking – I just didn't want to confront it. But now that I had seen her with my own eyes there was no denying that she was an alcoholic. If she had caught me watching I would have been thrashed to within an inch of my life. There was an almost death-defying challenge to being so close, so perilously close, to Mum as she took that drink.

I remember the arguments out on the footpath in Gerard Street when Dad would come to take me out for the day and I wouldn't go. I was still too scared. He just couldn't understand why I wouldn't get in the car with him, and I would never tell him that all the time Mum was telling me that if I went with him I'd probably never come back. Anyway, he didn't come around all that much. From when I was 12 it might have been only two or three times a year that he came and visited.

I knew no real family except that of my father's eldest brother, Leo, who had helped Mum get the job at Marist Brothers. When Leo promised my mother that he would never let on to Dad where we were it had caused a major rift between him and my father – but they had fallen out well before that when my father had billed several hundred pounds' worth of furniture to Leo, the battling father of seven children. The two men were like chalk and cheese. Dad was a cocky and brash, live-for-today petty punter who'd bet on anything. From playing poker and pontoon to gambling at any type of racetrack, my father was into it all, while Leo was the quintessential God-fearing Catholic. He was extremely strict and I'll never forget the thick, long leather strap that hung ominously on the kitchen wall, to be used if any of his six boys and one girl got out of line. Of course I was absolutely petrified of him. He saw in me a young boy who could easily go the wrong way if allowed to wander. I had never had any relative who was a good male role model for me and I think he was trying to be that, so he was very strict on me whenever I stayed with them. But I was old enough to recognise the goodness and well meaning in what he was trying to do for Mum and me.

His wonderful wife, Pat, was the cool-headed and easy-going balance to Uncle Leo. The family was good enough to take me on a couple of holidays with them to the south coast of New South Wales. Although they went out of their way to make me feel welcome I always felt as if I just didn't fit in. Maybe I had a chip on my shoulder; maybe I was envious of their solid family foundation. It wasn't until years and years later that Leo had any inkling of Mum's drinking problem. I said nothing to anyone about it for so long, for fear of losing Mum her job or getting another belting.

I was always on the lookout for places where I could feel like I was part of a family, even for a little while. I became very close to another family, the Mansfields, who lived nearby. I know a good family when I see one. They were blessed in every way – wonderful parents, balanced, healthy children. So the 'leech' immediately latched on. Around 12 I became good mates with their eldest daughter, Jo-Ann, who was a little younger than me. The family immediately accepted me as part of theirs, even though I did sweep through their iced vo-vos like a locust plague. I was probably about 13 when I arrived at their doorstep one Christmas in my dressing gown, uninvited, at 6.00 in the morning. I know I have the hide of an elephant these days, but even at 13! I proudly presented them with a blow-up Terry the Tiger punching bag which was on sale at our local Esso service station. Such was the relationship with this generous family, who knew I had problems at home but had no idea just how bad things were, that they accepted me as their own, and have continued to do so for 35 years. Not bad for 'a pasty-faced nothing'.

Thanks no doubt to her drinking problem, Mum rapidly went through a succession of jobs. From working in the personnel agency she went to a job at

Johnnie Walker's bistro, a steakhouse in Angel Place in the city that was frequented by the well-known and well-heeled. After that she worked as a receptionist in an office block in Circular Quay, and then she got a job at, of all places, a wholesale liquor outlet. Whenever we were *really* flat broke she'd also do some shifts as an usherette at Kings Cinema in Mosman. The good thing about that job was that I could get into the cinema for free, and get Mark, Terry and Geoff in too.

Mum and I were continually being thrown out of different homes as landlords realised they had rented to a drunk. We hadn't lasted very long at Gerard Street before we were evicted. We moved nearby to Lang Street, where we rented two rooms at the rear of an elderly lady's house. There I started going through an extremely insecure and obsessive-compulsive stage. I was 13 and for a number of years couldn't get to sleep at night because I continually believed the stove was on, that the front door was open, that there was someone coming into the house. I still had to share a bed with Mum and I would get out of bed a dozen times to check everything again and again. Even after checking that the gas was not on, I had to recheck it and recheck it before falling off to sleep exhausted. And because I had to get out of bed time and time again I got into trouble from Mum, depending on how drunk she was. If she was in a drunken stupor she wouldn't hear a thing, but if she had only had a few I'd disturb and annoy her. That's when it was dangerous, because I would get beaten. But I still couldn't stop myself checking everything.

We lasted about a year in Lang Street before being thrown out. We moved back to Military Road, into a tiny annex at the back of a family home. It was just a kitchen, a bedroom and a bathroom. It was a terrible place full of rats. We had to share a single bed, and there was a rat hole right underneath it. It was so depressing. The family was nice to us but it was a matter of how long they could put up with a screaming drunk and a little boy who would scream and fight back.

At one stage we shared a house with another sole mother and her daughter at North Sydney – the furthest we ever lived outside of Mosman, although it was only about three kilometres away. Once the woman realised she'd rented to an alcoholic she broke the lease and threw us out. On the one hand we were fortunate when another flat became available immediately, on the other it would prove the beginning of the end for my mother.

We moved to a one-bedroom flat at Spit Junction above a liquor store owned by the company Mum was working for in Brookvale. And after we moved in, the company gave her a job in the store downstairs. If there was ever a chance Mum was going to get off alcohol it disappeared when she started both working at and living above the liquor store. It was all over. She had already been a drunk for over 10 years but now she plummeted to the depths. She could get any amount of alcohol she wanted. Any hard liquor, any wine, anything for nothing. And there wasn't a damn thing I could do about it. She was still working, still managing to get up every day and work. How she did it for all those years

I will never know. She amazed me with her work ethic. She rarely ever missed a working day, no matter how much she'd had to drink the day before. She could also operate even though she might have had a couple of drinks during her working day. I can still smell the Lifesaver lollies she sucked on for 28 years to hide her alcoholic breath.

One good thing was that at last, at the age of 13, I had my own bed in the lounge room. It doubled as a sofa during the day and there was another rat hole under it. Sometimes I was too scared to get out of bed because I might stand on a rat, and the noise of the rats kept me awake at night. Once I woke to find a huge rat running across my bed, but at least it was my own bed. It was a start.

The other good thing was that the beltings now became less frequent because I was older and stronger, and because Mum was in bed drunk most of the time when she wasn't working. It got so bad that Mum would be drunk by about 6.00 most nights. But if she was still partly awake she'd be mean, as mean as a rattlesnake. What I would do is turn the clocks forward and tell her it was 11.00pm already when it was really only about 7.00. 'I'm going to bed now,' I'd tell her, and she'd go to bed. The moment she fell asleep I would climb out of the window over the shop's awning facing Military Road and down the 'no standing' sign pole, and I was out. I didn't get up to any real mischief – I used to go to friends' places or down to Balmoral to walk along the beach. I was just lonely.

The flat was so grotty that at first I refused to let anyone know where I was living, despite it being a 60-second walk from the local milk bar where I used to go and meet my friends after school in the afternoons.

'It took us ages to get to know you before you'd even let us know where you lived, let alone be asked to visit,' said Wendy Macken, a girl I had met down on the beach in front of Balmoral Beach Club. As time went on we became good mates and she would join me, Terry, Mark and Geoff down at the milkbar with her girlfriends. Wendy was the first girl I invited to the flat above the liquor store. I was ashamed of it and was always careful to try and not get embarrassed or hurt any more than I already had been.

'Oh yeah, it was a real privilege to get invited to go back to your place, which made all the other girls jealous,' Wendy said.

It was ironic, because all these girls were from well-to-do families and many lived in magnificent homes overlooking Balmoral Beach – and they wanted to visit *my* home. I suppose it was the novelty of seeing how the other half lives.

I was still constantly searching for other families to escape into, and thank God the Mackens – a generous family with 10 children, the eldest three all girls – lived just down the road. They became a lifeblood for me. In contrast to our couple of dingy rooms above the liquor store, the Mackens lived in this magnificent two-storey, eight-bedroom house that overlooked both Sydney heads and Balmoral Beach. It eventually became another home for me too, and they became my family.

Another escape for me was getting together with Geoff, Terry and Mark to ride our billy carts. We'd built them from wood offcuts, and for wheels we'd used car wheel bearings given to us for free by the mechanics who worked at the local Holden dealership. Each cart had an (extremely dangerous) foot brake – an old thong nailed to the front right axle – and a square wooden seat and a rope to help steer the front wheels.

We always started at Spit Junction, hurtled down the footpath past Mosman Council Chambers and the fire station, weaving our way between startled pedestrians, past the original Mosman RSL Club, through the public school and into Avenue Road for the final – and fastest – stretch down to the Mosman ferry wharf. It was almost a three-kilometre run and, apart from one short flat section, was all downhill. We'd annoy everyone on the footpath, not just because of our speed but because the ball bearings in our wheels made such a racket. Then again, at least pedestrians could hear our four billy carts coming and get out of the way.

Our 'rat run' wasn't just for fun though – it had a practical purpose, too. In Geoff's backyard there were hundreds of empty soft drink bottles, which you could cash in for five cents a piece. Just before we reached the wharf we'd call into Geoff's and grab two bottles each. We'd fly down the last 300 metres or so and head straight for the kiosk at the wharf. There we'd cash in our bottles and spend five cents each on lollies, saving the other five cents for the 10-minute bus ride back to Spit Junction, where we'd start all over again.

*   *   *

Around this time I started playing football. I was a very average footballer but pretty fast. Mum had no interest at all in football, but once or twice a year Dad would come to watch me play. Apart from that our chats now occurred during morning tea or lunchtime at school when he would unexpectedly appear. On one occasion he took off his watch there and then and gave it to me, and I kept it for many, many years. This was basically the way Dad showed his love. He would give me what he had there and then because next week he might lose everything in gambling. He once gave me an old set of about four or five golf clubs because he knew I did a lot of caddying at the nearby nine-hole golf course at Cammeray for extra money. I couldn't believe how lucky I was. My own set! I started playing golf at the course. But not long after, Dad asked if he could borrow the golf clubs for a weekend. I knew I'd never see them again. He probably needed them to pay off a bet or something. I never really went back to golf and still don't play it to this day.

Around the age of 13 all of the kids in the neighbourhood had bicycles except me. I was always having to run behind them, which was embarrassing and a damn nuisance. There was no way Mum could ever have afforded a bicycle so I started hinting to Dad: 'Gee, a nice second-hand bicycle would be good if that's possible.' But that just wasn't going to happen. Instead, one day he turned up with a second-hand tape recorder and unbeknown to me, my fate was sealed. It was the start of my journalistic career.

I immediately became fascinated with this old tape recorder, fascinated by how different my voice sounded on tape. It might not have been a bike but tape recorders weren't seen a lot – not in my circles anyway. It was a real novelty. I organised Mark, Terry and Geoff to perform group singing with me. So when other kids were out riding bicycles we were singing along to hits like 'Simple Simon Says' or 'To Sir With Love'. Over the next several years my tape recorder became my greatest escape of all. It gave me hours of enjoyment and allowed me to drift off into a completely different world.

It was the mid-60s. The race to put a man on the moon had started in earnest and the Apollo space program was well under way. It had captured everyone's imagination, me included. I would pretend that Mark, Geoff and Terry were astronauts going into space. I never wanted to be one of the astronauts; I was more than happy to be the reporter interviewing them. 'How do you feel about it, are you nervous?' 'What are you going to do when you get up there?' 'Is this something you've always wanted to do?' I'd even do the countdown – 10, nine, eight, etc – and then crackle paper into the microphone and do the takeoff, with all the sound effects. And then we'd play it back and roll around laughing at our voices. It was fantastic fun.

I then started to branch out and take the tape recorder up to the local shops at Spit Junction or Mosman. I'd go into the pie shop and interview them about how many pies they'd sold that day. Or if people were sitting at the bus stop I'd ask them: 'How long have you been waiting for a bus?' 'Are you happy with the transport system? How would you like to see it changed?' 'Are the buses running on time for you?' Or I'd go into the newsagency to find out what the top-selling books were at the time. 'What are your best sellers at the moment?' I'd ask.

I soon began to dress the part. My childhood friend down the lane, Jo-Ann Mansfield, would accompany me as my 'assistant' as I went about the neighbourhood playing 'reporter'. She reminded me that I used to wear an old coat that didn't look anything like a newsman's trench coat but was good enough to dress in for the role as we wandered in and out of shops and along the footpaths 'interviewing' people.

'You used to tell me that a good reporter never allows people to see the tape recorder or the cords,' Jo-Ann remembered.

I would put the tape recorder's carrying strap over one shoulder before putting on the 'trench coat' and feeding the microphone lead through my sleeve. That way our interview subjects didn't have to see the un-sightly equipment.

'You told me all this practice would help make you a good reporter,' said Jo-Ann.

As I got older the topics became broader, particularly when the Vietnam War was raging. Jo-Ann would be with me as I asked people along the shopping strip how they felt about the war and Australia's involvement in it.

'At one stage we were handing out moratorium protest badges to people after we interviewed them,' she laughed. So much for balanced and objective 'cub reporters'.

On occasion I would even hide the recorder and place the microphone near where Mum and a friend were likely to have a conversation. Afterwards I would retrieve the tape recorder and listen back to their private discussion. Little did I know that 20 years later I would be charged twice under the *Listening Devices Act* for recording private conversations during investigations I was conducting for the *Willesee* program and *A Current Affair*. But being charged under the *Listening Devices Act* would have been small potatoes compared to Mum discovering I was secretly recording her personal conversations. Had she found out life wouldn't have been worth living.

I only ever had one hour-long tape for the recorder and would record over it again and again. The lifespan of my recordings wouldn't be more than a couple of days because I'd fill up both sides of the tape and have to record over them again. Today I am a hopeless hoarder. I still have my first five scrapbooks from my career in newspapers, so what I wouldn't give to still have the recordings of those 'space launches' and 'interviews' about the transport system and the Vietnam War.

Where the hell was all this coming from? Singing songs into a tape recorder is one thing, but traipsing around the streets interviewing people on subjects of the day is very much another. Whatever it was and wherever it was coming from, it was a turning point in my life. Up until then I had been consumed with just getting through the next 24 hours. But now I had a plan, a goal. At 13 I decided it was journalism I wanted to do. I wanted nothing else but to be a newspaperman.

This was a time filled with discoveries. Down at Balmoral Beach Mark and I met a girl called Joanna who gave us the impression of being a forward, cheeky, experimenting type of young girl, though I think she was just as ignorant and scared of boys as we were of girls. Mark and I asked her one day to show us her breasts and she said she would, so of course we were salivating. But she said we first had to go for a walk. She led us along the beach all the way down past the baths, all the way across Balmoral Oval, up through the bush, into Middle Head. We thought, oh, this is where she's going to drop her top and show us her breasts. But she made us walk further, down Middle Head Road, past the HMAS *Penguin* naval base and into the army base overlooking Rose Bay. Kilometres had gone by, with us desperately trying to convince her to show us her bosoms. Finally she said, 'Okay, I'll show you back at Balmoral.'

We'd already been walking for an hour-and-a-half and were now confronted by having to walk for at least another hour-and-a-half back to Balmoral. Mark and I were seriously pissed off – but not so angry that we were going to risk losing our catch. We walked all the way back down Middle Head Road, through the bush, back across Balmoral Oval, to the baths at Balmoral Beach, and then she said, 'Okay, I'll show you under-water.' We really thought we were being ripped off here. We had put so much time and effort and patience into this but she would only agree to show us underwater, beneath the starting blocks in the baths, where of course it was full of shade. We begged her not to disappoint us like this after we'd been so patient. But it was to be the baths or nothing. Swallowing all pride we got into position. She undid her top and then on the count of three we all went under at the same time. Of course the glimpse was so fleeting and it was so dark underwater that it really meant nothing, but it was exciting – it was our first encounter with the other sex. We were 13.

Not long after this I actually kissed a girl for the first time. She was a bit older than me, probably about 14. I kissed her at the back of Sacred Heart Church. Very exciting stuff. Her name was Claudia, and after I kissed her I ran all the way home, straight home. I couldn't look at her. I couldn't say anything. I was so embar-rassed. I think she realised what an inexperienced and backward nerd she was dealing with and went on to bigger and better boys.

The next year, at 14, I fell very ill. I hadn't been feeling well for weeks, all through my mid-year exams. I didn't tell Mum because I knew I'd have to catch her when she was sober otherwise she would dismiss me as 'a whinger' or 'a hypochondriac', and because by now I'd become fairly independent. I had to be in order to understand the life around me. I was forever trying to

Mum, a vibrant, attractive woman with the warmest smile.

Much more than niece and aunt, more like loving sisters. Beryl and Vera, VP (Victory in the Pacific) Day, Market Street Sydney, 15 August 1945.

Dad courting Mum which all started because of a bet made by my grandmother (far right).

Dad and Mum on their wedding day, 20 August 1948. The beginning of the end.

Mum, Vera, Dad and Henry – happier days before Dad started ripping Henry off.

Mum with me at six months old.

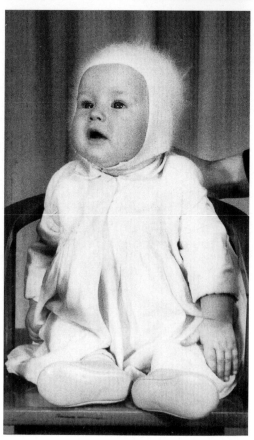

I was always a happy baby.

The only photo in existence of all three of us together.

Fourth class – lacking confidence and ability.

Befriending a stray in my backyard – the school grounds.

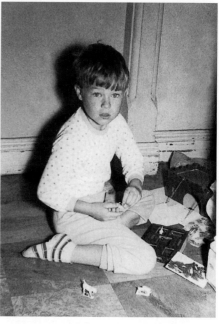

Christmas at Marist Brothers – they all chipped in to buy me a medieval castle and warriors.

Outside the school fence where I got to know Mister the dog ... and my father.

My cousin Gayle and her dog, Sooty. She always noticed the cuts and bruises.

My cousin Paul's wedding – the last family occasion with Aunty Pat and Uncle Leo (left of the bride) for many years to come.

The drunk's photo cage at Luna Park – Mark, me, Terry and Geoff.

turn negatives into positives; as long as I could do that I knew I'd be okay.

My urine turned the colour of tea and finally, one day at school, I collapsed in the toilet block and was rushed to hospital. Doctors diagnosed a severe case of hepatitis. I was in hospital for a week and bedridden at home for the next four months. The doctor told Mum rest was crucial if I was to make a full recovery and not suffer a relapse. As a 14 year old you'd think I'd have had a ball at home every day for four months. But I was so weak that my major exercise was going to the bathroom. As Mum was working downstairs in the liquor store she could at least keep an eye on me during the day.

The really frustrating thing was that I was not allowed to be in contact with anyone except Mum because the hepatitis was contagious. Mark, Terry and Geoff would have to visit me standing at our front door as I looked down on them through the window. They were very kind; most days at least one of them came around to visit and keep me up to date with my school work. It isn't until now that I realise how debilitating the hepatitis was. In the exams I did before I was diagnosed I got the best results I had ever had. They were only average – they probably positioned me somewhere around the middle of the class – but they were the last exams I ever did any good at. My schooling and marks really suffered because of the hepatitis, as well as my home life.

As a surprise treat for me after spending four months in bed recovering, Mum saved up and took us on the one and only holiday we ever had together – five days in the New South Wales Blue Mountains. We stayed at a small bed and breakfast called The Swiss Inn at Katoomba. We were both so excited, and while we were there Mum didn't drink nearly as much as usual, which meant we could spend more time together, enjoying the peace and beauty of the mountains.

4

All the time Mum's alcoholism was getting worse. She had become the manager of the grog shop, which meant she now had to answer to no one when it came to bottles of gin or brandy disappearing. And with the dramatic increase in the amount of grog she was consuming came an increase in her fury against me. I was a typical rebellious teenager and we began to argue more and more often about her drinking. 'You have to stop drinking otherwise it'll kill you, Mum,' I used to say. I think she wanted a break from me lecturing her, but the more she'd drink the more I'd lecture her and the more fed up she'd get with me, and then she'd tell me to pack my bag and get out. Such a catastrophic – and sometimes terminal – thing for a parent to say.

To infuriate my father, Mum would ship me off to his older brother Jack's house. Uncle Jack and my father hadn't spoken in years despite being inseparable growing up. In fact it was Jack, a professional gambler, who had introduced my father to the racetrack, and other types of gambling and confidence tricks. Both of them were overwhelmingly confident, brazen and willing to give almost anything a go. But because their family was so dysfunctional, it's no surprise that the two brothers never saw or spoke to each other for the last 20 years of their lives.

My father was incensed by the fact that I was too scared to go anywhere with him, though I would actually stay with his brother, whom he despised. I think Jack felt he was being the Good Samaritan, although he probably also felt some pleasure knowing how angry and hurt my father would be. Jack and his lovely wife Barbara would put me up until Mum was ready to take me back. Sometimes I'd stay with them for two weeks, sometimes for a couple of months. I stayed on and off at Jack and Barbara's over a period of a couple of years.

In the beginning I liked my Uncle Jack and used to daydream about what it would be like if he were my father. He was generous and led such an exciting life, calculating the prices and odds for a bookmaker, Bill Waterhouse, every Friday night in preparation for the Saturday races. He always dressed in expensive one-off suits, drove one of the latest cars and ate at all of Sydney's fashionable restaurants. He was a very success-ful gambler, even sometimes getting me to surrep-titiously put bets on for him because other punters would follow him and his betting.

Uncle Jack was generous enough to take me and the

son of another alcoholic on a cruise around the Pacific aboard the P&O liner *Orsova*. But Jack also had a cruel streak and this trip would be our last association for many years to come. I was 15 and Uncle Jack had long known about my goal to work in newspapers and how much it meant to me. Towards the end of the 10-day cruise he forbade me and the other boy from going ashore for the day in Suva, but being inquisitive, disobedient teenagers we naturally sneaked ashore for a couple of hours. As we came up the gangway back onto the ship my uncle was there waiting for us.

I didn't have to wait long for the king-hit. He showed me a handwritten letter addressed to his 'friend' Sir Frank Packer, Kerry's father, care of Sydney's *Daily Telegraph*, which the family then owned. He proceeded to read it out. In it he thanked the Packers for paying for my cruise around the Pacific to see whether I was suited to a career in journalism. As he read the words – and I can still hear them today – my heart sank. He said that it was certainly generous of the Packer family to offer me a position on the paper after I left school the next year. 'But I now find he doesn't have the discipline to obey orders,' he read on, as I started to cry. I was absolutely devastated. I was completely heartbroken that I had blown such a golden opportunity, all because I went ashore in Suva. But I told myself I still had another 18 months or so left at school and that anything could happen in the meantime. Negative into a positive equals survival.

My Uncle Jack let it sink in for a day or so. Then, just before we were to disembark at Circular Quay, he told me the letter was a sham, that he didn't even know the Packers and had made the whole thing up. I was so relieved, but did not speak to him again for 20 years. I lost all respect for him and only ever saw him a few times again. And after all the years of being surrounded by gamblers I still have nothing to do with any form of gambling – not because I'm scared of where it can lead to, it just bores me. Poker machines, horse races, Lotto and scratchies do nothing for me. I'd much prefer to pay off the mortgage.

My meagre family contacts were to shrink even further when we had a falling out with the relative who had always been there for us – Uncle Leo. When his eldest child, Paul, got married Mum and I were invited to the wedding, while Leo's own brother, my dad, was not. Then when the next son, Terry, was getting married, Mum was broken-hearted that we weren't invited to the wedding. They wanted to ask my dad this time. I think the family was only being fair but Mum took it very, very badly – and I took it worse defending her. From that moment on we were estranged from Uncle Leo for about 30 years. It would not be until I was hosting *This is Your Life* many years later that I would come into contact again with my cousin Terry. His wife, Maree, is the sister of the late and great Dr John Kelly, a highly respected humanitarian who ran Sydney's Taronga Zoo and the Western Plains Zoo in Dubbo. When we paid tribute to him on *This is Your Life* I met Maree and Terry again after all those years. We have since become family again, which is lovely.

As for Mum's side of the family, they had completely ostracised her. Mum's own brother, Billy, didn't even want to know us. I remember going to him and begging him to please come and help his sister as she had a major alcoholism problem. He never came. I have never forgiven him, and I've never seen him since. By the time I was in my mid-teens my grandmother, Eva, had died. But that made little difference because even when she was alive she refused to acknowledge Mum's drinking. My cousin Gayle, Billy's eldest child, remembers that my grandmother seemed to have a bias against Mum and me, and that I got into much more trouble from my grandmother than anyone else did. When we were children I had even told Gayle that I was being beaten by Mum. Years later she said to me: 'I remember a number of times seeing you with cuts and bruises. You told us when you were about 10 that your mum was using the belt buckle on you. One time I remember seeing you with a cut very close to the corner of your eye caused by the buckle. You told us that the belt would swing everywhere.' No one did or said anything about the abuse or Mum's drinking.

Having had no success with the family, I had also gone to the Church for help. I pleaded with the priests, and asked one in particular to come and speak to Mum to try and help her get off alcohol. The priest never once came to talk to her. She was a God-fearing, church-going woman. They knew her from being the housekeeper at Sacred Heart; they knew her problem. But of course we didn't have any money or influence in Mosman. If you didn't have any money, then you weren't worth fighting for or saving. This was a major turning point in my attitude towards the Church. I became disillusioned about actually attending Mass, though I continued to believe and pray. I now understood that priests were not infallible – they were only men.

I had just started Year 11 when I was struck by appendicitis and ended up in hospital. After having my appendix removed I charmed the tough nun in charge of the ward and talked my way out of hospital about a week earlier than I should have been allowed to go. I was still in a lot of pain but pretended I could walk normally. Within three days of leaving hospital I developed a shocking infection. I was in so much pain I could barely move. Late one night I was showering and smelt what I thought was sewage leaking from the toilet. It was the poison oozing from my appendix scar.

Mum was well and truly dead to the world; it didn't even enter my mind to try and wake her. I left her a note saying I'd gone to the Mater Hospital and caught one of the last buses that night to the hospital, which was about four kilometres away. I was doubled up in agony and pressing bandages against the wound to stop the flow of this foul-smelling fluid. You should have seen the wrinkled faces on the bus passengers. I was in hospital for the next few days being given antibiotics – which is what I should have allowed to happen in the first place – and was eventually discharged. I was off school for about three weeks all up – just what I needed going in to the two most important years of my schooling.

I got through the last two years of high school clinging to my dream of becoming a journalist. I was 17 when I finished Year 12. I went straight out to work in the magnificent old Hotel Australia in Castlereagh Street in Sydney as an assistant cellar man. My job was to restock all the bars in the hotel. I couldn't even drink legally but I was working in one of the most famous hotels in the country, which sadly is no longer there.

My confidence had really suffered when I'd got my final high school exam results. I had passed, but only just. Now I wondered whether I truly had what it took to be a pushy reporter. But Mum knew. She watched me earn a bit of money working as a cellar man and then started harping on and on about 'following your heart' and chasing something forever until you obtain it. All pretty corny stuff, but it started to work.

In February 1971 Mum finally said to me: 'Well, what are you going to do? Are you going to talk about journalism forever or are you going to do something about it?'

It's ironic, isn't it? Just when I needed a crystal clear direction, it came from my mother. It was one of the wonderful and caring moments when Mum let her gruff guard down. I think she often only pretended to be angry and hard. If she maintained that tough exterior there was less likelihood she'd be hurt any more than she already had been. In these rare times when she was sober, soft and measured she was the best mother in the world and I loved her so much it ached. But times like this when she openly and obviously cared about me upset me in a way because they made it even more frustrating that I couldn't help her get sober. I knew she was doing the very best she could for me, but I couldn't do anything for her.

I had had no real holiday but I hoofed it around to all three of the major newspaper groups in Sydney – Murdoch, Packer and Fairfax. I had decided I wasn't going to go to university. I was not a good student at school, the thought of another three years at university certainly did not enthral me, and in those days there was only one major journalism course in the country and that was at the University of Queensland in Brisbane. The only way to really get into journalism was to become a copy boy, running errands and delivering journalists' copy.

I went first to Fairfax's *Sydney Morning Herald* and they said: 'Good, okay, you're number 501 on the list to get a job as a copy boy.' Then it was on to Sir Frank Packer's Australian Consolidated Press in Park Street. They wanted to know (a) if I could play football and (b) how good a cup of tea I made. I was told that if accepted I would spend maybe two years in the advertising department before making it into the editorial department and becoming a copy boy for up to three years, before being lucky enough to get a three-year cadetship to become a reporter. That meant up to eight years before I perhaps became a D-grade journalist as it was called then. Finally I went to News Limited in Surry Hills.

They said: 'That's pretty timely 'cause we've just advertised for someone to start as a copy boy on Monday. We've got one person coming in for an interview who we'll have to see, but we'll see you now.' My father had bought me a suit and I was well dressed and presentable. They rang me later that day to say I had the job and started Monday, Februry 16, 1971 at 7.00am.

So began probably one of the most competitive periods of my career. I sat down that very first morning and, pointing to a man sitting behind a desk at the back of the room, asked one of the copy boys next to me: 'Who's that bloke? What's his name?'

The copy boy turned to me and said: 'I'm not telling you that.'

'What do you mean?'

'You've got to find that out for yourself,' he said.

The man sitting at the back was the editor, Neal Travis, who went on to become one of the most celebrated columnists in New York City, until his sad death in 2002. He sat at what is known as the back-bench, and the eight sub-editors sat at a long rectangular table in front of him. There were two or three copy boys and we sat at a little table in front of the sub-editors. When this copy boy wouldn't tell me the name of the editor sitting there in front of us I realised just how tough it was going to be.

For the first month I was assigned to work on *The Australian*, and if I'd continued working on that newspaper I probably would have become a broadsheet reporter and taken the more worthy and elitist route in journalism. Fortunately I was reassigned to the Sydney *Daily Mirror*, a fast, no-holds-barred tabloid putting out four editions every afternoon. I was surrounded by big names in journalism such as Ron Saw, Buzz Kennedy, Matt White, James Oram, Cirrel Greet and Gerri Sutton. I was 17 and it was the first time in my life I could say I was truly happy.

As a copy boy I took the reporters' copy to the sub-editors, then once the subs had edited them into finished news stories took them downstairs to be set into hot metal and printed in the paper. And I got the reporters' and sub-editors' cigarettes, put coins in the parking meters for them, picked up their dry-cleaning and got their lunches. I also did shifts in the radio room, from 3.00pm to midnight, midnight to dawn, or dawn to 3.00pm. I would sit in the radio room listening to police, ambulance and fire brigade calls, log the calls, take down the addresses and then let the news editor know that, for instance, a fire had erupted in the city. He would then decide whether or not to send a photo-grapher and a journalist to cover the story. I had to sit there and listen to those radios and never leave the room for fear of missing a big story. There were no second chances if you missed something.

This was a very exciting job because your tip-off might end up being a front-page story. I would ring up the police to get what information I could for the journ-alist, almost pretending to be the journalist: 'Michael Munro from the *Daily Mirror*, I'm sitting here in the radio room logging police radios. Can you tell us what happened?' And then I would pass that information on to the journalist. In my scrapbooks I often wrote: 'This story came from me in the radio room.' Of course I had nothing to do with it – I didn't go anywhere near the scene, write anything or take any photographs – but I was the one who told the journalist what was happening. For a copy kid this was being at the very forefront of journalism.

I spent three months on the copy boy's desk before learning they were going to assign three cadetships. There were five or six of us competing for them so it was an extremely traumatic and pressurised few weeks. On the 31st of May 1971 I got a call at home – Mum and I were still living above the liquor store – from the chief-of-staff, Gerry Kane. He told me I was now a first-year cadet journalist. I floated. Just floated on air. I was dizzy with dreams. I was on my way. It was one of the most memorable moments of my life, and was to be commemorated 30 years later when Network Nine Australia generously put on a wonderful party for many of my oldest and dearest friends and colleagues.

As a first-year cadet my job was to type out the TV programs each week. Channel Nine, 6.30am, *Playschool*; 10.00am, *Days of Our Lives*; 10.30am . . . right up until 11.00 at night. In those days there were only four stations – the ABC, Seven, Nine and 10 – and I'd type out the four stations, give it to the typesetter downstairs and it was put into the TV guide. Or I would do the shipping: *Australian National Line* coming in at 8.30am, or the *Fairstar* docking at 10.30am at Sydney terminal.

Then there was the weather, another 'fascinating' sideline as a cadet.

These were all really mundane jobs, but as a cadet you got to sit at the back of editorial, typing away with one eye on your typewriter and the other eye firmly on the people at the front of the editorial floor. I'd watch every move by the editor and the sub-editors, particularly if something exciting was happening. As a first-year cadet you weren't really involved in the major stories, but the excitement generated on the editorial floor was so infectious that you knew there was something unbelievably big unfolding. I still get goose bumps thinking about it. As I sat there at the front, my blood running and my heart racing, I wanted to be involved, wanted to jump up and say: 'Hey, I can do that!' I had to do these mundane jobs but was champing at the bit to be involved on a broader scale. It gave me a hunger. Slowly but surely I became primed and ready for when they would really let me loose to chase my own stories.

On days when there wasn't a lot happening I used to amuse myself very quietly, very secretly. I would have been fired on the spot had anyone known what I was up to. For at least a year or so I used to insert all my friends' names as stars in the movies in the TV guide. I'd write 'Channel Seven – 8.30pm *Sign of the Wolf*, starring Michael Whalen and Wendy Macken.' 'Who's Wendy Macken?' readers might ask. 'I've never really seen her, what's she been in in the past?' The *Persuaders*, with Tony Curtis and Roger Moore, was on at 7.30 or 8.00pm and starred some beautiful starlet. I swapped her name for the girl I was going out with at the time. There was a movie called *The Man in the White Suit*. I'd grown up with, and still know, Commodore Geoffrey Geraghty – now the Senior Military Attaché to London's High Commission. In those days Geoff was a midshipman at Jervis Bay at HMAS *Creswell* and was always dressed in his whites. There might have been a couple of well-known stars in *The Man in the White Suit* but so was Geoff Geraghty. It was a lot of fun but something I dare not share with anyone at work. Had I been caught my career might have been over before it began. I still have these clippings in my scrapbooks.

Now that I'd been made a first-year cadet I became a lot more confident. And with my new-found confidence came the odd practical joke. Some of us greenhorn cadets still had to get breakfast and lunch for the older cadets and senior reporters. Gerri Sutton adored a vanilla malted milkshake with her Vegemite and toast for breakfast. One day I asked Helen at the corner store to add three or four sardines to the milkshake. Naturally, Gerri was furious and chased me out of the newsroom, trying to get close enough to throw the vile concoction over me. It was a couple of months before I dared try it again on Gerri. This time I made sure Helen put a lid on the container so she wouldn't see the fish scales sitting on top of the bubbles. I watched from afar as Gerri sucked on the straw, spluttered, stood up and screamed out my name – you could hear her from where I stood, three open-plan newsrooms away. And senior reporters like John Hartigan and news editor Mark Day never really saw the funny side of a sardine tucked deep into the crevice of a pink-iced finger bun or inside a hot sausage roll.

I finally had to stop when the corner store refused to play along any more because people were beginning to complain. When you consider how foul these delicacies were it's remarkable that Gerri, John and Mark still call me their friend after more than 30 years.

Between June and August of 1971 the South African Springbok rugby union team toured Australia. In July the team was playing Australia at the Sydney Cricket Ground and I was chosen to accompany two journalists, John Hartigan and Gerri Sutton, to the game and run their copy back to the drivers waiting in the radio cars outside the ground. The drivers would then either deliver the stories back to editorial or read the copy out over the radio to a typist at the *Daily Mirror*. It was the very first time I had ever 'gone on the road' in journalism.

There were almost as many anti-apartheid protestors at the football as there were spectators. Police ringed the ground, inside the fence, on the playing field. Everyone entering the SCG was individually searched by police. Dozens of smoke bombs were ignited by the protestors and smoke drifted across the field, continually disrupting the game. The whole thing resembled a scene out of a doomsday movie; it was complete mayhem. It was also the most exciting introduction to being on the road that a young copy boy could ever hope for.

Hartigan gave his copy to me to run to the radio car. As I left the ground I noticed three or four policemen rushing through the crowd to a nearby group of people being questioned by other police. I followed the cops to see what the fuss was all about. I was gobsmacked when I overheard that the police had intercepted a live hand grenade in a shoebox which two fanatical anti-apartheid protestors had tried to smuggle into the ground. They were immediately arrested and carted away. I knew John Hartigan's copy was still ahead of deadline, so I ran back to him and told him about what I had just witnessed. He got on the phone to the police to double-check what I had told him. He was extremely generous with his praise, making sure he gave credit where credit was due. But I didn't care about credit because John Hartigan's hand grenade story made it onto the front page. Harto rightly received the by-line because he wrote the story, but I knew whose story it really was. If this was what being a reporter was all about, I couldn't get enough of it. I was on cloud nine.

I became swept up in the anti-apartheid movement after that Springbok rugby tour, which turned out to be the last one for two decades as South Africa was banned from playing any sport in Australia until the end of apartheid. The next year I entered the annual writing competition for cadet journalists, the Montague Grover Memorial Prize. The subject was whether or not racism existed in Australia. I began my 1,000-word essay with: 'Racism began in Australia the day James Cook set foot on Kurnell more than 200 years ago.' Young journalists from all over Australia entered so you can imagine how excited I was when I was awarded third place by the Australian Journalists' Association. Not only that, but I was presented with a cheque for the grand sum of $4.20. I still have that cheque, dated the 7th of September 1972, which I have never cashed.

Meanwhile, Mum's alcoholism had become even more chronic and she was deeply depressed and lonely. She had now even started to become dirty. I didn't want to go home. It was becoming harder and harder to live this life. It was only going to be a matter of time before the family who owned the bottle shop realised that their manageress had serious problems. It came to a head when she filled in for the manager of the company's outlet in Brookvale during his Christmas holidays. It was Christmas Eve and it had naturally been a frantic day of sales. I had helped Mum keep the shelves stocked as she served behind the counter. Out in a back room she had a bottle of gin hidden to help get her through the day. By the time she had finished up, counted the money, done the float and closed up she was well on her way. And that's why she forgot to lock up the premises when she left. After putting the burglar alarm on she closed the door but neg-lected to lock it. A breeze blew the door open around 3.00 on Christmas morning, setting off the alarm. We got a call from the furious owner of the liquor store chain wanting to know what was going on. He had been called by the police, who thought the store had been robbed. But when he and the police arrived at the business they found that the front door had not been locked.

'Get your mother,' he screamed at me when I answered the phone.

I put down the phone and went to Mum's bedroom, but as soon as I saw her I knew there was no way I could wake her from her drunken stupor. Even if I could partially wake her, she certainly wouldn't make any sense. My mind was racing. I went back to the phone and told him I'd forgotten that Mum was spending the night at her friend Bernice's place, and would be home in the morning.

'Get her to ring me as soon as she walks in,' he growled.

Not long after that Mum was fired from the job, and with that also went the flat above. We were out on the streets again. I thought it was a good thing because it would get her away from the limitless supply of grog – but the damage was now well and truly done. Mum would never work again. She was just too far gone mentally and physically to be in any way presentable to a prospective employer. She now became an invalid pensioner.

How she'd kept going for 20 years working while such a chronic alcoholic I'll never know. There had always been money coming into the house, most of the time there was food on the table, I had a full Catholic school education, and we always had a roof over our heads. Despite her alcoholism, until now, at the age of 50, she had shown no sign of slowing down or taking the easier welfare route. Though she'd never been set any kind of example of how to be a doting mother, she certainly knew how to survive and provide for her son under very tough circumstances. Her deep pride and immense work ethic got both of us through, and I like to think I've inherited both of those characteristics. There's no doubt I've been blessed with a strong desire to work hard in order to make a better life for myself and my family, but also to ensure that all of Mum's hard work for me was not in vain.

Even now that she was no longer able to find work she still had it in her to find us a roof over our heads. We moved to a flat behind a real estate agency not more than 100 metres from the liquor store, on another busy road, Spit Road. The tiny flat had an outside toilet and bathroom, but for the first time in my life, at almost 18, I had my own separate bedroom. It was a little sunroom that was almost falling off the back of the building. It was just big enough for my single bed. I couldn't even store any clothes in there it was so small; I had to hang them all in Mum's bedroom.

I had a second job in a barbecue chicken shop on weekends. It was a stinking hothouse in summer, run by a bitter and tight-fisted bloke who never had a nice thing to say about anyone. Although it was such an unpleasant place to work it was only a minute's walk from our flat and the extra money was crucial to our survival. With my two jobs I was earning enough money to buy food for Mum and me, pay the bills and buy us clothes occasionally. I couldn't give her cash because she'd spend it on grog.

I had only gone out with a couple of girls because it was so embarrassing to bring them back to our little hovel behind the real estate agency, particularly if Mum was drunk and nasty. And she was usually nasty to the few girls I went out with because she was so terrified of losing the only real thing in the world she ever had.

For a while I went out with Mary Macken, the eldest sister of my mate Wendy. But Deirdre, the third Macken daughter, who later followed me into journalism and is now a very respected and successful writer in Sydney, was constantly saying to me, 'You should meet my friend Lea, she's beautiful.' For two years I ignored her suggestion. Then on the 24th of June 1972, I walked into the main lobby of the Mackens' and here was this absolutely gorgeous creature. Olive skin, legs up to her neck and dressed in this white miniskirt. She had the highest cheekbones, the most perfect face and magnificent hair. She had light brown hair and piercing green eyes. My heart almost gave out. Deirdre had organised a blind date for us. We went to a party in nearby Cammeray then we went smooching down at Balmoral – nothing more because we were both shy. We've never stopped going out since that night. Lea was 15 but she looked 18. In fact she looked and acted older than me. She was 15 going on 19. I was 19 going on 14. And so entered the third woman in my life. Up until this point the two other women had been Mum and Our Lady.

From the moment we met I recognised a deep

strength of character about Lea and knew that if you were in need of good, sound advice from a wise and gentle soul, then Lea's your girl. That inner strength gives her the full confidence and honesty to speak her mind without giving a hoot about what people might think. Sometimes that sledgehammer directness has landed her in hot water; most times we applaud it. Unlike me, she actually thinks before she speaks. And more times than not it is with the infuriating wisdom of bloody Solomon! Right from those early teenage years together I noticed she was someone that people actively sought out for sound advice – and they have never stopped. Another of Lea's great strengths is that she always immediately looks for the best in people. Even if someone rankles her she'll still find far more good in them than the one downside. She's Irish loyal and never reveals a secret she's been asked to keep. Regularly over the past 30 years we've been together I've breathlessly run to Lea to tell her some hot gossip only to learn that she has known for weeks but was asked not to say anything. I had grown up with a mother who was a powerful influence and I think I needed to meet someone like Lea who was just as strong.

Our relationship grew up and deepened on glorious Sunday summer afternoons around the pool at Lea's family home. Her parents always put on great bar-becues, generously feeding not only me but also Mark, Terry and Geoff whenever they were around. Lea had a lot of friends on the upper north shore of Sydney while all mine were on the lower north shore, so our social life was pretty full on. Balmoral beach figured largely in our lives, whether it was an illegal fire on the sand late at night or a day at the slippery rock.

I certainly didn't hit it off well with Lea's father, though. Lea introduced me to him shortly after we met. He's a naturally quiet man, but he didn't talk to me very much at all at first. He made me conduct all the conversation. However, I'm about to enter this stage myself with my own daughter who's now 18, and if a brash 19-year-old first-year cadet journalist walked into my home saying he wanted to go out with my daughter, promising that one day he was going to become a journalist and work in New York, I'd be thinking: 'Good, could you leave tomorrow, but not with my daughter?' But regardless, Lea and I just fell for each other.

During the second year of my cadetship I was finally allowed out of the office with a photographer and a senior cadet who supervised me. We would go down to Australia Square, then the tallest building in the nation, to interview young people about the issues of the day. I'd ask people their names, ages, what they did for a living and what they thought of a particular issue. There were a lot of industrial disputes in those days so I might ask them about a beer strike, or a petrol strike. Then the photographer would take their photos, which would appear in a column called 'Under 25s' with their names, ages, occupations and quotes on the issue.

Every Thursday afternoon at 4.30 I went to lectures with about 15 other cadets from all the News Limited papers. We would be taught about Australia's defamation laws and what we could and couldn't say when reporting court cases. We learned that we could only report exactly what was said in court, no more than that. Yes we could report on the dress or actions of the accused, but could never give our own opinion or talk to anyone at the court involved directly in the case. It was an excellent foundation for accurate reporting, and we also became sort of bush lawyers. We knew our way very well around the court system – from the Coroners Court to the Court of Petty Sessions to the Supreme Court, the District Court, the Federal Court, and up to the High Court. Court reporting was a good introduction to getting great or really offbeat stories. Many years later *60 Minutes* reporter Peter Overton would remind me of the time when, as a school student on work experience, he came to Redfern Court with me while I covered an animal cruelty story. A man had been charged with biting the head off a budgie!

I was given the daily Coroners Court round – it was mine, and mine alone. Straight away I threw myself into an important aspect of journalism called 'making contacts'. In order to know about the good stories I had to ingratiate myself to the police prosecutors, the clerks of the court, the secretaries who typed up the depositions, and of course the coroners. Kevin Waller, the famous Chief Coronial Magistrate for New South Wales, became a very good friend. He was a well-respected, genuinely caring, concerned man. Between all these different people I would be tipped off about stories. 'Come into court two and keep an eye out 'cause there's a really unusual manslaughter in there today.'

In the Coroners Court the magistrate could decide whether or not a person who had been charged over someone's death could be sent to trial. The court also heard suicides. It may have been a depressing round but for a young, sparkle-eyed cadet journalist it was manna from heaven.

All the gory details read out in the Coroners Court prepared me for the more gruesome side of journalism. And the graphic photographs taken by police forensics at death scenes were always made available to the media to look over. I've never been squeamish so many of these details never bothered me. What did upset me was covering the deaths of children, whether accidental or deliberate. Two of the very early stories I covered at the court involved the tragic deaths of two little girls. The first was only 12 months old when she died. She had climbed out of her cot and onto a fifth-floor window ledge. Her poor mother came back into the room to find the little girl gone. When she looked out the window she discovered her daughter on the ground below, dying from shocking head injuries. Not long after that a coronial inquest was held into the freakish death of a six-year-old girl who had been out fishing on Botany Bay with her father, grandfather and two brothers. She fell overboard and her dad immediately turned the boat around, stopped about seven metres from his daughter, threw her a lifebuoy, dived in and swam to her.

'She had her arms tight around my neck,' the distraught father told the magistrate, Kevin Waller. 'When the boat was put in reverse to pick us up it just kept coming. I grabbed hold of it but was dragged under and lost hold of my daughter. When I came up she was mortally wounded.'

The little girl's grandfather, who had control of the boat's tiller and engine, said he did everything to stop the boat but couldn't.

Later that year I covered another interesting story, which involved the death of a patient who was discharged from a large Sydney hospital. The problem was she was discharged with a fractured skull. The 53-year-old woman was readmitted two days later but soon died from her head injuries and eventual brain damage.

Those early days at court also introduced me to a number of lawyers, one of whom happened to be John Marsden, who in recent years successfully sued Channel Seven over accusations made by two of the network's current affairs programs. At that stage I was driving a purple-and-black EH Holden I had purchased for $200. Over the next few years this bomb would cost me more like $4,000 or $5,000 in repairs. It turned me off cars for life. I'm not a car person – never have been, never will be – and it's largely due to that purple-and-black 1964 heap. I went through an orange light at the corner of Awaba Street and Spit Road just above Balmoral beach. I was going to lose my licence because

I was on my P plates. I didn't know what to do. The only solicitor I really knew was this helpful man called John Marsden who had tipped me off about a number of stories in the Coroners Court and who I got on quite well with. He was a good contact.

I said to him: 'What do you suggest I do here? I'm going to lose my licence.'

'I'll look after you, no worries. I'll defend you,' said Marsden.

'How much will that cost?'

'Look, don't worry, you don't have to fix me up.'

'No no, I'm happy to pay.'

'Don't worry about it, I'll just do it as a favour.'

And I thought: that's really good of him. We went to court and he won the case. I kept my licence and I was very grateful. But over the next three months I was constantly called by Marsden suggesting that we go to lunch, that I come out to his practice at Campbelltown and perhaps have dinner with him. It was so relentless. I thought: this is the last time I ask anyone for a favour. In that sense it was a very good lesson for a young journalist. It reminded me of author and former journalist Robert Ruark's advice to budding journos: 'Don't take no gifts from nobody.' This episode would become a great lesson in future years for me because it taught me to never ask for or to expect favours from *anyone* for *any* reason.

I was at the Coroners Court for about 12 months then I moved on to the Sydney airport round. My job was to cover any stories about airport security, construction and the airlines, and to interview celebrities, politicians and other newsworthy people coming and going through the airport. I had to arrive at the media room at the airport every morning at 6.30. I worked in a little cubicle, with journos from ABC TV and radio, *The Sun*, the *Sydney Morning Herald* and the *Daily Telegraph* newspapers, radio station 2UE, and Channels Nine and Seven in nearby cubicles. I was this callow, know-nothing, pimply-faced 19-year-old and I was up against two guys called Greg Newell and Ton Linson, both very professional and senior newsmen from *The Sun* newspaper, Sydney's other afternoon tabloid and our fierce competitor.

At the airport I again set about making contacts – with airline staff, federal police, customs and quarantine, even the tellers at the bank opposite the media room. Interesting times, and interesting people coming through: Diana Ross, Imelda Marcos, Bill Cosby, David Frost, Frank Sinatra and the Jackson Five, with their cute brother Michael Jackson who had a hit song at the time called 'Ben', about his pet rat. Nice kid and a nice family. Michael was only a teenager at the time. I remember looking at him and thinking what a handsome young boy he was – far more handsome than his brothers. Ironic, when you think what he did to his face all those years later. I also ran into the Hollywood actor Lee Marvin. My contact at the bank came in and gave me a quiet tip that he had just arrived and had cashed some money on his way to Cairns for marlin fishing.

This was my first taste of celebrities. At first I was

in awe of some of the bigger names but I eventually took it all in my stride, preferring to concentrate on researching the stars and preparing for my interviews rather than being goggled-eyed and monosyllabic. Once the interview was over I'd race back to my little cubicle to write up the story then read it over the phone to a copy taker who in turn sent it to a sub-editor who put the story in the next edition. Up until this point I had been writing my stories out in longhand before sending them through but when I started on the airport round I began trying to send each story through off the top of my head. After perhaps writing out the first two or three paragraphs I would ad lib the rest of the story, dictating it to the copy taker straight from my notes. This practice would become invaluable later on when I began reporting the bigger daily stories because those stories had to be filed very quickly for fear of being scooped by *The Sun*.

There was an advantage to working the airport round: Mum loved to hear about who had arrived that day. Sometimes we knew ahead who was coming in and I could tell her the night before. She could often fill in holes in my research thanks to her incredible knowledge of movie stars. Then the next night, after the interview, she'd be eagerly waiting to see how it went. She loved to hear how they reacted, what they were dressed in, how they looked after a 20-hour flight. But of course sometimes if she was drunk when I got home she wouldn't remember who I had been talking to in the airport media lounge.

Mum was a skeletal figure now, unkempt, scarred and limping from her many falls while she was drunk. Vera had never given up searching for her 'surrogate daughter' – over the years she had approached my Uncle Leo, but he had kept his promise never to tell anyone where Mum and I had gone. Then one day someone told her we were living in a tiny flat at the back of a real estate agency on Spit Road at Mosman.

'Someone mentioned it faced a seedy back laneway so I started looking,' said Vera. 'It took me a full day of asking people and following false leads until I finally located this miserable run-down dump with its outside toilet and bathroom. I knocked on the door and this person with matted hair answered it and I said: "Beryl?"'

'You're mistaken and have the wrong person,' Mum said immediately, still fiercely proud but also embarrassed about her condition.

Vera persevered: 'I said "No, I'm not mistaken Beryl, talk to me please." But she went to close the door in my face. I put my foot against the door so she couldn't close it on me, saying "Beryl, please let me come in, it's Vera."'

But Mum was determined and said: 'I think you have the wrong person.'

'No I don't,' Vera said. 'Please let me come in.'

Mum finally relented and let Vera in. They sat down together after almost 20 years to talk, but, of course, things had irreversibly changed between them. Mum was a shadow of her former self. Her mind had been drastically affected by so many years of alcohol abuse and her concentration and memory were shot to pieces.

'After she finally let me in she made an excuse to go and comb her hair but when she came back I could smell she had been drinking and the full realisation of her predicament hit me. I knew then I was years too late to help her,' Vera said as she started to break down crying. 'If only I could have got to her earlier I know I could have got her off the alcohol.'

It was hard for Vera to see my mother this way, when during their early years Mum had hated grog and only drank soft drink or soda water. I popped in on my way home from work the day Vera found Mum. She hadn't seen me since I was four but from that moment Vera and I became firm mates again.

'I'll never forget after you arrived,' Vera told me years later. 'Your mother again disappeared into her bedroom for another drink and when she came back out this time it was obvious she was now drunk. I remember you picked her up like a baby and took her to her bed and then drove me home.'

Vera did everything she could for Mum for the remaining years of her life but despite us both never giving up trying to get her sober it was no use.

There were some heady days at the airport and it's where I really started to get noticed by editors. I was on the airport round for about 12 months and during that time I was made a D-grade journalist. And again just floated. It was one thing getting the cadetship; the next great step was being made a D-grade journalist. Even if I was fired I was a fully fledged journalist now and no one could ever take that away from me. What's more, I hadn't even completed my full three years as a cadet. I had finished my cadetship in two years and four months – eight months earlier than most. And that was despite not having the required 120 words a minute in shorthand.

I hated shorthand, absolutely hated it, because it took me away from stories and was too much like school. Funny story. I was so bad at shorthand that I had to cheat to get to even 80 words a minute, which was the requirement to become a second-year cadet. The teacher was to dictate a passage to me that I had to write down in shorthand at 80 words a minute, and then translate it back into longhand. I discovered that at home I had the same book our teacher was dictating these passages from, so I arranged for one of my mates to call me at precisely the time the teacher would have finished dictating to me during the test.

On cue, the call came from editorial saying: 'Munro needs to come up here urgently, he's wanted for a story.'

The teacher said: 'Okay, you can finish at home tonight and bring it back to me tomorrow.'

No worries! I went home that night, found the passage and wrote it out – but not without the maximum of five mistakes. I was so bad at shorthand that if I'd come in with any less than the five mistakes allowed by our teacher she would never have believed that I had done it without cheating. Anyway, she passed me, which had enabled me to move into the second year of my cadetship with a modest pay rise. However you needed to be able to do 120 words a minute to become a third-year cadet, and I was never going to get to 120 words a minute. And you were meant to serve out 12 months as a third-year cadet before you could become a D-grade journalist. I was convinced I'd never get my D grading because of shorthand. But because I was out there suggesting ideas, madly writing stories, and even occasionally coming up with a front-page story, I had made myself well known around the editorial floors, so they gave me my D grading.

I was now a journalist. It was just unbelievable.

5

From the airport round I was put on the 3.00pm round. So now I found myself as a journalist in my own car with a photographer and a driver, and the copy boys in the radio room were feeding *me* information. Fantastic.

The 3.00pm round was certainly a hard news round but it was also one where you were supposed to go to a lot of cocktail parties and social stuff like that, which didn't interest me in the least. I tried to avoid the freebie drinks, movie and theatre premieres in favour of sniffing out news stories. I was able to scoop our opposition, *The Sun*, many times while their reporters were still enjoying the social round. More and more of my stories were appearing on the front page under the by-line 'Michael Munro' and our opposition 3.00pm realised that they too would have to chase the harder news stories like murders, robberies and car accidents, rather than the softer social round.

One of the most chilling stories I covered was about a family of new immigrants who had hired a small tinny to take out on the Hawkesbury River from a popular Sydney picnic spot called Bobbin Head. The boat had overturned with a five-year-old boy, his father and mother aboard. None of them could swim and the mother drowned. The father told police that he was so consumed by trying to rescue his son that by the time he started looking for his wife she had disappeared. I was the first newsman on the scene and was able to speak with the distraught man before he left with the police. There was really only time for him to give me his address and to promise to talk to me at length later that night. After he had given his statement to the police he returned to his home to join relatives in a communal mourning for his dead wife. The photographer and I arrived at his home at around 8.00 that night to interview and photograph him as he had agreed we could. I knew time was against us because the police had released the family's name and other reporters would soon be knocking on the door. Not only was there competition from *The Sun* but also the *Daily Telegraph*. The *Telegraph*, which Rupert Murdoch had only recently purchased from the Packer family, was a morning paper so it could easily beat us, an afternoon paper, to many stories.

The grieving father mentioned that he had had to leave his car at Bobbin Head after the accident and that the police had driven him and his son home. Seeing the perfect chance to offer help and to keep him well away from all the converging media, we drove him the hour-plus from his western suburbs home to Bobbin Head to pick up his car. All the way there he kept telling us how much he loved his wife, how he didn't know what he would do without her, and continually blamed himself for her death. Naturally the photographer and I tried to console him. Suddenly, over the radio in our car I heard the *Daily Telegraph* reporter, Norm Lipson, calling me, wanting to know where I was. I could hear him telling his boss over the same frequency that I had left with the widower in the *Daily Mirror*'s car to a destination unknown. They desperately wanted an interview with the man because their deadline was approaching. I had no intention of either answering him or letting anyone know where we were headed over the radio.

'Come on, Munro,' Norm screamed down the radio. 'I know you can hear me. Where the hell are you?'

Silence from me. In the end all the stalling worked and we had a great front-page story complete with photographs for the next day's afternoon edition. When the father had got home that night he had gone straight to bed and had seen no one.

But that wasn't the end of the story, far from it. Two days later the police charged the father with the murder of his wife. He had planned the whole drowning incident in a bid to collect on her life insurance. I then wrote another story about how well he had acted out his whole charade and how we had driven around with a murderer all night!

* * *

Without a doubt one of the most exciting periods while covering the 3.00pm to midnight shift was in July 1974 when one of the biggest names in the world, Frank Sinatra, arrived in Australia for a series of concerts in Melbourne and Sydney.

Growing up I was certainly no stranger to Sinatra because my mother adored him. I remember travelling on a tram at a young age to The Stadium in Sydney's Rushcutters Bay to see him perform on his first visit to Australia in the late 50s. My whole childhood I'd listened to the great crooner as Mum played all his classics. The little spare money Mum ever had sometimes went towards buying Sinatra's latest LP and later I'd buy her a Sinatra album for her birthday or Christmas. It was nothing unusual to come home from school, or later from work, to find Mum sitting down crying, drunk, listening to Sinatra belt out 'Fly Me to the Moon' or 'Night and Day'. Sinatra constantly reminded her of those wonderful and carefree days she'd spent with my father before everything soured. 'You'd never understand how I feel,' she'd always say as she wiped away the tears. There was never any movie in which Sinatra starred that we didn't watch on television. So it was only natural that I bought two tickets for Mum and I to attend one of his concerts.

With his arrival in 1974 the *Daily Mirror* pulled out all stops to have every possible angle covered. The great column writer, author and hellraiser, Jim Oram, was sent to Melbourne for Sinatra's first of two scheduled concerts. After being followed everywhere by reporters since his arrival in Australia, Sinatra was furious and let loose his legendary vitriolic tongue during his first Melbourne concert in front of 7,000 people. 'Gotta run all day long because of the parasites who chased us with automobiles . . . I say they're bums and they're always going to be bums,' Sinatra told his fans. But he then went further, a lot further. 'They're pimps, they're just crazy and the hookers, the broads who work for the press. Need I explain this to you? I might offer them a buck and a half, I'm not sure,' he told the Melbourne audience.

After this last comment where he insulted the media generally, and women reporters in particular, unions black-banned him. Sinatra was virtually held hostage when the ACTU and the powerful Transport Workers' Union refused to refuel his two luxury jets. Infuriated, Sinatra immediately cancelled his second Melbourme concert and fled to Sydney. According to Jim Oram's coverage, Sinatra left the then president of the ACTU, Bob Hawke, who had arrived minutes earlier to negotiate an apology or at least some compromise, at Melbourne's Tullamarine airport. 'There go my two tickets for tonight,' Hawke told Oram.

Sinatra's snub immediately became front page news around the world as he flew into Sydney airport and my 3.00pm round. At the time our news editor was Peter Brennan, now a successful television producer in America. Brennan was just as excited about the unfolding scandal as we all were and set up office at the seedy Au Revoir Bar at Sydney's international airport. I was in our rounds car with photographer, Frank Violi, and driver, Freddy Finch, and got the call from Brennan to drop everything and head out to the airport. None of us knew whether Sinatra would fly out of Australia on a commercial flight that night, wait until the next day to leave or stay and perform his three Sydney concerts. But there was no way he could fly out in either of his two jets because of the ban on refuelling them.

He and his entourage of about 20 arrived in Sydney a few minutes after the second Melbourne concert had been scheduled to start and high-tailed it to the Boulevard Hotel near Kings Cross in a fleet of nine limousines. His pilots were told to taxi their planes to parking bays near the Qantas cargo warehouse between the international and domestic terminals. So I thought I'd check out the planes.

Wearing our driver's large overcoat to hide the stills camera, Violi and I brazenly walked through the busy warehouse waving to various workers as if we were long-term employees ourselves. No one stopped us as we emerged onto the tarmac and found ourselves staring at the two luxury jets sitting 75 metres away. As we walked towards the nearest plane, we heard a low whistle from behind an airport vehicle. It was Neil Duncan, a photographer from *The Australian*, who had set up camp on the tarmac hoping to catch Sinatra when and if he returned. 'What are you two blokes doing?' he asked. 'We're gonna take a look at Frankie's plane,' I told him.

'Be careful,' he said, 'because there's security every-where.'

Violi followed me up the stairs into the plane which had its interior lights dimmed. Getting a photo was the first priority so I stood back behind Violi as he snapped off several pictures. I then left him near the entrance to keep a lookout while I took myself on a tour of this flying penthouse. The plane reeked of expensive perfume and cigarettes. Unwashed Scotch glasses and half-filled ashtrays still sat on several tables. The seats were covered in red suede in contrast to the black silk curtains over the windows. There was a marble bar and a giant double bed in the bedroom at the rear of the plane. The bathroom not only had both a shower and bath but a sauna as well. Just as I was furiously making notes, I heard Violi say there was a security guard heading towards the plane. We decided to wait right until he was at the foot of the steps before we emerged and started down the stairway. I recognised his uniform as being part of airport security and as we squeezed past each other on the stairs I put on my very best American accent and said, 'Mr Sinatra's private security.' He nodded saying, 'No worries mate.'

Resisting the temptation to bolt across the tarmac we calmly walked off until we heard him shout after us to stop where we were. No one needed to tell either of us that this was the moment to run for our lives. We shot through the warehouse to find our driver waiting with the motor running. We both literally dived into the backseat on top of each other as the driver sped off.

We went straight to report in to Peter Brennan who was still directing various reporters from the Au Revoir bar. Ecstatic over our 'exclusive', he gave us a pat on the back then told me to head to the office to write up the story for the first edition the next morning.

Over the next couple of days I worked 18-hour days camped outside Cranky Frankie's hotel covering negotiations between him and the nations' unions. While he refused to apologise for calling some women reporters prostitutes he did allow his final Sydney concert to be televised nationally to make it up to the Victorians he had cancelled on in Melbourne. It was this concert which I took Mum to. She was so excited about it that she went along stone cold sober. We had great seats so you can imagine our surprise when three or four songs into the performance he launched into a tirade about the 'idiots who sneaked onto my plane here in Sydney'. I was less than 40 metres from him and felt like jumping up and screaming out, 'That was me, it was me!' Of course, Mum completely sided with her idol, glaring at me as if Sinatra had insulted her personally. 'How could you do that? You're a disgrace!' she leaned over and said to me as Sinatra launched into another love ballad.

After finishing my 3.00pm to midnight shift, I was followed by Col Allan, who did the midnight to dawn round. Col had been working for the *Dubbo Liberal*, and had been sent to Cobar to cover a miners strike. John Hartigan, one of the paper's senior journalists, was there representing the *Daily Mirror* and was very impressed with Col. He enticed him to leave Dubbo and come to Sydney to work for the *Mirror*. Col came down and went on to the midnight round and we not only became extremely competitive but the best of mates. Many, many funny nights. We were always getting into blues and trying to protect each other. Neither of us could fight for nuts. In fact Col's nickname was 'canvas back' because his back always ended up on the canvas. Most of the time he'd start the fight – he'd be the first to admit it. He'd start a fight and then get his head punched in and I'd try to step in and end up the same.

In those days I was just starting to drink at the local pubs all the other journos frequented – the Invicta, the Evening Star or the Aurora – but I was quite wary because I saw every day what alcohol could do to you. I was scared to death that I too could become an alcoholic like Mum. And Col understood this having met Mum and stayed with us. He, like my boyhood friends, had been verbally abused by Mum when she'd had a few drinks. She was a complete Jekyll-and-Hyde character. Charming and hospitable as ever before a drink – vicious and insulting after.

This was a great period for Col and me. We looked up to the likes of John Hartigan and Mark Day who became our news editors and then editors. They realised they had two absolutely dedicated and driven young reporters. Our nickname became 'The Blue Heelers'. The 'Colin Allan' and 'Michael Munro' by-lines became daily events. We ran embarrassing rings around *The Sun* newspaper, of which Derryn Hinch was at one stage the editor. We nearly always had the story first, had the best pictures, and were rarely scooped.

After that year Col and I graduated to what were called the 'rounds cars'. There were two rounds cars – the senior daily reporter left in one at 5.00am; the number two reporter left in the other at 6.00am. Both went out with a driver and a photographer to be on call for any stories that broke around the city. Col's career now started to slightly pull away from mine. He proved he was certainly brighter, and definitely a cagier and more intelligent journo than I was. And I think a better writer. Much to my disappointment Col was put on the 5.00am senior car that chased the biggest local story of the day. I was in the second car but still had to spend time in the office whereas Col was always on the road, ready to move quickly.

We would often meet up with each other at our favourite watering hole, the Dunbar Hotel at Paddington. We could still have a beer on the footpath while listening to the car radio. It was relatively close to the office, so if a story broke in the eastern suburbs we were close by, if we needed to get to the north side it wasn't far from the Harbour Bridge, and we could quickly get out to the southern suburbs. The only difficulty was the western suburbs, but there was another office out at Parramatta anyway. The news editor knew that 'not too far away' meant we were at the Dunbar.

In fact, the news editor didn't always know exactly where we were. Sometimes we got caught out. One morning I told John Hartigan, who was the news editor at the time, that I was having breakfast with the driver and photographer in North Sydney but we were really in the city, on the southern side of the Harbour Bridge. An urgent job came up on the north side and Hartigan thought we were only 100 metres away and could get there very quickly. We got stuck in bumper-to-bumper traffic crossing the bridge.

'Where's Munro?' Harto asked.

I got the driver to answer the radio: 'Oh he's out of the car, he's just running ahead. There's been a bad accident, and we're stuck in very bad traffic. He's coming back to the car shortly but he's run up ahead to see what the problem is.'

And of course I hadn't even left the car. There were myriad stories straight out of Neil Simon's play *The Front Page*.

The John Hartigans and Mark Days of the world realised that they could not only pit Col Allan and me against *The Sun* but they could also pit us against each other. In those days the radio network covered not only the editorial cars for our paper but all the other newspapers as well, plus all the newspaper delivery trucks and the circulation department. Every-one heard every word spoken over the News Limited radio.

Harto might get on the radio and say: 'How you doing Munro, how you going at that story?'

'Not too good, they still won't talk. We're still wait-ing. We're still trying to get the picture.'

'Yes, right oh, well hang in there,' he'd say and then he'd call Col. 'How you going mate?'

'We're on our way back with the picture. We got the story. We got everything.'

And then Harto might say: 'Yes, yes, we knew we could depend on you Col Allan, better than that other bloke. Munro's still sitting on his fat bum getting nowhere.'

And of course I'd be bristling hearing this, knowing that every one on the radio network was hearing it too. The next day though it might have been my turn. I might have been returning with the story and the picture while Col was stalled waiting for his story to unfold. Mark Day might get on the radio and say: 'Good on you. We knew we could depend on you. Col Allan still has nothing.'

In many respects we should easily have become complete enemies, but I think we both knew that we helped each other. We rented together at one point in Mosman for a couple of years and I am godfather to Col and his wife Sharon's firstborn son. His name is Michael John Allan, named after myself and Harto. Col is today regarded as one of the most successful editor-in-chiefs ever of the *Daily Telegraph* and *Sunday Telegraph*. He was editor-in-chief for several years, making his mark with giant three- or four-word head-lines and popular public campaigns that always seemed to hit the mark. He was the most successful and contro-versial editor Sydney had seen for 30 or 40 years and is now posted in New York as editor-in-chief of Rupert

Murdoch's *New York Post*. He and his family moved there only there a few weeks before the disastrous World Trade Center terrorist attacks in 2001.

As soon as I started working in the rounds car, photographers became an integral part of my learning process. Most of the 'togs' were a few years older and more experienced than the new reporters. They helped teach us that mysterious but all-important ingredient called 'news sense' – recognising and knowing what a good story is and what isn't – and gave advice on how to deal with people in different situations. Some of the much older ones even showed us how to drink warm cans of beer at 7.00 in the morning. One of the most experienced photographers and newsmen I ever had the fortune of working with in newspapers was Graeme Fletcher, who's now in charge of all the News Limited photographers around Australia. He and I worked together for a number of years – eating, sleeping, drinking and reporting out of the rounds car.

One of our favourite places to go during the day while we waited for a story to break was the beautiful Mrs Macquarie's Chair near Sydney's botanical gardens, overlooking the Harbour Bridge and the Opera House. Having been up since 4.30am and perhaps having already completed and written a story for the first edition by 8.00am we'd often park at Mrs Macquarie's Chair and have an hour's snooze in the car if everything was quiet. One September day Graeme, the driver and I were blissfully sleeping in the car when we received a call over the radio that there had been a mass breakout of prisoners from the cells at the District Court on Oxford Street in Darlinghurst. Ten prisoners awaiting trial, most of them murderers and armed robbers, had busted out of the cells and made it to Oxford Street where they had spread out and disappeared. We were literally two minutes away. When we arrived on the scene the whole area had been cordoned off and there were dozens of police, people from the courts and passers-by running everywhere. It was absolute mayhem in the heart of Sydney.

'There's one hiding under the building here,' a cop screamed wanting back-up.

'Two over here in an old tool shed, quickly,' another yelled out.

Graeme and I immediately started our own search, while still keeping an eye out for any prisoners recaptured by police because that was obviously *the* picture to get for the next edition. At one point a policeman screamed out that there were three prisoners hiding in the grounds of St Vincent's Hospice. The gates were locked so I climbed over this high metal gate. Never one to be flustered, Graeme snapped off a photo just as a cop and I went over the top of the gate. It's a fantastic picture and remains one of my favourite professional photos of all time. The entire court complex was closed and trials postponed during the manhunt. The police flooded the area and rounded up most of the crims within a few hours but a couple of them remained on the loose for a week or so before being recaptured.

But exciting stories like that were mixed with the

dreaded 'death knocks' – going at 6.30 or 7.00 in the morning to knock on the door of someone who'd lost their loved one, knowing that they hadn't slept all night, knowing that you wouldn't have slept all night if you'd lost someone. None of us liked having to do these – but they're still done, they still have to be done, and someone has to do them. Usually a reporter from the opposition newspaper was there too and if you didn't go in they would. If they went in and got the picture and the interview and you didn't you were in big trouble.

In later years, if no one from the other newspapers turned up often I would pretend that I had knocked on the door but there had been no answer, or the family had refused to speak to us. We were required to try knocking not just once but two or three times.

The news editor would say: 'How many times have you been in now?'

'Oh, twice.'

'All right, just go in one more time.'

Well, we were actually parked just around the corner. I hadn't knocked once. I just couldn't bring myself to do it any more. It was too hard and too depressing and I'd done it for too long. But if our opposition was also at the home of the grieving family neither of us really had any choice but to knock on their door.

I was starting at 6.00 each morning. In winter I woke freezing because of the holes and cracks in my bedroom – and then I had to brave the outside bathroom. But when I got into the car and left for work it was glorious, just on dawn. I remember with great fondness driving across the Harbour Bridge knowing I was on my way to work and somewhere I really wanted to be. I was able to finish at around 3.00 in the afternoon, just in time to rush back across the bridge to pick Lea up from school at Loreto Kirribilli and drive her home. The nuns would see her being picked up in this purple-and-black EH Holden by that drunk's kid. I always stood out like a you-know-what and they would ring Lea's mum, Lois, and say: 'Oh, just letting you know that that boy in the purple-and-black car has picked your daughter up again.'

Lois would reply: 'Yes, thank you Sister, I'm aware of that and I'm sure he'll bring her straight home,' which I always did of course. When you look back, the nuns' concern is quite ironic really. Outside that very same school gate 20 years later we'd pick up and drop off our own beautiful daughter, Amy.

During the Christmas holidays Lea would go to Queensland to holiday with her family. I managed to convince first Geoff, and then a year later Terry, to drive there with me to see her – there's no way my car would ever have made it. On one occasion we arrived at 3.00 in the morning. Lea's mum and dad were not impressed, and who'd blame them. But I came bearing gifts, mainly for Lea, who was now 17. I had already told her I'd bought two presents I knew she'd just love. I brought one of them to Queensland, saving the better one for when Lea returned home. When I gave her the first treasure – a Juicy Lucy electric orange squeezer –

she never let on in any way just how disappointed she was. Years later she told me that she had seriously wondered what sort of a mummy's boy dag would give a 17-year-old girl an orange squeezer. Together we reasoned that I must have been desperate to latch on to any form of domesticity and stability.

But back in Sydney I had an even better gift up my sleeve. It was gloriously wrapped in a fashionable tea towel in the shape and colour of a $20 note. This *pièce de résistance* was no less than an electric can-opener. The moment Lea saw this second Christmas present she knew she was going out with someone very strange indeed.

By this time we had been going out for two years and Lea was certainly aware of Mum's alcoholism and the difficulties at home. In fact poor Lea was verbally abused by Mum most times she came to our tiny flat. It was a credit to her strength of character that she withstood such a barrage of insults for so many years. One moment she'd be at home with her loving parents, sisters and brother; the next she'd walk into my nightmare, and what's more, cope with it. Her relationship with Mum was strained because most of the time Mum had been drinking. Then, during the times Mum was sober, they didn't really know each other well enough to converse.

Lea would come to dinner at Mum's, but basically just to please me. Then, having agreed to come over for dinner she was often confronted with being called anything from a 'slut' to a 'whore' to a 'bitch'. Of course the next day it would all be forgotten by Mum. While

Lea naturally found it harder to forget, she was able to withstand the onslaught of abuse she faced. She rarely ever criticised Mum to me, choosing instead a dignified silence. I think the way Lea handled my situation at home drew me even closer to her. My respect and admiration for her grew more and more every day.

To Mum, it wouldn't have mattered if I was going out with one of her Hollywood idols, like Vivien Leigh; no one would have been good enough. She was the classic clinging mother, and took it all out on Lea. And of course the more serious and prolonged my relationship with Lea became, the more vindictive Mum became.

Being as Irish as she is, Lea's never taken too many steps backwards, and when she was 17 we had a raging argument brought about in part by my mother's drinking. We were having dinner at Mum's place and Kim, Lea's older sister who would eventually marry my childhood mate Terry, had joined us. We were having takeaway Chinese and the four of us were going to squeeze around the kitchen table which was only meant for two. We guessed that Mum had already had one or two drinks. Lea was extremely disappointed that once again she couldn't stay sober, particularly with her sister visiting, and I wrongly accused Lea of calling Mum a 'bitch'. Mum and Kim were in the next room watching television when our argument erupted but as soon as they heard the ruckus they moved into the kitchen. Lea told me she had used no such word but I was convinced she had. Neither of us would give an inch – and then she dumped a whole container of chicken and almonds over my head. All the four of us could do was laugh as the dish slowly slid down my hair, face and ears. I think Mum even slightly warmed to Lea after that.

Lea's parents had bought a couple of units by the beach on the Gold Coast and decided to move there and go into semi-retirement. Their four children stayed in Sydney, Lea deciding to train to be a nurse at the Mater Hospital at North Sydney. I must admit, from where I stood, having no real family, I couldn't under-stand why her parents were leaving. When I heard that they were moving, in my naivety I bought Lea a sheep-dog puppy, which she named Q. I had wanted to give her something very special apart from a Juicy Lucy and an electric can-opener, and I thought it would be good if she had something to care for and call her own after her parents had left for Queensland. I also thought that if she had the responsibility of looking after Q she would stick to her nursing to ensure her upkeep. Well, her parents, particularly her father, were furious because it meant that she would no longer be able to stay in the safety of the nurses' quarters. She would have to rent a house. Her father was ropeable and he and I had a major argument at their farewell, which took us years to recover from.

Up until this point I'd done everything I could to remain at home with Mum despite hating it. But now I realised I had to make a break and began spending more and more time with Lea, who had moved into a house in Beauty Point with her brother Jon, and Deirdre and Wendy Macken. These were wonderful days in a great house and we had some unforgettable parties!

Meanwhile, I was desperately trying to get Mum to go to Alcoholics Anonymous and was spending a lot of my wage making sure she was in the top private health cover so that I could always afford to send her to a good hospital to dry out. I felt sure that between me and Our Lady one day we would get her sober. There were a number of clinics in Sydney, most of which included four or five AA meetings per week in their treatment program. But of course when you're in complete denial you tell yourself that 'these places are not for me', as Mum always told me. I would ask her how she could not be an alcoholic when she was drunk most of the time and always hid her grog as if she was ashamed of it, which deep down she was of course.

'I'm just lonely,' she'd say. 'What sort of life do I have? You're never here any more now that you're spending all your time with that Lea. The rare drink I have is my only comfort.'

Very occasionally she admitted that she may have had a drinking problem – and when she did I would stay on the offensive and try to persuade her that her life could be very different if she just tried to get sober and attended AA meetings on a regular basis. For a long time during my teens I had attended Alateen. Those group meetings for the children of alcoholics had helped me come to terms with what I was up against and had given me a chance to talk to other kids who were going through exactly what I was going through. At the meetings I had also learnt how to handle Mum and talk to her about her alcoholism.

The first time I had booked Mum in to dry out I was only 17 or 18. I had been to see a psychiatrist about Mum and even discussed the prospect of committing her temporarily to an institution to force her to dry out. The psychiatrist had explained that because I was under age I couldn't sign the relevant papers and would need a police officer who knew Mum and would be willing to stick his or her neck out to actually commit her. There was no one like that, but I did manage to convince her to 'have a holiday' at Allanbrook, a psychiatric clinic in Mosman that catered for alcoholics. It had beautiful gardens full of jacaranda trees, she would be near home, and I'd visit every day. I'd been pestering her for weeks to give it a go when she had a bad fall at home. She fell down the three steps at the front door, splitting her head open. She was admitted to hospital and from there I convinced her to go to Allanbrook.

She was to stay for two weeks, during which time she would attend at least four AA meetings a week. She only lasted a week before discharging herself, saying: 'I don't belong here with these people, I'm not like them. I only came to recover after my fall.'

When Mum came home that first time I was on a high believing that this could be it. She had dried out for the first time in almost 15 years. But she lasted only a few days before she was back on the booze.

Her next dry-out came a couple of years later, when

she had given herself another particularly bad battering with the grog – emotionally as well as physically. This time she flatly refused to go back to Allanbrook because it was too local. Since her stay at the clinic she had kept running into people she had met there, whether patients or visitors. I promised her she wouldn't have to go locally and suggested a clinic called Hydebrae, which was a magnificent old Federation mansion sitting on a couple of acres at Strathfield, about a 30-minute drive from our suburb. This stint would be for a month and she promised me faithfully that she would stay for the whole time. I'll never forget taking her there with her pathetic belongings. She wasn't able to look anyone in the eye; she was so embarrassed.

'I'm just here because I've been so run down lately,' was her excuse to anyone she met. Those who had been sober for some time had heard all the old explanations time and time again. She was shown to her room, only to discover that she had to share it with another woman, which horrified her. But the staff were gentle and understanding and made her feel as comfortable and wanted as possible.

As I left her we hugged and broke down crying in each other's arms.

'I'll try this time, I really will,' she whispered to me.

'You can do it Mum, you can,' I said. 'You have a wonderful life ahead of you, you just have to get sober.'

I'll never forget the look on her face when I left her. Alone, scared and with an almost impossible feat in front of her. I rang her every day and tried to visit at least every second day. I prayed so hard during this period and believed with all my heart that this could be it. Four weeks at Hydebrae meant at least 16 AA meetings – far more than the total number of meetings she had ever been to. If she could find herself a reliable and loyal sponsor; if she could really connect with one of the speakers at the AA meetings; if she could examine herself in the cold reality of sobriety. There were lots of ifs, but I was really positive and believed this was the time she might just make it. When I visited she appeared relatively happy. Although she always complained about being there she knew deep down that it was for the best. These were the times when I loved my mother most – when she laughed and offered sound advice. I had this overwhelming feeling that I was discovering my real mother, and all the joys associated with that.

She lasted the whole four weeks there. My hopes soared. When she was discharged she promised me and hospital staff that she would continue to regularly attend AA meetings around our area. I moved back to live with her full-time to keep an eye on her during this crucial period and took her to a couple of meetings that first week she was out. Eight days went by and still she was sober. 'I think we've made it,' I kept telling Lea and myself. On the ninth day I came home from work and found her flat on her back on the lounge room floor. She was so blind drunk she was almost unconscious. I was devastated.

Yet I continued to try and get her to go to AA meetings. On one occasion Mum had spent the day at Bernice's home at Seaforth so I knew that she'd be sober.

I went and picked her up from Bernice's, but instead of going home I drove her straight to an AA meeting at Mosman.

She was saying: 'I'm not going, I'm not going.'

'Well, if you're not willing to go, you're going to have to get out of the car at 60 kilometres an hour because I am not slowing down; I'm taking you straight to AA,' I said. She did threaten to jump out of the car at one stage.

When we arrived Mum sat there absolutely fuming, refusing to really believe she was an alcoholic, denying there was a reason why she should be there.

'I'm not like these people,' she'd say.

I, on the other hand, was absolutely inspired by these people. They were so brave to get up and introduce themselves and talk about these deep and personal issues. They revealed everything, almost performing character assassinations on themselves. I remember at one stage being so inspired that I almost wished I was an alcoholic so I could get up to speak to these unbelievably strong people. But not Mum. She would not admit she was an alcoholic, which of course was the first crucial step of the 12 steps to sobriety. She sat through the whole meeting genuinely believing she didn't belong there. At the end we stayed for tea and biscuits, but Mum was so sober she had the tremors and couldn't hold her cup of tea. And while she was shaking she still had the temerity to tell all these hard-core-sober alcoholics that she was not one of them. I had to walk away and cry. It absolutely broke my heart when she couldn't hold that cup of tea. She put it down and walked away in complete denial, still in complete denial. I took her home and no sooner did we get in than she went straight for the cupboard where her grog was hidden.

6

After the early morning rounds car I was given a shot at the political round by Mark Day who was now editor of the *Daily Mirror*. Mark, who had been a very good political correspondent for the *Adelaide News*, had taken me under his wing.

When I became the Mirror's chief political roundsman Tom Lewis was the New South Wales Premier and Neville 'Nifty' Wran was opposition leader. It was an open secret at parliament house and in the press gallery that Wran was separated from his wife but it would be big news when he went public. His office had promised me the exclusive story when he was ready to announce the split. His press secretary, Brian Dale, had told me: 'Don't worry, you will get it first.' But what they did was give it to me late on a Friday afternoon when the deadline had passed and the only place we could run the story was in the 'Stop Press', the last 'hole' on the back page of the paper, the place where the late-breaking news was printed and where not many readers bothered to look. The 'exclusive' amounted to just one paragraph on the back page.

Mark Day was absolutely furious that we'd been dudded. And he was even more furious when he learned that the *Daily Telegraph* would have the story on the front page the following morning.

Mark told me: 'You go back and tell Neville Wran that if he doesn't give us this exclusive story his relationship with this newspaper will greatly suffer.'

I couldn't have been any older than 23 and had to take this message back to such a powerful and successful politician.

He said: 'You go back and tell Mark Day to get f@#*&!.'

So then I went back to Mark Day and told him Neville Wran's reply, and he said: 'You go back to Neville Wran and you tell him this is his last opportunity, his last chance to come through with the goods.'

The pressure was just mind-boggling for a young journo. I felt like a ping-pong ball being whacked back and forth. In the end all we got was the lousy 'Stop Press' and it was on the front page of the *Daily Telegraph* the next morning. We had lost that round.

I never liked covering politics. It meant sucking up to too many politicians and public servants. There were far too many agendas, far too many policies, too many sheep, and to really get into it you had to drink, eat, walk and breathe that lifestyle. I was just not prepared to do that.

* * *

I pulled one of my more elaborate practical jokes during the *Daily Mirror*'s 'Lovely Mothers' Day Contest'. At that stage Mark Day was the editor of both the *Daily Mirror* and *The Australian*. To a young reporter, Mark was the most God-terrifying cyclone of a man you would ever want to get mad. I always did enjoy pushing the envelope, but I didn't know this joke would go on for about three weeks, or incur his wrath to such a degree.

I called Mark one day and, putting on my best feminine voice, told him I was an attractive and lovely mother who would make it 'worth his while' to let me win the Lovely Mothers' Day Contest. Exactly what form the payment would take was never discussed; it was just left hanging. I asked him to think about it and said I'd call back. During our second call Mark gave the 'woman' a dressing down for making such an inappropriate and unacceptable proposition. But as a good reporter he smelt something and suggested he meet me for coffee. I said I would get back to him.

I was based at parliament house then, so I had a mate back in the office watching Mark's every reaction after he'd spoken to the 'lovely mother'. He told me later that Mark had walked out of his office scratching his head and told the deputy editor, John Canning, the whole story.

'Oh, that'll be Munro for sure,' said Canning.

Either my reputation for being a poor mimic had given me away, or someone had dobbed me in. Anyway, now Mark knew it was me, and, thanks to my spy in the office, I knew Mark knew it was me. The real chase became all about him trying to catch me in the act. I sat right next to David O'Reilly from *The Australian* in the press office at parliament house and as a precaution, every time I rang Mark as the 'lovely mother' I took David's phone off the hook. I didn't want Mark to get someone to try and ring that number and catch me out with the phone ringing right next to me. And sure enough, the next couple of times I called Mark I was told he had people madly ringing the other phone – but they only received an engaged signal. Mark and I finally arranged to meet at the Aurora Hotel, one of our three local pubs.

What Mark didn't know was that I'd arranged with Wendy Macken, my old mate and surrogate sister, to actually play the lovely mother. She'd prepared a whole spiel. It didn't matter that while Wendy may have been lovely she was certainly no mother. On the big day Wendy was down at parliament house with me, ready to go. I rang Mark, putting on my sexiest voice. One problem. For the first time I had forgotten to take the other phone off the hook. After almost three weeks I had forgotten.

Anyway, I'm talking away to Mark, chatting him up: 'Yes I'll see you there. Looking forward to meeting you. Can't wait to see what you look like.'

Then suddenly the other phone rings. There's silence from both of us.

The next thing he says is: 'Munro, you're fired. Get back to the office right now.' And then he hangs up on me.

I still had this suicidal urge to salvage the joke, so I rang the news editor and said: 'Mark Day has just gone off his head at me and he's fired me. And on top of that I've got a woman down here at state parliament who says she's a "lovely mother" in our Mothers' Day contest and has an appointment with Mark.'

I waited for the reaction. He said: 'Sure you do, why don't you put her on?'

So I did. Wendy got on the phone and handled it beautifully, saying: 'Yes, I'm a Lovely Mothers' Day contestant and I'm hoping to meet the editor but I've come to the wrong place.'

Despite all the holes and inconsistencies a genuine woman's voice completely scrambled the news editor's logic.

'I don't know what's going on,' he said, 'just get back here!'

So we marched into Mark Day's office. Both of us had pledged solemnly that we would not give each other up, that we would go down fighting and denying everything. Shoulder-to-shoulder childhood mates. But what we didn't count on was Mark calling us in separately. Wendy went in first. Under the glare and firepower she completely broke down and spilled her guts in about 12 seconds flat.

Then Mark hauled me out in front of everyone on the editorial floor and said: 'Sardine milkshakes are one thing but lovely mothers are very different and a definite no-no. Who are you going to play a practical joke on next – Rupert Murdoch?'

He told Wendy and me to leave and to still consider myself fired. I went home completely distraught. I thought: I've come so far and now I've lost the job that I've lived and breathed and dreamed about since I was 13. It was all over.

Thank goodness, after letting me sweat it out for a day or two, Mark relented and told me to come back to work. Thirty years later, and with Mark as our son Sean's godfather, we still laugh about it. And within 20 years of that Lovely Mothers' Day Contest incident I'd be hosting a national television program built around a surprise or practical joke sometimes costing many thousands of dollars.

After two years on the political round I went back to the daily rounds car. By this stage John Hartigan was editor. Two plum jobs came up in New York as News Limited's foreign correspondents in America, writing for newspapers in Australia and the UK. The postings would be for at least two or three years, or as long as you could talk the editor in to allowing you to stay. Three people were vying for them: Sally MacMillan on the *Daily Telegraph*, and Col Allan and Michael Munro on the *Daily Mirror*.

Col and Sally got the postings. I was absolutely devastated. I'd always wanted to go to New York. In fact as a copy boy I had pestered Rupert Murdoch to let him know that I was alive, very enthusiastic and wanted to work in New York one day. For months I had written

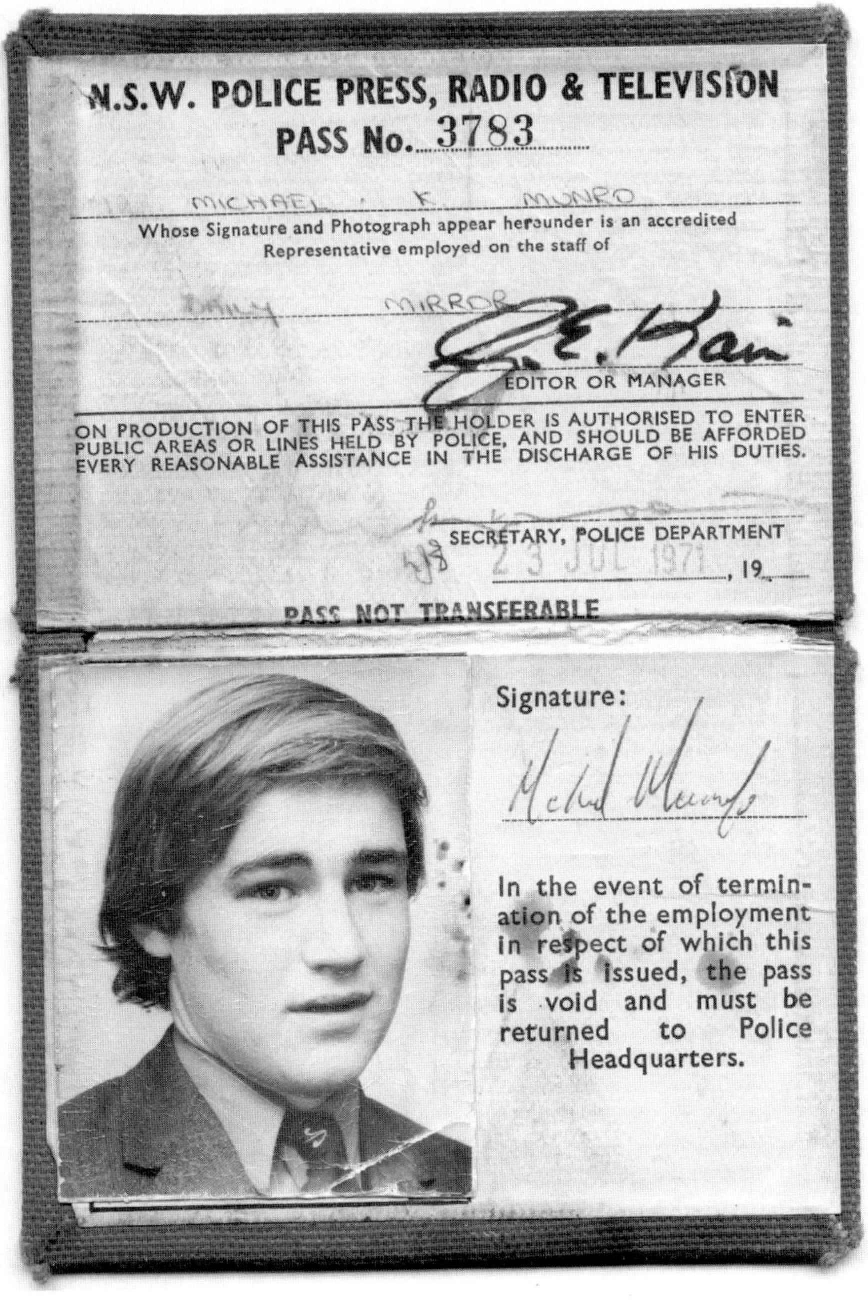

N.S.W. POLICE PRESS, RADIO & TELEVISION PASS No. 3783

MICHAEL F MUNRO

Whose Signature and Photograph appear hereunder is an accredited Representative employed on the staff of

DAILY MIRROR

G.E. Bai

EDITOR OR MANAGER

ON PRODUCTION OF THIS PASS THE HOLDER IS AUTHORISED TO ENTER PUBLIC AREAS OR LINES HELD BY POLICE, AND SHOULD BE AFFORDED EVERY REASONABLE ASSISTANCE IN THE DISCHARGE OF HIS DUTIES.

SECRETARY, POLICE DEPARTMENT

23 JUL 1971 , 19

PASS NOT TRANSFERABLE

Signature:

In the event of termination of the employment in respect of which this pass is issued, the pass is void and must be returned to Police Headquarters.

My pride and joy – my first press pass.

The Beast and the Beauty – get a look at that body shirt!

Dad gave me a 21st birthday party and a cheque for $200 – but told me not to cash it.

Jon, Lea's brother, and Deirdre Macken with me and Lea at Lea's final year Formal.

My favourite photo – journalism in action. (Photo: Graeme Fletcher)

On tenterhooks waiting for the next big news story.

Sporting a perm for an undercover story in an attempt to get picked up by a gang kidnapping drug addicts and stealing their dole cheques.

Mis-directing during Koo Stark's arrival at Sydney Airport.

Our first fall of snow after arriving in New York

Thanksgiving in New York with Ira Berger and Helen Dalley.

Patrick and James Kenniff, my great-cousins and perhaps two of Queensland's most famous bushrangers.

to him once a month and phoned his secretary every second day, until he agreed to see me. He was very understanding and patient, and asked me how I was going with my typing and shorthand, whether I was attending my cadet lectures, and if I wanted to specialise in any particular field of journalism in the future. I told him that what I really wanted was to work in New York. He told me that if I kept working hard, one day I'd make it there. Now, I was 24 and a B-grade journalist. I hadn't got one of the New York postings. And I had always promised myself that I would be an A-grade before I was 25, but for budget reasons John Hartigan couldn't upgrade me at that stage.

Over the past 18 months Tom Barnett, the news director at Sydney's Channel Ten News, had been getting other journos at state parliament to suggest that I give him a call about giving television a go. In those days newspaper journalists looked down their noses at television journalists and I did as well. I thought: television? Forget it. They were all a bunch of pretty boys who were more concerned with which way their hair was parted than a good story. They wouldn't know a breaking story if you hit them over the head with it. Though I'd been flattered by these hints I hadn't really seriously considered them. But now Col had left for New York, Mark Day had left the paper to become Kerry Packer's first editor of Australian *Playboy* magazine and I wasn't going to get my A-grade by the time I was 25 at the *Daily Mirror*, so I met with Tom Barnett. He offered me an A-grade plus $40 a week in expenses. I thought, okay,

I'll give it a go. So in September 1978, having spent seven years at the *Daily Mirror*, a tough, no-nonsense training ground in journalism, I resigned.

I was worried about leaving the first work 'family' I'd ever known. I would miss them greatly – the editors, the other reporters, the car drivers, the photographers, the copy takers. I was apprehensive about being on camera. Taking the job was not about getting my ugly head on TV but, as always, it was about reporting the story, whatever the medium. I had no inclination whatsoever to be a 'star'.

It was naturally very difficult the day I left the *Mirror*, but I left full of confidence, believing I could make the transition to television on my ear. How wrong I was. Writing for a newspaper and reporting for television news are worlds apart. From writing a 2,000-word five-part series at the *Mirror* I found it hard to adjust to writing a 90-second, 270-word piece for the nightly news. And there was no one to teach me the difference.

I still have a VHS copy of the very first television story I did. It was about Ma Evans Wonder Hair Tonic, a 'miracle' hair-growth liquid. It was one of those offbeat stories that run at the end of the news bulletin. The cameraman I was working with was an old hand who'd been around for a long time and knew he had a very green and gullible kid on his hands. He suggested a 'great idea' might be for me to take my shirt off for the camera and get Ma Evans to sprinkle my impotently hairless chest with her magic tonic. I can laugh now but for years I couldn't believe I did it.

Most of the time though I was back on 6.00am starts, chasing the main stories of the day, only now with a cameraman and a sound recordist. The first thing I noticed when I moved into television was the size of some people's egos. Most were fine and great fun to work with but a few of the on-camera people had very large heads. I preferred the company of the camera crews and when I wasn't in an editing room or typing up a script I was hanging out with them in their common room off the newsroom.

Lea and I had known each other for six years, but we had never spoken about marriage. Of course, coming from the background that I did, I was scared of marriage. I mean, I had walked down the street with these two parents screaming at each other in public. Almost every day of my life my mother had told me what a scoundrel and a scum bag my father was.

But while I was scared of marriage I had also seen Lea's lovely strong family. At the time, her parents had been blissfully married for more than 25 years – they had also been together since they were teenagers. I knew there were success stories, but I knew you really had to work at it. To have any real hope of making it work I've always believed in the two Cs: commitment and compromise.

Lea and I had gone out with each other for about four years and then on and off we'd lived together for the last three years, so we had a fair idea that we were pretty compatible. Ever since our first meeting on the 24th of June 1972, we had never once split up. Came very close on one occasion, but never broke up, even temporarily.

I planned a romantic dinner with Lea at a restaurant called Barrenjoey House, near Palm Beach in Sydney. Lea had no idea that I was going to ask her to marry me. I waited nervously until after the main course.

'You have become such an important part of my life . . . I would be so happy if you agreed to marry me,' I blurted out clumsily.

'I'd love to,' she simply said.

We had a nine-month engagement, and were married five days before Lea's 22nd birthday. I was about to turn 26.

The wedding went off without a hitch. It was at Sacred Heart Mosman where I had gone to school, where I had lived, where I had been an altar boy, where I had stolen the unblessed communion hosts, where I had drunk the altar wine behind the priest's presbytery door. When the guests filed into the church, Mum, being the matriarch on my side, met my guests and showed them to their seats. Lea's side of the family were in far greater numbers than mine. I only had a handful of guests on my side of the church. Down the aisle came this bloke and Mum asked if he was with the bride or groom. The man said he was with the groom's side and Mum directed him to a pew, proud that there was someone she could actually usher into our side of the pews. And guess who it was? It was

Dad, and she hadn't even recognised him. Despite Lea's sister Kim staying with her on the morning of the wedding to make sure she remained sober, Mum had still managed to sneak a couple of drinks and was pleasantly tipsy when she arrived at the wedding. Because of the grog and the fact she hadn't set eyes on him for probably 10 years she didn't recognise him at all.

Dad had changed a lot. Being in his mid-50s, naturally his hair was greyer, and his face was very blotchy because he too was now drinking heavily and suffering from cirrhosis of the liver. I was seeing my father more often now, although we had very little in common. We would occasionally have a lunch together but we were father and son in name only. Dad had recognised Mum, and was absolutely shocked and horrified at the way she looked. But God love her, she told him, with her best smile, to please take a seat and that they'd chat after the wedding.

At the end of the ceremony I told Mum that we were going to have family photos taken and she said: 'Is your father here?'

'Yes, you were talking to him before the ceremony,' I said.

She said: 'I was not!' She'd hate to think that she'd say even one word to him.

I pointed him out to her. And she was furious at herself. But when we had the photographs taken she had no qualms about looping her arm through my father's. They never said another word to each other as long as they lived.

We had about 120 guests at our reception at East-lakes Golf Club – all my old journo mates were there. Lea and I paid for the grog and her mum and dad chipped in for the food. We had a band and it was a wonderful night. We managed to prevent Mum from having any more to drink so it was a great party.

Having saved long and hard, Lea and I were able to have a two-week honeymoon in Hong Kong, Malaysia and Singapore. At last there was some normality and a feeling of belonging coming into my life. And all due to Lea.

I wasn't happy in television. I missed the world of print and the knockabout rough diamonds in newspapers. The final straw came when Tom Barnett took my $40 in weekly expenses away as part of across-the-board budget cuts at the network. I resigned after just eight months.

But I had come very close to being fired before I could resign. Prince Andrew's gorgeous, sexy girlfriend, Koo Stark, was coming to Sydney for an interview on the *Michael Parkinson Show*, which was being produced in Australia at the time. The fact that the show was on my network, Channel Ten, didn't mean anything to me – I wanted an exclusive with her, and I wanted her to tell me all about her recent steamy affair with Prince Andrew. I still had good contacts with customs and immigration officials from my airport round days, and one of them told me Koo Stark was going to try to bypass the phalanx of 50 or so media waiting at one end of the arrivals concourse and leave via the other end.

It was nothing for me to wander in and out of customs and immigration just as long as I looked confident enough and wore my Channel Ten ID pass, which coincidentally resembled a customs ID. So I marched into customs with my Channel Ten ID pass showing prominently and, quite rightly, told Koo Stark that I was from Channel Ten and that I could get her past all the pesky media outside and take her to the station. I took her out of the door at the opposite end of the terminal to where all the media were waiting and got an exclusive interview. Anyway, about two minutes later, the media saw her from about 75 metres down the footpath, and turned into an absolute herd of charging elephants. Cameras, cables, people tripping over, screaming abuse at each other, flashes going off, cameras being dropped. By the time she reached her white Rolls Royce it was just crazy and no media had any chance to see or speak to her. Very few photographers got any pictures. It was a classic steal with an exclusive interview.

Later that morning Greg Coote, who was then in charge of Channel Ten, was rung by Koo Stark's publicist, who demanded that I be fired. She said that I had completely screwed up all the publicity for her airport arrival and they would have to take her out in public again for media coverage. So many of the media were complaining that they didn't get anything. No photographs – only a half-view here or a badly angled shot there. That afternoon Koo Stark had to take a stroll through a shopping mall so they could get some shots. Fortunately, while Coote considered firing me, Tom Barnett went into bat for me and saved my job – although I was to resign shortly afterwards anyway.

I had three months' notice to work out. I rang John Hartigan and asked him to take me back. He agreed to have me back, and as an A-grade. After 11 months in television I left, believing I would never return.

The most exciting – and downright frightening – story I covered when I went back to the *Daily Mirror* concerned Russell 'Mad Dog' Cox and Eric 'Houdini' Heuston, then the two most wanted criminals in the country. The men, who were extremely dangerous and heavily armed, had escaped from prison, robbed several banks in Sydney, and were now hiding out.

The *Daily Mirror's* legendary senior police rounds-man, Bill Jenkings, was tipped off by Sydney detectives that there was a major undercover operation under way to catch Cox and Heuston at South West Rocks, near Kempsey on the mid-north coast of New South Wales. John Hartigan sent me and a photographer, Graeme Noad, to South West Rocks, telling us to check in to a motel and sit tight until Jenkings got a further tip-off from his superb Sydney police contacts about when the police were going to spring Cox and Heuston and arrest them. Even the local Kempsey Detectives were not aware of the operation.

Graeme and I drove up to South West Rocks,

checked into a motel, went for a brief drive to check out the area, and stopped to have some lunch in a restaurant. There were two couples sitting in the park across the road from us. I recognised the two men – they were Detectives John Hamilton and Kim Cook. It turned out that the undercover police from Sydney were staying at the same motel as us; their rooms were directly above ours. They left the motel at all hours – sometimes 3.00 or 4.00 in the morning. Graeme wanted to follow them, but I decided to sit tight and rely on Bill Jenkings getting another tip-off. My patience paid off, and we eventually got word via Bill that the police were about to raid Cox and Heuston's hideout. We were advised to go straight to Kempsey Police Station as once the crims had been captured they would be brought there under police guard. We took off. Little did we know that we were driving a car similar to the one Cox and Heuston were driving . . .

Speeding to get there in time, we approached a small bridge – only to be confronted by two police marksmen, aiming their weapons directly at us. We stopped the car. Immediately, two more policemen appeared, one placing a gun to the back of my head, the other pointing a .38 pistol at Graeme.

A fifth policeman appeared from below a roadside embankment and said 'Don't move an inch or we'll blow your heads off.'

'We're newsmen with the *Daily Mirror*!' I screamed.

'Identification,' was all the cop said.

I reached inside my pocket for my press pass and

suddenly the scene resembled something out of a Hollywood movie, all five heavily armed cops making a lunge at me in case I was reaching for a weapon. Once they saw our press passes they relaxed – then told us to get the hell out of the area. It didn't take much to convince us!

With his uncanny sixth sense, Cox smelled a rat and disappeared just before the police raided the hotel that he and Heuston had been hiding out in. Heuston, however, was not so lucky, and was arrested. We were at Kempsey Police Station when Heuston was brought in under police guard. He took one look at Graeme shooting away and karate-kicked his professional Nikon camera, smashing it and splitting the lens in half – not before Graeme managed to get off three photos, though.

We went to our car to get the portable darkroom out, only to discover that the developer and fixer chemicals were missing. Just then, the two 'couples' who had been staying at our motel arrived at the station. They told us that they had broken into the boot of the car and had taken some of our equipment 'just for insurance'. Uncertain of what we had been up to, they thought they might need something to use as leverage against us. It turned out that on our first day at South West Rocks, Detective Hamilton had looked across from the park and recognised me in the restaurant, and that another afternoon, while we were lazing by the side of the motel pool, the cops had come into our room and gone through everything. Graeme and I looked at each other, both thinking that we had found ourselves in some spy novel. After we got our photographic chemicals back Graeme developed the pictures and sent them to Sydney. One of those shots appeared on the front page later that afternoon. Graeme and I joined the four undercover cops at the pub for a few beers. Russell Cox wasn't sighted again for years, but was eventually re-captured.

It still remained a dream of mine to work in New York. A position became available at News Limited's New York bureau working for the over-the-top US tabloid *The Star* magazine, writing for Murdoch newspapers in England and Australia, and also doing some reporting for Australian TV.

At the same time I was able to get my own working visa for America. I asked Mark Day, the editor of Australian *Playboy* magazine, for help and he agreed to write a letter introducing me to the US consulate as we had both agreed that I would also be a contributing journalist for Australian *Playboy*. Now that I had a working visa I could go to News Limited and say: 'Well that's it, I'm going.' I knew they didn't want to lose me, but I was determined to get to New York. We had to pay our own way to get there, but News was good enough to pay for a hotel for one month after we arrived until we found an apartment.

Of course the most heart-wrenching thing about leaving Sydney was leaving Mum behind. I spoke at length to her doctor, Dr Harvey Turk, about keeping an eye on her. He had a lot of time for my mother, always describing her as a 'wonderful and caring woman'. For years he had gone far beyond the call of duty for her. He would often pop in on Mum to see how she was coping. She would sometimes ring him so drunk and incoherent that he would immediately rush to her aid. Many times Dr Turk had admitted her to Mosman's local community hospital for, as he would always describe it, 'a little R & R, some good food and a break from the bottle'. In her mind her health problems had little to do with alcohol – it was always 'just the flu' or more often 'that damn bronchitis returning again'.

Lea and I left for New York in May 1980. Saying goodbye to Mum was much harder even than I imagined it would be. It was all because of her that I was now able to go off to New York and work, yet Mum had never been out of Australia all her life. She was relatively sober on the day of our departure and was fairly quiet. I think she was going through all sorts of emotions. She was already desperately lonely and my departure would make things even harder. Foremost in my mind was the thought: 'Will this be the last time I see my mother alive?' I was still programmed to always expect the worst – if it didn't happen, it was a bonus. If it was hard for me and Mum, it was just as hard for Lea and her family. They were extremely close, and here I was taking her away to one of the most dangerous cities in the world.

It was a subdued departure, but the following two

years were to be two of the best in our life together. We were to grow individually, we were to grow as a couple, and I was to grow professionally.

We went to New York via Los Angeles. A journo mate of mine had booked us into a place in Santa Monica, a real dump of a motel. It was terrible. The walls were so thin we heard screams and gunshots during the night; we were petrified to come out of our room. We thought we were going to be mugged or murdered in our bed. We had the TV on all night and literally only fell asleep by accident. This was our introduction to America and ever since this time I have despised Los Angeles. Years later, with *60 Minutes*, I would go to Los Angeles a dozen times a year and every time it was the same – a concrete jungle that is shallow and artificial.

We had a wonderful drive up Highway One, with the Pacific Ocean on our left as we drove north, past Malibu and the Hearst Castle, Big Sur, Carmel and then San Francisco. We had a couple of days in San Francisco, did Alcatraz, and then flew to the Big Apple. Col Allan, who had already been there for a couple of years, met us at the airport that night in a hired limo, making our arrival in New York as exciting as possible – and it *was* so exciting! At last I had made it to New York City. The housekeeper's kid had made it to the toughest city in the world, having just turned 27.

We found an apartment in Gramercy Park. It was heavily populated with gays and therefore a clean and safe neighbourhood. We lived in a block of 120 apartments on 22nd Street between Second and Third Avenues.

I worked on Third Avenue at 45th Street so it was basically a kilometre-and-a-half walk to work every day. And
Lea and I could do it together because not only did Lea
score a job in an office supplying nurses to private homes
around New York City but her office was right opposite
mine on Third Avenue. The visa I had normally wouldn't
have allowed a wife a social security number, and therefore no opportunity to work, but for some reason when
we entered the country they gave Lea a social security
number. Every other wife travelling on her husband's visa
couldn't work, but Lea could, and it was a real bonus,
making life much easier for us. In the end we were the
very first News Limited couple in 11 years to return from
New York still married! The city used to really take its toll
on marriages – one giant adult playground that raged
25 hours a day. Because most wives weren't working they
became dangerously bored, and of course most of the
Aussie and English journos worked and played very hard.
But during our time there we were lucky to be able to
walk to and from work every morning and afternoon, and
we began to draw much closer. Our relationship was deep
before we left and in New York our love was only
strengthened.

It was such an exciting time, despite the fact that we
had to struggle on a joint wage of about US$30,000
a year. Almost a third of that went on rent for our tiny
one-room studio. The apartment had two doors only –
the bathroom door and the front door. But we could not
have been happier.

Still wary of alcohol, I didn't get involved too often in

the hard, all-night drinking sessions among the Australian, British and New York journalistic community. The poms and the Aussies hung out together in three particular bars – Fleet Street, the very famous bar Costello's, known for the James Thurber cartoons and drawings that once lined the walls, and a bar on Second Avenue called Eamonn Doran's. While Lea and I did a bit of all-night partying, we didn't get right into it. We were too busy saving up to go to Broadway plays and musicals, or going to museums, brunch on Saturday and Sunday, and the Orchard Street Markets, where you get all the designer brands at half the price.

We also became very close friends, and still are today, with Ira Berger, a photographer who I travelled with to more than half the states in America on various stories. Ira went on to become pictorial editor for *People* magazine. Born and bred in Brooklyn, he lived at Park Slope, which is the Central Park of Brooklyn. His mum and dad were Orthodox Jews but Ira was no longer that strict. He was always very generous with his time and his adoration of New York City, introducing us to the real New York City outside Manhattan – Brooklyn, with its 155 nationalities, Queens, the Bronx and Staten Island. All five boroughs. Even some New Yorkers we knew who had lived in New York all their lives had never been to Queens or Staten Island. He showed us all over the city and introduced us to Arabic, Russian and Lithuanian neighbourhoods, and the Hasidic Jewish community in Brooklyn. In this Orthodox community the women and men are separated in the synagogue – only the men are allowed on the main floor and the women, who wear red wigs, sit in the gallery above. Only on one night of the year could the men drink alcohol, and didn't they tuck into it, making up for lost time!

Lea and I also made friends with a lovely woman named Eve Kandor who worked at News Limited as a junior reporter. She also happened to be Rupert Murdoch's niece, and when she decided to return home to Melbourne, Rupert and Anna Murdoch invited us to an intimate family dinner at Windows on the World, the 107th-floor restaurant in the north tower of the World Trade Center. Before dinner our party of eight met in Rupert Murdoch's office at the *New York Post* on South Street, overlooking the Brooklyn Bridge. There was a very early model of an Ansett Airlines passenger plane on his coffee table. News Limited had recently acquired a major shareholding in the airline and Rupert was deciding what colour scheme his planes would be. The model plane was white with a yellow stripe along the fuselage and the southern cross on the tail.

Anna Murdoch said: 'The new-look planes will have a southern cross on the tail and a white fuselage but Rupert wants a yellow stripe down the middle and I don't particularly like the yellow stripe. I'm trying to talk him out of it.' Well, history will tell you that Anna got her way.

We headed off to dinner, but there were no fancy limousines for Rupert. He was fast becoming one of the most successful and powerful men in the world but he still called four or five cabs for all of us to go to the World Trade Center. From our table at the restaurant we looked straight up Fifth Avenue to the north end of the island of Manhattan, and looked down on light aircraft and helicopters – that's how high those magnificent twin towers once were.

At one point Rupert Murdoch leaned across the table and said: 'I told you, I told you you'd get to New York one day.' It just blew me away because I didn't think he'd ever remember our meeting 10 years earlier. During the meal he also announced to the table: 'Robert Stigwood and I are thinking of making films together. We're going to call it R & R Films. Our first movie, we think, is going to be about Gallipoli.' Of course the movie *Gallipoli* has become an Australian classic.

Later on we went to a very famous jazz bar in Greenwich Village called Bradley's. Lea and I, and the rest of the Murdoch party, sat around listening to wonderful jazz. It was a very special night.

While I was in New York I was fortunate enough to be able to do a number of stories for Australian television. They included the attempted assassination of President Ronald Reagan and a health scandal involving suspect meat exports to the US in 1981. But a truly unforgettable assignment fell on my birthday, the 12th of April 1981 – the first launch of the space shuttle Columbia at Cape Kennedy. It remains one of the most amazing experiences I've ever had.

The launch had been scheduled for the 11th of April and the countdown had got to within a minute or so but was stopped because of computer problems. The launch was postponed for another 24 hours. As the new launch time approached it was nerve-racking because Channel Ten wasn't prepared to pay for me to stay for another postponed launch. It had to be now or never. Fortunately the launch went ahead. I was part of the 3,000-strong media contingent standing about a kilometre away from launch pad 39A. Even when the shuttle was probably a kilometre in the sky you could still feel the ground beneath your feet shaking. It was just awesome. Earth-shattering. And of course I couldn't help but remember that 13 year old with the tape recorder during the Apollo missions, interviewing his three 'astronaut' friends. If anyone ever asks me what story I would love to do most it would be to go into space. It would be some experience. It was tragic not only to lose so many young lives in the Columbia explosion in early 2003 but she was also the pioneer shuttle of the 20-year space shuttle program.

Although both Lea and I are of Irish ancestry, we knew very little about our backgrounds. All I knew about my history was Mum's labelling of me as an 'Irish thief' and sometimes even 'murderer'.

While we were in New York something drew us to get in touch with our roots and take one of our annual holidays in Ireland. We flew to Shannon Airport near

Limerick with a group of tourists from New York. Lea and I wanted to see all of Ireland, including the north, but when we told our American companions that we were going to hire a Republic of Ireland car and actually drive it into the north they all thought we were crazy. They had no desire whatsoever to go anywhere near 'the troubles'. When we arrived, in May 1981, the situation was particularly volatile. We had arrived the very week that the famous 'hero' of the IRA, hunger striker Bobby Sands, had starved himself to death. Both the north and south were extremely tense, with clashes and bombings by the IRA and the Protestant paramilitaries occurring every day.

It was into this whirlwind that Lea and I set off in our little car from Dublin, via Armagh, and into Belfast. Most of the republic was draped in black mourning flags. Driving from the south to the north was like going from heaven to hell. We were dumbfounded by the difference, from the relaxed easy-going country green of the south to the grey depression and war zone of the north. But as a journalist with an Irish background I was drawn to see all facets of this intriguing and beautiful country. I felt as if I belonged.

Back in New York, one of the big stories I covered for the newspapers was the assassination of John Lennon in December that same year. Within an hour of the shooting I was outside Lennon's home, the Dakota apartment building, with God knows how many hundreds of reporters. The Lennons lived on the top two floors of the Dakota, a creepy old building overlooking

Central Park, where the horror movie *Rosemary's Baby* was made. I camped out the front for the next three days, only coming home for a shower and a change of clothes.

It was obviously a massive story – and of course the one and only interview to get was with Yoko Ono. And at one stage I got very close. I took off my coat and tie, went across to one of the supermarkets, bought a box full of groceries and tried to make myself look like a delivery boy. I got through the first line of security without having to tell a lie; they took me as a grocery delivery boy, no questions asked. I got through the second line of security, then the third line of security.

I was almost knocking on Yoko's door when the last bloke said, 'You're not a reporter are you?'

I was almost right in there. I said, 'Yes, I am.'

'Good try, now out you go.'

I was also working for the *Michael Parkinson Show* while in New York, organising guest interviews in Australia, including one with Shirley Temple. Each time I organised a guest for the Australian show from America I was paid $1,000. One of those $1,000 pay cheques went towards sending Lea home to surprise her sister Kim at her wedding. Lea was originally asked to be a bridesmaid but because we didn't think we'd be able to afford to go, she turned the offer down. But then I was able to get a cheap airfare for Lea. She knocked on the door of the family home the day before the wedding. Her mum was so beside herself she went and hid in the closet.

The baby of the family would be at the wedding after all. And what's more Kim was marrying one of my longest and dearest mates, Terry. After knowing each other for 23 years – since we were five – we were now becoming brothers-in-law!

While I had the opportunity to work on many exciting stories for Australian TV and newspapers, about 70 per cent of my time was spent working on *The Star*, which was just like *The National Enquirer*, a shocking rag. My beat was anywhere in the United States or Canada where gee-whiz believe-it-or-not survival stories occurred or there were profiles to be done on sportspeople or Hollywood celebrities. I was never overly happy working on *The Star* because accuracy and facts weren't exactly regarded as priorities. I remember having several arguments with editorial executives who wanted me to exaggerate or 'beat up' stories I had written. Because I refused to do so I was never very popular. That was why I always loved writing for the News Limited bureau, which telexed its stories to Murdoch newspapers in Australia and the UK. It was also a great bonus to be able to do those television stories because, although I didn't know it at the time, they were enabling me to keep in touch with television reporting and production techniques that were soon to become valuable to my career.

In addition to being dissatisfied with the kind of stories I had to do for *The Star*, after many years in newspapers I was now also coming to the realisation that when it came to writing, I was no Ernest Hemingway. And Lea and I were ready to start a family but didn't want to raise children in New York. So after almost two years in New York I came to consider a return to television. Channel Ten's News Director, Tom Barnett, had contacted me and offered me a job back on Sydney television. I owe Tom a great deal for seeing in me what I didn't see – a future not in newspapers but in television.

'We'll pay you $32,000 a year to come back but on that generous wage you'll have to be on a three-year contract,' he said.

'I don't want to be on a three-year contract,' I said. 'I'll come back, but I only want to be on a two-year contract, otherwise I'm going to stay here.'

After agreeing to my demand for a two-year contract he arrived in New York – and put a three-year contract in front of me! I had already resigned from my job and my boss in New York was not a happy Vegemite. There was no turning back. I was absolutely trapped and had to begrudgingly sign the three-year contract.

Lea and I arrived back in Sydney in 1982. We had become very close because we had only had each other. When we came home we were a bit put out by so many people wanting to see us, so many people ringing us. We now could no longer enjoy just each other's company – we had to share ourselves with friends and family. We hadn't wanted to arrive back home with an American accent but to our surprise Lea did. Her days were spent working in an office full of New Yorkers and despite fighting it she slowly developed a slight American twang. Because I had worked mainly with Aussies and poms I wasn't affected at all. To her relief, Lea soon lost the accent though.

Personally, socially and culturally New York had been fantastic. I had grown up a lot and changed forever, and Lea and I had cemented our decade-old relationship. About six months before we were married Lea and I had bought a two-bedroom unit near North Sydney, and rented it out. We now planned on selling it, buying our first house and starting a family, but would stay with Lea's mum and dad, who by now had moved back to Sydney, until we found the right house to buy. It took us six months to find a house and, as such times always are, it was trying for both the in-laws and us, but nevertheless it worked. We looked throughout the north side of Sydney. Lea had been brought up on the upper north shore and I had been brought up on the lower north shore, so there was never any possibility of us going to the eastern suburbs or anywhere else. By now Mosman was far too expensive for us so we settled on leafy St Ives. We found a lovely old 1940s single-storey home that needed a lot of work and would eventually have to be rebuilt. It was a large block with a private, lovely back yard and lots of trees. We paid $127,000 for it, and after we sold our unit we had $50,000 worth of equity in it.

By April Lea was pregnant; naturally we were both over the moon about it. This was not only the beginning of our family but also the culmination of our decade-long love affair. From teenage sweethearts to parents it had been an awesome ride. Lea's pregnancy went fairly smoothly and she had no morning sickness at all. The only real hitch was that the baby got himself into a breech position and had to be delivered by Caesarean. We named him Sean.

Mum had been admitted to hospital two or three times while we were in New York but I always knew Dr Turk was watching out for her, because we had spoken on the phone when things were looking more grim than normal for Mum. When I arrived back home I was dreading what Mum would now be like. I had written to her every week for two years. I had also spoken to her once a month – or at least when she was sober enough to answer the phone. It was very hard because you could try at any hour of the day and she'd either be out or drunk.

Even I wasn't prepared for how she looked when we got back. She had lost a tremendous amount of weight and her walking was much less steady. She had obviously had many falls because there were a number of particularly bad scars around her eyes. It was not a good look, and she was now slightly brain-damaged from the years of grog. She was still a closet drinker, but now she was into the real cheap wine.

I knew that if I didn't get her sober soon she wouldn't last much longer. It was heartbreaking to see this wreck of a woman. She was a walking corpse. Deep in my heart I knew she probably didn't have a lot longer to go. Each time she went into hospital it was for a longer period of time and the damage to her liver, kidneys and most of her other organs was just getting worse. I felt so helpless because there was nothing I could do. It was agony to sit there and watch my mother slowly die.

7

As well as always calling me a pasty-faced nothing all my life Mum had referred to me as 'only being from a family of bushrangers and murderers'. For the first 30 years of my life I had no idea what she was talking about. I just ignored it, like all the other abuse, believing it was just the grog and her lifelong bitterness towards my father talking.

After we returned from New York my father sat me down one day and told me the whole family history. He floored me by starting with the fact that our name was not really Munro – it was originally Kenniff. Then I was gob-smacked when he told me that two of my great-cousins were perhaps Queensland's most famous bushrangers, one of whom was hanged in Boggo Road Gaol at the turn of the 20th century for murdering two men. For over 30 years Mum had known the whole story but had never told me – just abused me with it without explaining. Naturally I was fascinated when

Dad told me, and began years of researching and collecting anything to do with my bushranger family history.

My great-great-grandfather, Patrick Cunniffe, arrived in Australia from Tipperary in 1862 with his wife Mary and their 10 children. Free settlers, they moved to northern New South Wales, near a tiny town called Kaaraak Flat near the Upper Manning River. My great-grandfather, William, the couple's seventh child, was six years old when they arrived. His older brother, James, the second eldest of the 10, was almost 20 years older than him. He was a wily and tough character who, with his wife Mary, had 11 children. Because so few people could really read or write, their name soon started to be spelt phonetically – not 'Cunniffe' but 'Kenniff'.

The family had arrived in Australia from Ireland to start a new life as honest hard-working stockmen. They originally settled around Taree on the mid-coast of New South Wales. After James (Snr) and two of his sons, James and Patrick, had several brushes with the law, they left New South Wales and headed for the Carnarvon Ranges near Roma and Mitchell in Queensland.

The Kenniffs managed a small property called 'Ralph', which adjoined one of the biggest and most profitable stations in the district, 'Carnarvon'. The brothers, Patrick and James – my grandfather's cousins, and my great-cousins – didn't stay out of trouble for long. They were both superb horsemen and were soon renowned in that part of the state for being able to steal the most cantankerous and flighty thoroughbreds around. Stealing racehorses was their speciality but the two men also dabbled in quite a bit of cattle duffing. Soon after arriving in the district Patrick and James were sentenced to three and two years' gaol respectively for stealing two racehorses. In the late 1890s they were out of gaol but the prime suspects in the theft of more than 1,000 head of cattle from the neighbouring property, Carnarvon. The manager of Carnarvon, Albert Dahlke, was furious but couldn't prove his claims, so he persuaded Carnarvon's owners to buy the Kenniffs' grazing lease on Ralph out from under them and then evict the whole family.

Once the bog Irish family were evicted they roamed the district stealing whatever supplies they needed, using several hideouts as their bases. At a local race meeting Dahlke beat Patrick in a fight. Patrick openly threatened the station manager, saying, 'I'll get you for this Dahlke, just wait and see that I don't,' in front of several punters.

Just before the turn of the century the Kenniff brothers were often seen openly and defiantly riding while heavily armed. Locals and senior police in Brisbane became so concerned that a new police station was constructed. Called the Upper Warrego Police Station, it was built on the exact spot where the Kenniffs' home and yards had once stood, infuriating the family even more. The scene was now set for one of the great murder mysteries in Queensland history.

Around the 25th of October 1901 a thoroughbred

pony was stolen from a small town called Springsure, and the Kenniffs were the prime suspects. That was quickly followed by the news that 'Sunnyvale', a small station at Merivale, had been ransacked and burnt down. It appeared the Kenniff brothers had gone way too far this time. On the 21st of March 1902 police at Roma took out a warrant for the arrest of Patrick and James Kenniff. A week later, on Good Friday, Senior Constable George Doyle left the Upper Warrego Police Station with Albert Dahlke and an Aboriginal tracker, Sam Johnson, to find the Kenniff brothers. Constable Doyle was the only one of the trio who was armed – he was carrying a police-issue Webley revolver. Dahlke carried only a stockwhip while Sam Johnson, who was responsible for the pack-horse, was unarmed. Constable Doyle didn't see anything wrong with taking unarmed civilians with him to catch the Kenniffs – he was probably relying on the fact that the Kenniffs had tried to resist arrest only once before and would probably be taken easily again. But he couldn't have been more wrong. The tiny posse had no idea that the night before they had set out, Patrick and James had ridden to Dahlke's homestead demanding to know where he was, and threatening his staff.

Doyle, Dahlke and Johnson rode to Mt Moffatt, where a local told them he'd seen fresh horse tracks heading north to Kelman's Gap, in the Carnarvon Ranges. Doyle knew it had to be the Kenniffs riding for their favourite hole in the wall, Lethbridge's Pocket. The three men spent the night at Mt Moffatt before riding down into the valley of the dry Lethbridge's Creek very early on Easter Sunday morning. What happened next is best described by Johnson, the only one of the three to survive. Later in court Johnson would be the only witness for the prosecution:

I went first leading the packhorse and Doyle and Dahlke came along close together. We went about six miles like that and then we saw the Kenniffs. I saw them first. They were Tom Kenniff, Pat Kenniff and James Kenniff. They were coming on, walking their horses back towards us. I saw them and I pulled up and said to Doyle, 'There they come.' Doyle was just behind me. I let the packhorse go. Doyle raced after the Kenniffs who turned round and raced away. Dahlke went after them too. Pat and Tom Kenniff went one way together and Jim Kenniff went another way. Doyle and Dahlke raced after Jim. I galloped a little way after Tom and Pat and then I turned around and came to Doyle and Dahlke. I rode right up to them. Dahlke was on his horse holding Jim Kenniff's horse by the rein of the bridle. Jim was on his horse and Doyle was pulling him off. When Doyle had pulled Jim off his horse he said to me, 'Go back and get the packhorse.' The handcuffs were in the pack. From where the packhorse was I was out of sight of Doyle, Dahlke and Jim Kenniff. There were too many trees for me to see them. Before I got to the packhorse I heard one shot fired. When I got to the packhorse I heard another shot fired. I caught the packhorse and after I caught him I heard three more shots, five shots altogether. They were all loud shots, none louder than any other. I know Mr Doyle's revolver that he had with him that day was in his pouch. I did not think the shots came from Mr Doyle's revolver. After I heard the shots I continued to lead the packhorse. I saw Pat and Jim Kenniff coming towards me riding on horseback. They were coming fast, galloping. They did not sing out to me. I let go of the halter of the packhorse when I saw them coming and I cleared. I cleared because I could not see Doyle or Dahlke. I have never seen them since.

After riding to the police and raising the alarm Johnson returned to Lethbridge's Pocket to find only Doyle's and Dahlke's horses and the packhorse – minus the saddlebags. Albert Dahlke's saddle was covered in blood. There was no sign of either man.

Because of a lack of available police horseflesh and the tyranny of distance, police didn't arrive at Lethbridge's Pocket until two days later, Tuesday the 1st of April. Constable Millard, from Carnarvon Police Station, was led back to the scene of the shooting. He discovered the ashes of three large fires; alongside one was an amount of congealed blood. Then he found Doyle's and Dahlke's spurs. But it wasn't until the next day that he made the gruesome discovery of what appeared to be the men's remains in the bags from the packhorse.

A medical practitioner, Dr Voss, examined the packs and later gave this evidence in Rockhampton Court:

The pack-bags were full of ashes and on examining these I have sorted out various fragments of human skull and vertebrae. The fire charred one portion and the flesh was still adhering to it. There were portions of bones of the palm and fingers and a number of broken teeth. There were buttons, a piece of a stud, two peculiar pins and metal rings, which were a pair. From my examination of the body portions, thickness and size and state of the teeth I concluded they were fully grown males. I am unable to say the cause of death of the men but they were subject to a great deal of heat and a good deal of force.

More than 60 police officers now joined the search for the Kenniffs, but the brothers, in true Kelly Gang style, were being helped by many Irish sympathisers and friends as they moved closer and closer to the Great Dividing Range. On the 19th of April the Governor of Queensland offered a £1,000 reward for information leading to the recapture of Patrick and James Kenniff. The first confirmed sighting of the pair occurred at Hutton Creek on the southern slopes of the Carnarvon Range. Senior Sergeant Roddy Byrne from Toowoomba Police Station surprised the brothers at dawn one day, just as they were about to leave with two horses, a pack-horse struggling under the weight of supplies, fresh food, a Winchester, a Colt and plenty of ammunition. But just as police charged the camp, the Kenniffs disappeared into the dense scrubland on foot.

April passed, May went by, and midway through June the Kenniffs had still not been captured. But there were often sightings of the men, as well as tales of horses disappearing and stores being stolen. Public pressure was mounting on the police, who were now being led by Sub-Inspectors Dillon and Malone, Senior Sergeant Byrne, six more sergeants, 43 constables and 16 Aboriginal trackers.

After a farmer at Back Creek reported two of his horses and a bag of wheat stolen Sub-Inspector Malone set out with three constables and two trackers. Just on dawn on the 16th of June they came across a campsite with four horses and some supplies. But Pat and Jim were camped 30 or 40 metres away. The Kenniffs had lived in the bush long enough to recognise the sudden uneasiness among their horses. Pat was the first to see the law, and screamed out a warning to his brother. Police shot dead the Kenniffs' two already saddled horses, forcing the men into dense prickly pear scrub. Unarmed, Patrick was caught quickly. Jim, however, disappeared with two loaded rifles.

The police confiscated the Kenniffs' stockpile of fresh food, tea, sugar, wheat, flour, clothing and two loaded Colt revolvers, then set out with the captive Patrick for the town of Mitchell. They couldn't believe their eyes when later that day they saw Jim Kenniff about half a kilometre ahead. One of the constables told him the police had his brother, and Jim said he'd only surrender if Pat hadn't been shot and was still alive. Once Pat was produced and the brothers could see and talk to each other, Jim gave himself up. The Kenniffs had been caught 10 weeks after the remains of Doyle and Dahlke had been discovered.

The Kenniff trial created a sensation in Queensland.

Pat and Jim maintained their innocence throughout. Their barrister argued that because no bodies were ever found there was no evidence proving Doyle and Dahlke were even dead. He also tried to discredit Sam Johnson's evidence and asked whether the jury was really prepared to take the word of an illiterate Aborigine who wasn't even a Christian! But the Kenniffs' main defence was that they were with another man at the time of the murders, and had been roaming the ranges for three months without any knowledge that the police were hunting for them. The prosecutor tore apart the Kenniffs' alibi and showed their only witness – the man who said he was with them at the time of the murders – to be unreliable. He scoffed at their story that they were unaware of the huge police hunt for them.

In summing up the trial to the jury, Chief Justice Sir Samuel Griffith, former Premier of Queensland, made no secret that he thought they should arrive at a guilty verdict for both men. The jury deliberated for only one hour before handing down their verdict. Court reporters later wrote that Patrick appeared nervous while Jim just stared at the jury. Both brothers were found guilty. The chief justice's associate asked Patrick if there was anything he'd like to say.

'Yes,' he answered, 'I know the sentence that is going to be passed on me. Before Your Honour passes it, I would like you to understand I am an innocent man. I hope that before you depart from this world you will find I am an innocent man.'

The chief justice was visibly angry.

When James was given the chance to speak he said: 'I wish to comment on your summing up in our case today. I think you never gave me one item of justice. I have no other witness to call except the Almighty God that I am an innocent man today. He is the only one I can call and I call on Him today.'

The chief justice glared at him and said: 'I think it is my duty to say that I entirely agree with the verdict of the jury and I fail to see how they could give any other verdict. You will both be returned to your former custody and, at a time appointed by the governor-in-council, each of you will be hung by the neck until you are dead. May God have mercy on your souls.'

But there was real sympathy among the public for the Kenniff brothers and people now questioned why they should be hanged when the evidence against them was only circumstantial. Donations poured in from all over the state to pay for an appeal. Begrudgingly, Chief Justice Griffith postponed the execution of the Kenniffs until the case could be heard by the Full Court of Appeal in Queensland. After a heated and controversial deliberation the four judges decided that only Patrick should hang, while Jim should have his execution commuted to life imprisonment.

Right to the gallows Pat maintained his innocence. He released this statement just before he was hanged in Boggo Road Gaol:

I have told you twice before I am an innocent man. I am as innocent as the judge who sentenced me. I must thank my warders for their kindness towards me. And to my well–wishers I say goodbye. May God have mercy on my soul.

Patrick Kenniff was executed at 8.00am on the 12th of January 1903. Jim served only 11 years of his life sentence and was released late in 1914. He died in 1940 at the age of 66, having spent his final years as a tin miner and recluse around Charters Towers and Cloncurry. Just like Pat, Jim maintained to his dying day no knowledge of what happened at Lethbridge's Pocket. It's little wonder the Kenniffs are often referred to as 'Australia's Last Bushrangers'.

My grandfather, who was much younger than his cousins Patrick and James, faced a real problem – he had been named after Patrick Kenniff. He was 22 years old when Patrick was executed, and having the infamous name of Patrick Kenniff in Queensland made it difficult for him to get a fair start in life. Nevertheless, he married Elsie Considine in 1917 in Rockhampton and the pair had a baby. For anonymity they moved to Taree on the New South Wales mid-north coast, near where the Cunniffes had first settled 30 years before. They moved on to a property called 'Munrook' and from that moment my grandfather began to call himself Henry Munro. Why he had to choose a Scottish name instead of an Irish alias I will never know! Henry and Elsie Munro had five children, the youngest of whom was my father. Henry had never made his name change official so Elsie and the children were illegally named Munro.

When Henry died in 1945 a death certificate was issued under the name of Henry Munro, finally legitimising his change of name.

Exactly 50 years after Patrick Kenniff swung from the Boggo Road gallows I was being baptised in a tiny church in Sydney. Dad had pleaded with Mum to name me Michael Kenniff Munro, to which she agreed. But at the very last moment she whispered to the priest, telling him to make it Michael *Kenneth* Munro, and I was so baptised. Thirty years after my baptism Lea and I were to baptise our son as Sean Cunniffe Munro – and no one is more proud of the name than he. Even as I write this he is fortunate enough to be spending a year at an Irish monastery and boarding school as part of an exchange program. The school is smack bang in County Tipperary, not far from where our ancestors originally came from. Through Dublin's Genealogy Society we've even been able to find the tiny lots of land they leased and worked on before moving to Australia.

So I started at Channel Ten the second time with a greater understanding of my working-class bog-Irish background, and a whole new perspective on who I was.

However, I was wary about working in the television industry, because of the financial promise that had been broken the first time I had worked in TV, the promise regarding my contract that had not been fulfilled this time, and most of all because I didn't really understand the medium. No one was teaching me production techniques so I had to learn as I went along.

I gradually developed an understanding of film, audio, how to speak, timing, and how to appear on camera, how to feel comfortable and be myself. I always thought the latter was very important. A lot of people tried to talk me into having voice training or lessons in how to walk on camera, how to behave, how to tilt my head, or what to do with my hands. I've always believed that as long as you're accurate, balanced, and look and sound credible then you can't go wrong. The crucial thing is to honestly and objectively tell people a story, as the person you really are. If you're false the viewers pick it. They're not stupid. They know wankers when they see them.

In an interview with a big movie star or personality you need to see their interaction with the reporter, but generally the journalist is nothing more than the storyteller. You're just the reporter telling the story; the public don't necessarily want to see you. I think some reporters pretend they're the story and try to appear in as many sequences in the report that they can. Perhaps a few of the younger reporters think that the more they're seen, the more famous they'll become, and the more they'll succeed. Not true. If the audience sees a really good, balanced story by a reporter they feel comfortable with, they're going to remember him or her next time. Not because of his tie or her hair, but because they did an interesting, accurate and objective report.

Between 1982 and 1984 I was very proud that Tom Barnett gave me my head, letting me do many investigations. One of the highlights was busting a large heroin gang in Darlinghurst. We hid out on rooftops for days at a time filming heroin being sold outside the Tradesmans Arms Hotel. The police investigated our report, insisting on putting me under 24-hour guard for a few days until things quietened down.

But my first-ever investigation for television had been a five-part exposé of Sydney nursing homes, for which I worked undercover in several homes. At one nursing home I used a tiny hidden stills camera to take photos of residents who had wrapped themselves in blankets because the heating was almost nonexistent. I also took photos of filthy bathrooms and some pretty questionable food. The male matron called it 'cattle food'. 'You wouldn't feed this to your cattle,' he said one day dishing out lunch. When I had gone for the job interview I had used my real name, but the matron had said 'Oh, you can use another name if you want', presumably so I could avoid paying tax. The first day I was there he even asked me to hand out drugs to the patients. I flatly refused. He knew I wasn't qualified to hand out drugs, and it was a dangerous practice. After my report had aired and I'd made an official complaint to the New South Wales Health Department, the department closed the nursing home down.

Another nursing home I worked undercover in wasn't quite as bad, and one was quite good. But even in the one that was quite good they still locked up the food so the residents couldn't take any. It was like Fort Knox when it came to everyday food items. I snuck out one day to stand on the footpath to be filmed by a cameraman and sound recordist hidden across the road. I had a small radio microphone on. Anyone watching me would have to have thought I was crazy because it looked like I was talking to myself – or to an egg and a biscuit that I had in my hands. I'd taken an egg and a biscuit from the padlocked pantry and was holding them up saying: 'An egg and a biscuit which we all take for granted in most of our households, but in nursing homes like this they're locked up.' And then I turned around, ready to walk back inside after finishing my piece, and there was the matron glaring at me.

'What are you doing?' she asked.

'Um, I'm talking to an egg and a biscuit,' was all I could lamely manage to say.

She looked at me as if I was absolutely stark raving mad and said: 'Just get back inside and finish your work' which I did, and got away without being caught out.

That was the first investigation I ever did for television and one of the most graphic investigations into our crumbling nursing homes the country had ever seen. *Good Morning Australia* and Channel Ten News in Sydney and Melbourne aired it, and it caused a huge stir.

It also earned a nomination for a Logie for most outstanding current affairs report. I was so chuffed but was up against *60 Minutes'* George Negus, who'd been nominated for his unbelievably beautiful story on

Annie, an intellectually disabled girl who later became the subject of a full-length movie.

At the 1983 Logies I was an absolute nobody and over the moon about being nominated. It was Lea's and my first Logies; we had flown to Melbourne for the night and had been put up in a flash, expensive hotel. It was a very big deal. Lea looked gorgeous all dolled up in her new gear. Nervously we walked up to the entrance and handed in our tickets. They didn't have a seat for us! With all these people walking in behind us we were ushered to one side. The organisers were just as embarrassed that one of the nominees didn't have a seat. We just wanted to go home and die.

Eventually they found us two seats on the *Cop Shop* drama table with Paula Duncan, John Orcsik and the rest of the cast. It was certainly generous of all of them to allow two nobodies to squeeze on to their table. Anyway, the big moment comes and the award is about to be announced. Because I had never been to anything like this before I didn't see the camera already pointing at George Negus 10 seconds before the announcement so the live telecast could get his reaction. John Orcsik slapped me on the shoulder and said: 'Oh mate, you've lost. See, the camera is on Negus.' And just at that moment Negus was announced the winner. When I went up afterwards to congratulate Negus, just being near the *60 Minutes* table gave me a chill up my spine. To a television novice like me these guys were the ultimate in news and current affairs.

At that time I used to sail with a *60 Minutes*

cameraman who had a half-share in a yacht. Vernon Moore and I became very close friends and still are to this day. Back then we used to get out on the water together and through Vernon I was invited to a *60 Minutes* barbecue. I was extremely apprehensive about going because I didn't want to appear to be endearing myself to the program. I couldn't bear to think that I might seem like a crawler trying to get on to the show using a friendship. So I deliberately never went near Peter Meakin or Gerald Stone, the senior producers of the show. I kept right away from them. Had someone told me that within two years I would not only be at Channel Nine myself but also be one of the four reporters on *60 Minutes* I would have thought them crazy.

When I'd been at Channel Ten for two years, which is when I'd wanted my contract to end, I received offers from Channel Seven's *Terry Willesee Show*, which screened in New South Wales, and from Michael Willesee and Peter Meakin who were to be co-executive producers of a new national current affairs program called *Willesee*. I was furious because I couldn't legally leave Channel Ten and they wouldn't let me go. It was very frustrating and I was not happy. And it was often very obvious I wasn't happy. My will to work just wasn't there; I no longer had any real enthusiasm for the job.

Anyway, it was all settled for me one slow news day when I was horsing around with the crew in the cameramen's room. We were bored and were throwing a chair to each other, the idea being that we had to catch it before it hit the floor. I threw the chair and it flew up into the ceiling and knocked out a couple of cheap particle-board panels. Just as it happened the chief security guard walked into the room.

'I've got you Munro! I've got you now! Caught red-handed,' he said.

'You beauty! Good, do something about it,' I said.

They did. They let me go. After two years and six months at Channel Ten I opted to join *Willesee* on Channel Nine because of the station's supreme reputation in news and current affairs, and the journalistic prowess of Willesee and Meakin. Channel Ten's lawyers didn't want to make it easy for me to get away. They sent me a bill for $80 worth of damage to the ceiling and a letter trying to stop me from appearing on Channel Nine until my three-year contract with Channel Ten was up. The lawyers at Channel Nine just laughed at them and told them where to go – and they did.

So in June 1984 I appeared on *Willesee* for the first time. Going to Channel Nine was the next major move in my career since first joining newspapers and going to New York. Not only did I find myself working for the great pioneer of Australian television current affairs, Michael Willesee, but also Peter Meakin, who helped launch the original *A Current Affair* in the 1970s and who would eventually become the Nine Network's director of news and current affairs. He is largely responsible for the enormous success of not only news and current affairs at Channel Nine but infotainment programs like *Money, Good Medicine,*

Getaway and *RPA*. He would eventually offer me *This is Your Life*. He also played a major role in establishing *60 Minutes'* dominance in the early 1980s. Meakin hired others for *Willesee* like Stephen Rice, who now runs the *Sunday* program, Janet Eastman, who became one of the best producers *60 Minutes* ever had, and John Muldrew, one of the best writers and producers, who over the years has written for Michael Willesee, Jana Wendt, Ray Martin, and who wrote most of the introductions for me on *A Current Affair*. Robert Penfold, the Nine Network's longtime and respected foreign correspondent in the US and the UK, was also a reporter on *Willesee*. All of these people were not only wonderfully talented but also generous enough to share what they knew with a know-nothing like me. My days at *Willesee* were among the happiest of my whole career.

What I had been doing at Channel Ten news I found fairly bland. A reporter's voice over the pictures, a grab from an interview with one of the subjects involved in the story, and a piece to camera by the reporter. It wasn't rocket science, and as I had come from writing 2,000-word five-part features and news stories over the years it wasn't very satisfying. I needed something more. I had told myself that if the move to *Willesee* didn't work I would never again entertain the thought of trying television journalism. But at last I was being taught how to write and produce for television. Voiceovers, timing, structure, how to keep it pacey and not put people to sleep – and of course to keep it accurate and fair.

Suddenly a whole new world of journalism opened up to me. It was as if I was starting out all over again. It was just fantastic. I very quickly found myself going from being wary of this third foray into television to realising that this was where my future in journalism lay.

In the first year I was there we did a major investigation on a child pornography ring in Kings Cross. Producer Shane Maguire posed as a sleaze wanting to buy photographs of children, some as young as nine and 10. We were eventually able to buy some photos and rented an apartment to which they could be anonymously posted. Those photos would eventually convict the 60-year-old man who had taken them – all the sofas, rugs and wall hangings that appeared in the photos were found in the first floor 'studio' where he photographed children in various degrading poses. When the investigation aired on national television it caused an outcry. Police immediately raided the premises and we handed over all our videotapes and other evidence. The man concerned was charged, convicted and sentenced to six months in gaol.

I think one reason for Channel Nine's success is the fact that most of the programs' offices are housed in cottages around the perimeter of the main station building. Staff can work on their own show in their own cottage without the interruptions and politics of the main building. *Willesee* was in a cottage at number 2 Scott Street in Willoughby.

Lea and I were madly trying to pay off our home, save up to renovate, and bring up Sean, who was now two. New home, first baby, new job – it was all happening. I also needed a new car, but finances were obviously tight. I bought a Mini Moke, which I would drive for the next 10 years. I'd always wanted to own a convertible and I figured that the only convertible I was ever going to be able to afford was a Mini Moke. It cost me $1,900 and ran on the smell of an oily rag – Peter Meakin would always joke that one of my on-camera suits was worth more than my car!

The only problem was that it didn't have a roof and we couldn't afford to buy one. Fortunately, number 2 Scott Street had a carport that I was able to park under when it rained. Michael Willesee, however, didn't have a car spot in those days so when it rained the $1,900 Mini Moke got precedence over his $300,000 Bentley. Michael was very good-natured about it and always joked about the Moke getting priority.

I became known around Nine as the madman driving the red Mini Moke, wearing various hats to keep my hair clean if I had to do a piece to camera. In winter I also wore an old blue ski parka with a high collar, which came up to my nose. I looked like the abominable snowman. Sometimes it would start raining while I was driving in a suit. I ruined a couple of suits over the years from being caught in downpours on the way to or from work.

As I discovered a whole new world of journalism at *Willesee* I also became a lot more confident within myself. I was surrounded by talented, funny and dedicated people who loved working on substantial and relevant stories and investigations. We all worked hard – and now started playing hard. I would hit the pub on Friday nights with a wild group of cameramen and reporters, all good blokes. We went to the Channel Nine hotel – the Bridgeview Hotel at Willoughby – and it used to rock. I was becoming more and more my own person as I approached my 31st birthday. I suppose it had probably taken me this long to break that fear of alcohol. And once I had gotten over that fear I had no qualms about being one of the last to leave most Friday nights. It was as if I was making up for lost time. Friday night drinking sessions began turning into Saturday morning marathons. Not only was I more confident about drinking but I also enjoyed the company of everyone I was working, and drinking, with.

The person I was hurting most was Lea. I was leaving her alone at home with baby Sean most Friday nights, when something I had always abhorred about Australian men was their Friday night drinking ritual. This period didn't last too long. Lea read the riot act to me and I quickly pulled my head in. The debate over whether alcoholism is genetic or a person can develop it also ticked away in the back of my mind. I certainly had no desire to find out one way or the other. I still had the occasional big night, but not nearly as often.

Around this time I started to get quite a reputation as the 'walk-in merchant', chasing down villains, politicians and other con men. Incredibly, I have never been punched once. Have had to duck and weave from a few, even had a shotgun fired over my head once when I worked in newspapers, but I've never been hit.

It was a very exciting time because tremendous innovations were being made on the show. We take the credit for developing what is called a 'simsat', a technique used when the interviewer and interviewee are in two different places. The interviewee wears a hidden earpiece connected to a telephone, through which the interviewer asks them questions. The interviewee answers, while being recorded by a camera. The video footage is then sent to the TV studio via satellite. The interviewer records the questions on video and they are edited together with the answers to recreate the interview. Today this technique is used in television all over the world, but only since *Willesee* developed it. It meant that we could get interviews from the most isolated locations, so long as there was a telephone and we could get a camera crew there.

I believe another reason for Channel Nine's dominance of Australian television is that management, all the way up to Kerry and James Packer, have always taken the time and patience to develop the on-air talent and production staff. To watch them and plan for them.

Within 23 months of joining *Willesee*, Peter Meakin asked if I would be interested in becoming a *60 Minutes* reporter as George Negus was leaving. I was absolutely blown away by the offer: me, a *60 Minutes* reporter?

It was a decision that I never dreamed I would have to make. Only two years earlier I'd been hiding at the back of a *60 Minutes* barbecue, just grateful to be there and staring goggled-eyed at the likes of Jana Wendt and Ian Leslie. Now, at the age of 32, I was being offered a position as one of the reporters on the program. It was 1985 and I was told that the position would probably come up around the middle of the next year.

If I took the job I would be away from home about eight months a year. Here I was, a person who'd had this difficult childhood and was always determined to have a wonderful, close-knit family, being offered one of the best jobs in a career I'd always wanted, knowing that it would take me away from that same family. Since leaving home and marrying Lea I had become a home-body. I knew I wouldn't travel well. Lea and I had a great deal of talking and soul-searching to do over the coming months.

Around this time I asked Lea if she would be okay with Mum moving into the house with us. Could she put up with that?

Lea had been abused and called some outrageous names by Mum for years – all under the effect of alcohol – so you can understand how she felt about inviting such a chronic alcoholic into her home, especially when I might be joining *60 Minutes* and be away from that home for up to eight months every year. Even after we had arrived back from New York and had just bought our first house Mum had continued to abuse Lea over the phone. Only now while researching this book has Lea told me that Mum would ring her wanting to know what time I might be at home and then when Lea told her that I would be late Mum would turn on her, believing Lea was just making it up. It was then that Mum would abuse her, still calling her a 'slut' and a 'whore'. Lea didn't tell me about it because she didn't want to make things worse for me, and because she knew, like me, that it was just the grog talking.

Lea sought her mother, Lois's, advice. When younger, Lois had shared her family home with her mother-in-law for 10 years and it had not been easy for her. She didn't want her daughter to have to face the problems she had to. She said she didn't think Lea could cope with my Mum and Sean, who was only about two. At the time I was bitterly disappointed that Lea's mum had advised her against Mum moving in. She had always tried to make me feel welcome in their family so I couldn't understand why they didn't want Mum to come and live with us as a family. But now, as a parent myself, I can understand Lea's mother's point of view, looking out for her youngest daughter.

Lea said no to Mum moving in. It was a very difficult decision for her, and it was a heartbreaking one for me. The fact that I didn't push the issue has plagued me for many years now. Perhaps if Mum had come and lived with us I would have had a better chance of encouraging her to sober up. There would have been no alcohol in the house and she couldn't have gone very far to buy any. And perhaps she would have survived. I couldn't forget how much Mum had done for me over the years and how much I owed her. But looking back I can see that it probably wouldn't have worked with Mum living under the same roof as Lea, Sean and me. I think it would have been impossible for Lea and would have had a drastic effect on our marriage.

Instead Mum moved into a Housing Department unit in a large complex on the north shore of Sydney. It was less than half a kilometre from Sydney's Royal North Shore Hospital where, within the year, Mum would die.

8

In 1985 the *Willesee* investigation that had smashed a child pornography racket earned me and the crew a nomination for the Logie for the most outstanding public affairs report. I was also nominated for the Logie for reporter of the year. This second Logie experience was very different to my first. Although I still wasn't that well known on Australian television, the organisers did at least have seats for Lea and me this time. We felt as if we belonged.

Willesee didn't win the Logie for best current affairs report – but my name was called out as the winner of the reporter of the year Logie. Lea and I couldn't believe it. I'd only been in television journalism for just over three years so winning anything was a complete surprise. My one and only regret was that I forgot to mention my mother in my acceptance speech. In fact, I almost forgot to mention Lea. I thanked all my work mates who had helped me and was about to walk away when I remembered, and stepped back to the microphone to 'thank my best friend and soul mate, Lea, for all her support'. But I forgot to mention my mother.

To make matters worse, Mum had once again been admitted to hospital after collapsing and hitting her head. Doctor Turk had found Mum at home and had admitted her to hospital while we were in Melbourne at the Logies. I returned and went straight to the Royal North Shore Hospital to visit her. She was the worst I had ever seen her. Pale, in a lot of pain, and with stitches in her head from when she fell. She was also having major problems with her liver and kidneys. Despite this, she had lost none of her venom when it came to me forgetting to mention her at the Logies. I was already feeling guilty about it when she launched a verbal attack on me in the hospital ward: 'You can thank that Lea and say how wonderful she is but couldn't even mention all that I've done for you all your life. You're an ungrateful wretch.'

Mum loved her television. Apart from alcohol and me, towards the end she had no other life but television. We would often talk for hours about what she had been watching on TV. And here was her son accepting an award at the biggest television awards of the year thanking his wife but not thanking her. I'll never forget the look on her face as she said: 'Well you could have thanked me.' At this stage I had just told her that I had been asked to join *60 Minutes*.

About three months later, in July 1985, Mum went into Royal North Shore Hospital again. By now her whole body was giving up, falling apart. I knew it was bad but I didn't think she was going to die. To me she was never going to die. She was tough and resilient and yes, things were going downhill, and yes, she was getting worse, but I really thought she'd get through it again.

Mum was only in hospital for about a week before she passed away. The doctors rang to tell me that virtually every one of her major organs was barely functioning. I had only seen Mum the night before in her hospital room but now I found myself rushing to intensive care. She was lying unconscious in a large, cold impersonal chamber-like room in which a nurse monitored her vital signs. I couldn't really tell her exactly how I felt because the nurse couldn't leave the room. In tears, I whispered to Mum how much I had always loved her and that I knew how much she had given up so that I might have a better life. I tell myself she heard me but there was no sign that she did. The nurse walked over and gently said, 'She's going.' I burst into tears and held her, again telling her how much I loved her.

I regret so much that I didn't get a chance to speak with her before she died. I think that if we had both known she was about to die we would have spoken freely about our feelings for each other for the first and only time in our lives together.

Once she had passed away I told myself she was at peace at last. No longer racked by loneliness, no longer in constant pain from her failing kidneys and liver. I told myself that, but deep down, until that moment I had never given up the belief that one day, one day, I would get Mum sober and she would revert to that happy, always laughing, bubbly personality she was in her late teens and early 20s, before things began to sour with my father.

Mum had died 10 months before I was to join *60 Minutes*. She would miss the successes that followed, including my years at *A Current Affair* and *This is Your Life*. We would never be able to discuss my interviews with Dolly Parton, Bette Midler, Katharine Hepburn, Sean Connery, Madonna, Julia Roberts and Michelle Pfeiffer – all stars of the big screen that her son had met. It was a sad and tragic thing that she had given so much and was not going to see any of her hard work pay off, particularly being someone who loved her television so much.

Over the years Mum never told me once to my face that she was proud of me or loved me, but I would always hear it from everyone else: 'Oh, your mother's so proud of you'; 'She never stops talking about you'; 'She loves you'. Only on one occasion I knew of did Mum actually tell me she loved me. She said it one night when she thought I was sound asleep. It was when we were living above the liquor store and I remember it as if it were yesterday. At the time I wanted to jump out of bed and wrap my arms around her shouting, 'I knew it, I knew it!' Instead I managed to wait until she had gone before I burst into tears. Happy tears.

But even as a toddler, and then certainly in later years, the thing that had kept me going was the absolute belief that Mum did love me. That I really wasn't just a pasty-faced nothing. And maybe I really didn't come from thieves and bushrangers. I grabbed hold of every positive I could to get me through the darker times. Why else would Mum work so hard holding down two jobs on occasions to make sure we always stayed in the same area and had stability? Mum had always deliberately sought out jobs and housing in a three-kilometre radius of my school and my friends – that was her plan all along and she stuck to it zealously. I owed the whole foundation of my life to her. Now, the only blood relative I'd ever really known and loved was gone.

I had always thought that if anything would get her sober it would be being a grandmother to Sean. She tried for a while after he was born but it didn't last. And now that she was gone she would never get to see her beautiful granddaughter, Amy. Ames was born just 13 weeks after Mum died. And, to my eyes, Amy has been the spitting image of my mother all her life. The same hair, mouth and nose. Mum would have absolutely adored her.

Mum's funeral was held at Sacred Heart, Mosman, where she had attended church for almost 30 years. My Uncle Leo and his wonderful wife, Pat, were there as were two of their children, Terry and Colleen. Lea's family were all there as were my childhood mates, Mark, Terry and Geoff. For most of the Mass, Sean, who was then two-and-a-half, played around underneath Mum's coffin, which was raised on a stand. I remember thinking how ironic it was because although Mum adored him we could never leave the two of them alone together or allow Mum to babysit him in case she got drunk or fell over. It was nice watching him quietly play. Naturally Vera was there to say farewell to the 'baby sister' she found too late to help. Vera took Mum's death very hard, almost blaming herself for not finding her sooner. But there was only one person in the world who could've helped Mum and that person was herself. Tragically, she never admitted that.

After much discussion, Lea and I decided that I should take the position at *60 Minutes*. I was given the choice of replacing George Negus in May 1986 or replacing Jana Wendt in August, when she was to leave and begin her reign at *A Current Affair*. I was keen to get going and opted to start in May. It was hard to believe but in less than two years of joining the Nine Network I was a reporter on *60 Minutes*.

Sean was three years old while Amy was only seven months. It was a lot to ask of Lea to run the household with two babies while I would be away for up to eight months a year. So we decided to employ a live-in nanny until everyone's routines settled down. Lea hired a lovely young woman from Melbourne called Sharon, who became a major part of our family right from the start. She was kind and patient towards the children, who adored her. She also became a good friend for Lea while I was away. Sharon stayed a little over a year, when she decided to return to her own family. But at least her time with us gave Lea the breathing space she needed to sort out our new lifestyles.

The first story I did was an investigation into a

Melbourne doctor who had killed two or three patients through negligence. The story never went to air because the producer gave the doctor the right to veto the story if he didn't like the way the interview went or the way the story was put together. The story was always going to be very critical, and of course he didn't approve of it. It was a surprising introduction to the program for me because I had not seen *60 Minutes* as being the kind of show where villains were given control over stories. Gerald Stone, the executive producer, erupted angrily when he found out; an interviewee was not given the power of veto again in the next seven years that I was there.

I left Melbourne and went straight to Italy to do a story on the Pope. This was my very first overseas trip for *60 Minutes*. We were to film the Pope travelling through the Ravenna region on the Adriatic Sea then back to the Vatican, where we would have an audience with him. A great colour story. I wasn't overawed by the event; I saw it more from a journalistic point of view than a religious one. Regardless, I almost never got to set eyes on the Pope because I was almost killed in a car accident while driving in a hire car from Bologna to Ravenna. It had been several years since I had driven on the right-hand side of the road and I was driving around hairpin bends blissfully and stupidly unaware that I was on the wrong side of the road. And just as I realised and swerved back to the correct side, this huge truck came barrelling around a bend, literally a second or two after I had corrected myself. My *60 Minutes* career had almost ended before it had even begun.

We followed Il Papa for several days then returned to

Rome, where it had been arranged that I and cameraman Nick Lee and sound recordist Michael Breen would meet him after an outdoor Mass at St Peter's. We were told he would be brought to us but there was to be no sound recording. Only the pictures would carry the moment, and I had to try and make that moment last as long as possible. So when he was brought to us I began telling him my history as an altar boy. How I used to serve Mass for Bishop Muldoon. 'Do you know him?' I asked the Pope. He was very patient and charming despite my obvious stalling to keep him there for the camera. He even grabbed my arm and in the end he stopped and chatted for about two minutes. For years since, Peter Meakin has always joked that the only reason the Pope stayed so long chatting was that I was standing on his foot to make sure he didn't go anywhere. The Pope was then directed away from me along a row of pews for dozens of five-second greetings with overseas visitors and dignitaries.

Anyone who thinks the Vatican isn't a business should think again. As the Pope had approached me he was trailed by two of his own camera crews and at least three photographers. Every person the Pope ever meets is photographed and videotaped from at least two angles. And for no small amount of money the videos and photographs can be delivered to your hotel within three or four hours of them being taken. The Vatican is certainly a well-oiled machine.

* * *

When I began at *60 Minutes* it was in the days before bean counters started running the world and when the Aussie dollar was healthier. If we needed a helicopter for filming purposes we hired one. We stayed in the best five-star hotels in the world, with thousands of US dollars in travellers cheques and credit cards that had limits of tens of thousands of dollars. I remember putting US$80,000 down on my corporate American Express card to cover hotel bills and extra airfares for a seven-week trip.

The way the program operates is that crews made up of a reporter, camera operator and sound recordist leapfrog around the world meeting up with producers, doing stories and sending the pictures and sound back to Australia for broadcast. The crew would travel together for a period of anywhere between three and eight weeks. Once all the interviews have been filmed for a story the producer and reporter lock themselves away in their hotel rooms for a couple of days to look closely at the interviews and see how the story is shaping up, then spend another day writing a script for the voiceover. While this is going on, the camera operator and sound recordist might be out and about shooting any further shots needed for the story – or just taking some time off for sightseeing. Once the reporter and producer have finished writing the script the sound recordist completely rearranges the furnishings in his hotel room, using mattresses, pillows and cushions to create a makeshift sound booth. I'd record my voiceover script and that, together with all the pictures, other sound recordings and editing instructions would be flown back to the *60 Minutes* office in Australia and be put together to go on air.

I only ever saw my completed stories if I was back home when they went to air. I was often too busy or just wanted to spend time with Lea and the kids, rather than sit down and watch tapes of four or five stories that I'd missed go to air while I was away. Of the 150-plus stories I did for *60 Minutes* throughout the late 1980s and early 90s I've probably only ever seen half of them. No point in watching something on television which you've already actually lived through. Plus I have never been comfortable – am still not today – with watching myself on television.

The average cost of an overseas story in those days worked out to be about $50,000 each – a story produced in Australia cost around $20,000. Usually we'd spend five or six days on each story. Once we had finished, the producer would start researching and developing another story, while the camera operator, sound recordist and I would travel to the next location to meet up with another producer who had already laid the foundations for our next assignment.

Although there were always four of us on the road together it could be lonely. Returning to the hotel room, no matter how nice it might be, was the hardest thing for me to do each day. At the end of long trips away you'd look back at the first couple of weeks and the stories we did and they seemed like we had done them years before rather than only weeks earlier. It was incredible to look back over those longer trips and realise how much we'd packed into them; how many very different people from worlds apart we'd met and interviewed and then moved on and out of their lives forever. By the time I got home I felt I'd been away for six months instead of six weeks.

It was a completely unrealistic lifestyle and you had to be careful not to be suckered in by it. One day I'd be swimming alongside Madonna in a pool at one of the most expensive hotels in the world, the next day I'd be back home with Lea and the kids, getting roused on by Lea for leaving my wet towel on the bed after a shower.

When I took the job several people warned me about the 'recognition factor' of working at *60 Minutes*. But nothing prepared me for the sudden light in people's eyes when they recognised me being from *60 Minutes*. It was obvious not only to me, but also, uncomfortably, for Lea and the kids. That's when I took to wearing caps and sunglasses. I had never worn sunglasses in my life and wasn't a particular fan of baseball caps but now I rarely leave the house without them. It wasn't that people weren't always friendly and flattering. It was just embarrassing for us as a family. It was obvious pretty early on that *60 Minutes* was going to be like no other job in journalism I had ever had before, professionally as well as personally.

Having finished with the Pope in Rome, I went to Vancouver in Canada to interview David Coombe, the High Commissioner for Australia in Canada, and former

Secretary of the Australian Labor Party. It was quite a controversial interview as he was very critical of the way the Labor Party had forsaken him, and one of his children spoke out against the way the party had treated his father. I was back in Sydney by late May, having been away for only two weeks. The idea had been to get the new reporter up, running and established as soon as possible with a couple of big stories.

I only stayed home for two weeks before heading for Athens, the Greek island of Mykonos and Israel. One of my stories was an examination of security at Athens Airport and on Israel's tight-as-a-knot airline, El Al, as there was an ever-growing threat of international terrorism and there had been a lot of hijackings and terrorist activity in Greece. It was an interesting story in the light of the disaster of the September 11 terrorist attacks in 2001, because even then, in the mid-1980s, El Al's security was unbelievable. Twenty years before any other airline started doing it they searched your suitcases before you even took your ticket to the counter for check-in. Once you had checked in they searched your bags again, pulling everything out of them onto large tables. Then security searched all your hand luggage again before you boarded a bus to take you to your plane out on the tarmac. On the bus we actually saw one passenger's carton of cigarettes being opened to make sure the carton contained only packets of cigarettes. The first two packets in the carton were also opened. The Israelis don't muck around.

On the way from Athens to Tel Aviv we filmed two

of Israel's air marshals, a term most of us have only learned about since September 11. Sitting across the aisle from me was a heavy-set bloke pretending to read the paper. In front of him, directly above the pilot's cabin, was a magnified mirror that looked directly down the aisle of the whole plane. He could see anything that might occur within three-quarters of the plane. There was another marshal sitting down the back of the aircraft. Both men were well armed.

When we arrived in Tel Aviv and were waiting to clear our equipment through customs we filmed airport security moving through the crowd making sure there was no unattended baggage. I deliberately stood away from my briefcase. In a matter of seconds two Israeli soldiers were standing over it, asking people nearby to whom it belonged. We immediately claimed ownership and filmed the sequence unfold. The four of us then drove up to Jerusalem and stayed at the historic King David Hotel where dozens of British soldiers were blown up during Israel's fight for independence in the late 1940s. There we scripted the airline security story.

And that was only the first month or so of *60 Minutes*! Things started to move even more quickly after that. It wasn't long before I went to America to interview Dolly Parton, which was to result in one of the many famous interviews on *60 Minutes*. Raw, untried, callow young reporter flirting with Dolly Parton and asking her the size of her bust; sort of half knowing that she wasn't going to tell me but feeling confident and brave enough to ask anyway.

Married at last after seven years of going out together – you can never be too careful.

Mum and Dad's first meeting in almost 20 years.

Lea's parents, Viv and Lois. A loving relationship very different to that of my parents.

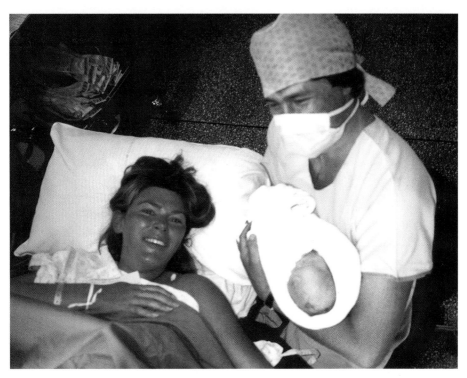

Sean's birth – a smiling dad and an exhausted mum.

Sean's first birthday party – I thought if anything could stop Mum from drinking it would be her grandson.

Amy at 10 weeks – our
beautiful little Quaker baby.

Sean and Amy – best of
mates as toddlers and still
best of mates today.

My two great mentors – Mike Willesee and Peter Meakin.

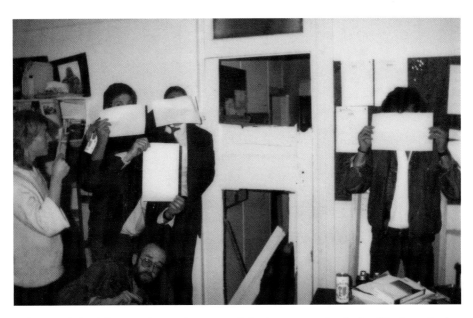

What was left of the 60 Minutes door … and the 'anonymous' culprits. That's me in the coat and tie.

I didn't ever have to stand on the Pope's foot to keep him chatting.

'People say I should carry a .45 rather than wear one!' (Photo: Warren McStoker)

'Don't be one minute late or I won't open the front door!' (Photo: Ben Hawke)

'Up yours buster,' was her much-celebrated reply.

But after the interview, once the cameras were turned off, Dolly Parton did tell us the size of her bustline. She admitted that it went up and down with her weight but that at present her bust line was 45" – and she only stood at 4'11½".

'Everyone says that I should carry a .45 rather than wear one,' she said in her southern drawl.

That was my first-ever major celebrity interview. Being such a novice and so critical of my work I said to Warren McStoker, the producer with us in Tennessee, that I didn't think the interview was that good. He gave me a quizzical look and said, 'You should be pleased with it.' After we had written the story Warren took it straight back to Australia while the crew and I moved on to London. When Gerald Stone, the executive producer of the program at the time, saw the interview he remarked to those in the room: 'This is the sort of interview that reputations are made on.' Gerald had this uncanny gift for knowing what stories would work. And of course he was absolutely right. Even now, all these years later, people are still kind enough to say how much they enjoyed 'that cheeky interview with Dolly Parton'.

Despite these early tinglings of success I was already desperately homesick. On the way to interview Dolly Parton in Los Angeles I completely broke down on the phone to Lea because I missed her and the children so much. I was an absolute blubbering sook and wanted to come home. Lea, as usual, was a rock and calmed me down. My other major problem was sleep, or the lack of it. Maybe it was psychological, maybe jetlag, but every time I went away I could only ever grab a few hours of sleep in the first four or so days. And I have never been able to sleep on aeroplanes. Until we were well into a trip I was often a walking zombie.

I wondered whether I'd made a mistake in moving to *60 Minutes* because I was desperately missing home; it was a very hard time for Lea and me. I wasn't drowning my sorrows in grog, but I guess sometimes it did help me to sleep. While I still wasn't a big drinker by any means because of Mum, when I did drink I made the most of it. I might not have one drink for a fortnight and then have a huge night. It never made me violent, just loud and playful. But on one occasion I completely flipped out. I was just about to leave for a six-week trip through Europe and Africa. It was a Friday night, the birthday of one of the senior producers, and we were having a barbecue in the *60 Minutes* compound within the Channel Nine complex. We all had a few drinks at the birthday party, and by 7.00 or 8.00pm there were about five or six desperates still going strong. I had started wearing a particular brand of cowboy boots while living in New York and had worn them ever since. Now, in the *60 Minutes* office, I was being goaded into kicking in an old wooden door that took up too much room. A couple of the guys were egging me on, screaming at 'foot-in-the-door' Munro to kick the door in. In my hazy stupor I gladly obliged. In fact, not only did I kick it in, there was very little left of it except hunks of wood and splinters all over the floor. As if that wasn't enough we all then posed for a photograph in front of the door.

At that point I'd had more than enough and left to catch a cab home. As I walked down the pathway I passed Gerald Stone on his way back to the office, said goodnight and told him I'd talk to him in six weeks, after the trip. I certainly didn't think he'd be screaming at me down the phone and threatening me with the sack within 30 minutes of me arriving home. Naturally he was irate about the door in the office. People had always spoken about Gerald Stone's famous 'Force 10' temper. I now found myself smack bang in the middle of the cyclone.

'No little scumbag from the *Daily Mirror* newspaper is coming in here and destroying my program and everything we've worked for,' he bellowed down the phone.

Still playful and thinking like a practical joker, I thought maybe everyone at work had put him up to it as a joke. So I said to Gerald: 'Are you joking?' Well, didn't he go off then! He told me he wasn't sure if I'd be leaving for the trip on Monday, or any other trip for that matter. He told me to call him after I had completely cleaned up the mess in the office the next day.

I thought: this is great, I've been at *60 Minutes* only a matter of months and already I'm going to be fired. And probably deserved to be. Fortunately Gerald calmed down and let it pass but it was a timely wake-up call. From that moment on I pulled my head in and quietened down. I stopped having big nights out – I had a four-year-old and one-year-old at home with the best and most loving wife anyone could ever wish for.

9

One particular interview was to stand out during 1987: an interview with Jan Murray, the then wife of the Federal Tourism Minister in the Hawke Government, John Brown. The angle to the story was that they were a high-profile power couple. He was the good-looking, popular politician and businessman while she ran a successful public relations business. We had filmed them in Canberra and Sydney, and had one last interview to do with Murray in her office. She struck me as a no-nonsense and upfront woman who always told it just like it was. While cameraman Nick Lee was changing film during a break in the interview Jan began telling us that after John Brown became a federal minister the two of them decided to make love on the ministerial desk in parliament house – to christen it so to speak. So mischievous and cheeky were they that they decided to leave her panties in the ashtray on the desk for the staff to notice. She said they loved each other very much and didn't care if the whole world knew about it. She had us in stitches with tales of their escapades during that brief break in the interview. I told her that the story indicated how much she and Brown loved each other and proved just what an 'innovative' couple they really were. I suggested that now we were ready to roll the camera again she should actually tell us the story during the interview. I meant what I told her, but I also knew we were on to a sensational and extremely controversial story.

Anyway, being the good sport she is, Jan Murray did relate the story during the interview. When the profile aired it caused a huge fuss and made the front pages of newspapers all over the country. John Brown was hugely embarrassed and furious over her kiss and tell. These days the couple are no longer together. Jan Murray often appears on television panel shows and fights for causes close to her, a couple of which she has suggested to me as stories. Wherever she or John Brown goes the incident of making love on the ministerial desk is never far behind them.

That same year, in April 1987, I was fortunate to meet two giants in the multi-billion-dollar animation industry, Bill Hanna and Joe Barbera. Hanna-Barbera were responsible for giving life to mega hits like Tom and Jerry, The Flintstones, Yogi Bear and The Jetsons. And because they had a very successful production operation in Australia they had a soft spot for Aussies, particularly Bill Hanna, who had spent a lot of time in their Australian office. We filmed their whole animation and studio complex in Los Angeles.

One sequence we filmed for the story really stood out. When they first started out together almost 50 years before, they sat on opposite sides of the same desk. Bill Hanna would write the music for the cartoon while at the same time Joe Barbera would draw the pictures for the animation. Their first cartoon – Tom and Jerry in *Cats Concerto* – remains a classic today. Tom plays an eccentric concert pianist performing at Carnegie Hall in New York, and poor Jerry is bedded down on the keys inside the piano, trying to get some sleep. Naturally, Tom's performance is a disaster because of the pesky little mouse who refuses to move out of his 'bedroom'. Anyway, one of the sequences we filmed was the men re-enacting how they originally wrote, composed and drew *Cats Concerto*, Bill writing the music while Joe drew the pictures. I kept their pencilled work from that shoot and nursed it all the way home, knowing that these two guys were right up there with the likes of Walt Disney. I framed each of their first pages from *Cats Concerto*, which they had signed for me, and they are hung in my office. Sadly, Bill Hanna passed away in 2001 but the laughter and legacy he and Joe Barbera leave behind is incalculable.

My father had contracted cancer. He was 58. He was already a diabetic but still a heavy drinker. Cirrhosis of the liver didn't help either. He spent the last few months of his life living with us at home. Although I was travelling a lot we did manage to become a little closer than we had been. We both knew what a lousy father he'd been and there wasn't much more to be said.

Each afternoon he'd walk up to the local shops with Sean, promising not to spoil his five-year-old grandson, and of course headed straight for the milk bar and let Seany pick what he wanted. They were quality days in which Sean and his grandfather really got to know each other.

I was overseas when Dad became so bad that he was moved to a nearby hospice. I saw him a few more times before he passed away in October 1987, two years after Mum. They're now buried together because I always believed Mum loved Dad until the day she died. She was so hurt by his womanising and gambling that she could never bring herself to forgive him or make him a part of her life again, but I reckon she still loved him.

Almost immediately after Dad's funeral I had to leave for one of the longest trips I would ever do at *60 Minutes* – a seven-weeker through the US and Central America. I would do six stories, starting with an interview with dictator and president of Nicaragua, Daniel Ortega. Central America is a breathtakingly beautiful part of the world but harsh and cruel. It was heartbreaking seeing children begging outside our four-star hotel as we came and went during filming each day.

From there we flew to Miami. Around this time Don Johnson and the television cop drama *Miami Vice* were hugely popular around the world, and the real vice squad was trialling a new police technique called 'the reverse sting'. Others might call it entrapment.

Undercover cops went into heroin, crack or cocaine enclaves offering to buy drugs. Once a dealer agreed and a deal was done the dealer was busted. The squad took the *60 Minutes* team on raids in one of the poorest, drug-ridden ghettos of Miami called Liberty City. It was on these raids that I realised just how addictive this new drug called crack was. After only two or three smokes you were hooked. Whole families – two and three generations – were wiped out, lying in filthy, rat-infested, condemned houses. I'll never forget the fear in the eyes of the cops as they searched people's pockets, fearful of being pricked by a syringe tainted with HIV-infected blood.

From one extreme to another, we moved on to New York to do a story on the explosion in the international popularity of Aussie models such as Elle Macpherson and other Australian models working for international agencies operating out of Manhattan. We had another story planned in New York, but it was less of a certainty. For years before I had arrived at *60 Minutes* the program had been trying to get one of its own reporters an interview with Katharine Hepburn. Morley Safer from the American CBS *60 Minutes* had been the last reporter to interview her, several years before. Because I had grown up watching all those Katharine Hepburn and Spencer Tracy movies with Mum (and Bill Collins), almost as soon as I arrived at *60 Minutes* I wrote to Ms Hepburn and asked for the opportunity to interview her. She was in the middle of writing a book about the making of *The African Queen*, in which she starred alongside Humphrey Bogart. She wrote back to me saying she was busy with the book, but to keep in contact. She signed off with: 'As you know I'm very fond of Australia.' I have the letter framed and hung in our home office.

I did keep in contact and developed quite a good rapport with Bridget, Ms Hepburn's housekeeper. I had told Bridget when we would be in New York and that we would like to interview Ms Hepburn if she was available. I had even rung from Nicaragua – it took about two hours to get through – and confirmed the dates. I still hadn't spoken to the legend herself but as soon as I reached New York I phoned, and when she answered, the voice was unmistakable.

'I can't talk to you now. I'm about to be arrested in the street!' I can still hear those exact words today.

I asked what I could do – did she need help, a doctor?

'Ring me later. If I'm not in some cell in the local precinct,' she said as she hung up the phone.

I ran out of the Plaza Hotel, where we were staying, and caught a cab to Second Avenue and 49th Street. I was expecting to see cops, camera crews and crowds, with the great Katharine Hepburn in the middle of it all. There was nothing. Dead as a doornail. So I caught another cab back to the hotel and rang the Hepburn house. Bridget answered and told me that Ms Hepburn had had another argument with New York's parking police. In Manhattan you can't park your car on the same side of the street two days in a row; you have to change sides. Ms Hepburn had refused and been threatened with arrest. When Bridget told her that I had come charging down to try and help her, the great lady was so taken by the gesture she agreed to be interviewed.

She stunned us with her professionalism, inviting me and cameraman Nick Lee to her magnificent four-storey brownstone walk-up a couple of days before the interview so we could check the layout. Because it was such an important interview we needed enough room for two cameramen, a sound recordist, lights, me and the producer. She showed us her main sitting room where other interviews have been done in the past.

We chatted for more than an hour as she plied me and Nick with tea and brownies she had made herself. We kept looking at each other as if to say: 'Is this real or are we dreaming?'

She eventually showed us out with one last message, in true Hepburn style: 'Don't be late, or I won't open the door.'

Back then her Parkinson's shake was not that noticeable but was even less so in the mornings – sufferers' symptoms generally get worse as the day goes on and they get tired. The interview was set down for 11.00am. And we were painfully punctual.

She was generous with her time, allowing me to interview her for a full hour. I didn't expect her to talk about the one great love of her life, Spencer Tracy. She never had before, why start now? Nevertheless, as a journalist I had to ask. I couldn't believe it when she suddenly opened up about him. She said she believed he was the best actor she'd ever seen and that because of her love for him she had never been able to bring herself to watch *Guess Who's Coming to Dinner*. He had filmed his powerful and emotional monologue about racism for the film only days before his death, and she could not bring herself to watch the film. I nearly fell out of the chair. I was winding up the interview when she announced she wasn't finished yet and called for Bridget to fetch one of her paintings. It depicted Barrenjoey Lighthouse overlooking Palm Beach in Sydney.

'I climbed up the cliff face with my old friend Sir Robert Helpmann. And then I painted this,' she proudly said, offering it to our camera.

Just when the crew and I thought the day couldn't get any better Ms Hepburn invited us all to stay for a lunch of antipasto. I thought: this is what this job is all about. I really did have to pinch myself as Katharine Hepburn, next to me at the table, talked about Bogie's drinking during the making of *The African Queen*, and how she had him around her little finger, and about the relationship between Bogie and Lauren Bacall. I very subtly lowered my right hand and pinched myself firmly on the bum. Yes, I *was* awake.

We were to spend the next few days with some of the most beautiful young women in the world but we were all mesmerised by a woman in her 80s. My experience has shown that it's the true, triple-A-grade stars who are the nicest and easiest to deal with. Sadly, Katharine Hepburn died in her Connecticut home on 30 June 2003 aged 96.

* * *

Producer, Ben Hawke, took those first four stories back to Australia while the crew and I went to Chicago to do a story on the growing scandal of priests breaking their vows of celibacy in the Catholic Church. We did one final story back in Los Angeles and returned home. I was only in Sydney for a few days before I had to head to Papua New Guinea, Tasmania, Uluru and the Philippines.

After the Philippines I was lucky enough to come home for five whole weeks before heading to a small, bland little town called Medjugorje in what was then Yugoslavia and is now Bosnia-Herzegovina. For years the Virgin Mary has been appearing to several visionaries – children from the local village – every evening in a church loft, overlooking the altar. Each year tens of thousands of people from all over the world make pilgrimages to this tiny town, where rosary beads change colour and other miracles are said to occur. Driving there from Dubrovnik on the Adriatic Coast, we stopped and interviewed the local bishop in Mostar. Because the hierarchy of the Church can take hundreds of years to recognise miracles and divine appearances he dismissed the visionaries and their claims. But with my upbringing and my relationship with the Catholic Church I didn't need much convincing – in fact, for me this was an excellent opportunity to get a lot closer to someone I still prayed to and had adored all my life. The cameraman on this trip was a gold-plated atheist. Although he respected the beliefs of the pilgrims, he thought the whole story was a bit of a joke. But as it progressed and he came to know the visionaries he softened his stance a little. He found it hard to argue with certain points put forward by one of the visionaries, 19-year-old Maria. In our interview Maria asked: 'Why would I do this? Why would I admit to the visions and ruin my life? I can't walk outside my front door without American tourists wanting to throw $100 bills at me. I've never accepted any money. I ask them to donate it to the church. There are people knocking on my door around the clock. I can't go to church without being followed by 20 or 30 tourists. Why would I do this? Why would I ruin my life?'

During the interview she told me how the Virgin Mary had taken her to heaven and hell, and she described what she saw there.

According to folklore, during the war in Bosnia bombs were dropped on Medjugorje to lower the Croatian morale but the bombs mysteriously didn't explode, and some bombs were said to simply bounce off the church. The question is also often posed as to why the Medjugorje church, built around the turn of the 20th century for a village of about 100 people, is big enough to accommodate today's believers, whose crowds number up to 3,000.

We left the Balkans for Tel Aviv in Israel, where we interviewed quadriplegic soldiers maimed in the never-ending conflict. They were using highly trained spider monkeys to assist them lead as normal a lifestyle as possible – turning on lights, putting on a CD or fetching and holding a book for them to read.

* * *

Up until this point I had never been called anything but Michael all my life, mainly because that's what Mum had always called me, and she would have a crack at anyone who dared to call me anything different. During my decade in newspapers my by-line had always been 'Michael Munro'. When Mark Day was editor of the *Daily Mirror* he wanted to change my by-line to Mike but I convinced him otherwise. Michael contained three more glorious letters to look at in print than Mike. And for the first year or so at *60 Minutes* I always called myself Michael at the beginning of the program, when the reporters introduced themselves. Now the executive producer, Gerald Stone, asked me how I'd feel about calling myself Mike. I knew Mum would've hated the idea, but Stone was right – I was a rough diamond knockabout and more a Mike than a Michael. We compromised. For the next six years or so I was Mike at the beginning of *60 Minutes* but Michael in the final credits, out of respect for Mum.

In 1987 the most notorious female prisoner in the nation was to be released from prison . . . once again. Her name was Julie Cashman Wright and she had been in and out of gaol most of her life. She was known as 'the angel of death' because she always managed to survive while those around her died in extremely violent circumstances. She had lost two men in her life, one during a shootout with police. She and I had first met at Parramatta Gaol in the mid-1970s when I was working in newspapers. She was the first woman in a New South Wales prison allowed to keep her newborn baby with her in gaol after she gave birth. I covered the story, which, at the time, was big news too – but she was only a kid herself and yet to go on and make a name for herself running with some of the most feared crims in the country, including Russell 'Mad Dog' Cox. Her release from Silverwater Gaol in Sydney was a major story and everyone wanted the exclusive. Because we had met at the birth of her beautiful little girl, Jade, she trusted me now, a dozen or so years later, and agreed to be interviewed.

She had spent many years in New South Wales and Queensland prisons for armed robbery, but had impressed all her case officers, counsellors and shrinks, who believed she had been fully rehabilitated and would never go back to crime if she were released. Jade was now almost a teenager and needed her mother, after having lived with her loving grandparents for most of her life. In her *60 Minutes* interview 'the angel of death' was certainly convincing. She had turned the corner and would never again return to gaol – for Jade's sake if for no other reason. She may have even truly meant it when she said it. I certainly believed that here was an intelligent woman who wanted to get off the criminal merry-go-round so that she could save herself and give her daughter a better life than the one she had led. After the story went to air I received many letters from viewers who thought I'd been too easy on her. I felt she really had rehabilitated herself – but within a few years Cashman was in trouble with the law again, this time over drugs. Julie Cashman died in February 2003, a free woman at the time.

By the end of 1987, my first full year with *60 Minutes*, I had worked on 25 stories and covered hundreds of thousands of kilometres. In all the 16 years that I had been a reporter I had never worked so hard in all my life. There were only four reporters but around a dozen producers. And a dozen producers divided into four reporters just doesn't go. Whenever you finished a story with one producer there were perhaps 11 producers waiting and vying for you so they could start the story they had been working on. It was relentless.

Lea's and my relationship naturally went through a fair bit of upheaval as we adjusted to spending long periods apart. Up until I had taken this job we had never been apart for more than a couple of days. The wife of a former *60 Minutes* reporter once told me that pressure would always mount between she and her husband a few days before he left for a trip. Well, the same thing happened to Lea and me. I was always so anxious about having to leave that we'd argue over the smallest thing. I provoked most of the arguments because I was so unhappy about having to go away. I was just on edge knowing I would probably miss Amy's very first steps – and I did. Lea's and my birthdays are only two weeks apart but for four years in a row we didn't get to spend a birthday together. After having dreamed all my childhood of having a happy, loving and stable family around me I was conscious of every minute I was missing with Lea and the kids. But isn't that human nature? Whatever we have, we're never completely happy.

At least for the children it was still early days so our farewells weren't too painful – in the years to come, as they got older and more aware of what was happening, our farewells would become tearful nightmares.

Lea and I faced and talked about our difficulties – hers at home and mine away. Working through them together was good because it helped me understand just how much she had on her plate having to cope as a virtual single parent for weeks on end. I endeavoured to focus more on the benefits of working on *60 Minutes* – the incredible professional opportunity it offered, and the better education and more comfortable life it would help us provide for Sean and Amy. I tried to concentrate more on the scripting process, interview techniques and research, and reflected on all the amazing places the job would take me.

10

K een to spend as much time at home as possible I slowly but surely whittled down the time I needed to spend away. I had come to realise that we didn't need to spend five or six days on a story – it was too time-consuming and expensive. When I first started at *60 Minutes* I might have done five stories in six weeks, but now I aimed to do five stories in three weeks.

And while production normally ceased at the end of November each year I started working right through to mid-December. Sean was about to start school and I wanted my annual break to coincide with his, and eventually Amy's, school holidays. Executive producers Gerald Stone, and later Peter Meakin, always accommodated our family in that respect. Probably because they knew how loopy and obsessive I was about missing them – a 24-carat sook.

When I returned to work in 1988 I headed straight to the Kimberley in the north-west of Western

Australia, I would then go on to Kathmandu, London, Spain, New York, Las Vegas, Miami, Los Angeles, Sydney, Brisbane, Melbourne, Los Angeles again, New York again, London again, Paris, Spain again, Pakistan, the Great Barrier Reef, Sydney, Texas and Mississippi, and finish the year back in Sydney.

Early that year producer Janet Eastman suggested a profile on the increasing popularity of polo, led primarily by Kerry Packer's love for the sport. We really needed Kerry to take part in the story for it to work. No Kerry, no story. Fortunately he agreed to a full sit-down interview, one of a handful he's ever given.

My first question to him was to be: 'Mr Packer, why polo?' But instead it came out: 'Mr Polo, why Packer?'

There was a moment's silence before he calmly asked me: 'Do they pay you much to do this sort of thing, son?'

Luckily for me, Kerry did not own the Nine Network at that time. He had yet to buy it back from Alan Bond for $500 million less than he had sold it to him for.

Although he had agreed to an interview he wouldn't allow us to film on his magnificent property, Ellerston, near Scone, which has polo fields and facilities that equal any in the world. Most of our filming took place at the polo field at Warwick Farm, in south-western Sydney. I took Lea and the kids out with me. Kerry was extremely cordial and charming, even inviting me for a private visit to Ellerston later in the year. At first I thought he was just being polite but he actually mentioned the invitation three times. I told him I'd always loved horse riding but had about as much style as

Norman Gunston. He said that October might be a good time to come up to Ellerston for a ride, but that was as far as the story went . . . until I next saw him a couple of years later, after he'd bought the network back. The CEO, David Leckie, was hosting a boardroom lunch with Kerry Packer, Nick Falloon, then General Manager, Peter Meakin, all the sales heavies and a couple of on-camera people like me.

Whatever people think of Kerry Packer, he is a mesmerising speaker. He not only has the sort of clout that makes you think you'd better listen, but at his most charming he's thoroughly entertaining. I light-heartedly chipped him about not following through with his invitation to Ellerston two years before. The whole table of 12 stopped dead.

'You even mentioned October at one stage, Mr Packer,' I then blurted out.

Now there was audible coughing and spluttering around the table; you could almost hear everyone thinking what a complete idiot Munro was.

As quick as you like Kerry shot back: 'I didn't invite you because I probably knew you were going to do that ridiculous chemical poisoning story you covered last Sunday night.'

60 Minutes had got a medical team to test more than 40 employees at a chemical company who were thought to have been poisoned at work – but the outcome, which we reported, was that they tested negative to any poisoning. Kerry's comment was half-joking, and I think at that stage everyone relaxed. Two weeks later he invited me to go quarter-horse riding at Ellerston for a day. I was pretty chuffed about the invitation, particularly because he'd taken my jibe the right way. Others thought I had a death wish.

In March we did a profile on Julio Iglesias, the great Latin crooner whose album sales are up there with The Beatles and Elvis. In Spain I interviewed Julio's former butler, who had recently written a hot and steamy kiss-and-tell book about how for years he had juggled all the women in Julio's extraordinary love life. On one occasion the butler had three women in different rooms of Julio's house, keeping them separated from each other, while a fourth was on her way from the airport with the chauffeur. In his interview he told us how over the years he had bought thousands of pairs of under-pants and had them monogrammed with Julio's initials so that when Julio was staying in hotels around the world 'the housekeeping and laundry staff could steal them and cherish them'.

I wasn't all that fussed about Julio. I thought he was a complete whacker. But the great thing about doing the profile was that he agreed to us filming him not only on stage on the last three nights of his 10-night run at Caesar's Palace in Las Vegas, but also later in the Green Room, his private entertaining room backstage. Each of the three nights we went backstage the same two young women were there. One was in her early 20s, had the most sensational figure you've ever seen, and each night wore a rubber dress. The other woman was in her early 30s and was a bit of a 'Miss Prissy' type from Foghorn Leghorn fame. A complete eccentric. The two of them would disappear with him every night after the performance back to his room. They were 24-hour-a-day guests of this man who had boasted that he'd made love to over 3,000 women.

Julio is one of the world's great wine connoisseurs. He has his own wine buyer in Los Angeles and air-conditioned cellars in Los Angeles, Miami and Argentina, where he mainly resides. At this point in my life I was still mostly a beer drinker but someone suggested I try a red wine backstage, which I did. I knew next to nothing about wine – but enough to know that this was a pretty decent one. It was a very easy red to drink.

I drank the red each night and kept asking: 'What wine is this?'

The wine merchant would always laugh and say: 'Oh, just the house red.'

Blissfully ignorant, I thought: if this is only the house red God knows what a top French red wine tastes like. At the end of the three days in Las Vegas we flew with Julio in his private jet to Miami. We took off at midnight – with the *60 Minutes* crew and Julio's entourage there were 14 of us. The seatbelt buckles and ashtrays were gold-plated and there was a bedroom at the back of the plane – it was a different world, even for *60 Minutes*.

Julio asked me: 'Where is your wife, I shall ring her for you?'

'Yes, sure Julio,' I said.

So he picked up the phone and rang Lea in Sydney: 'Mrs Munro?'

Lea said: 'Yes.'

'This is Julio Iglesias, here is your husband. Lovely to talk to you, I put you on to your husband.'

I'm now speaking to Lea 14,000 metres – 4,000 metres higher than a jumbo – over America while she's rushing to get the kids ready for the day. She was not overly impressed.

During the flight we were still drinking this 'house red' and Julio said: 'I can tell you love your red wine.' I'm thinking: Julio, I don't even know red wine, but I do like yours. He told me red wine was 'like a beautiful woman – something to be caressed and consumed. And I can tell that you also have that relationship with red wine.' I desperately tried not to burst out laughing. 'When our final interview is finished I shall give you a very special wine to take home to your beautiful wife,' he said.

It was a nice offer but not one I took seriously, knowing that in our interview I'd be putting some of his estranged butler's juiciest allegations to him. So I just smiled politely and we charged our glasses. It was then he told me that we'd all been drinking Château Lafite Rothschild 1979. If you can find it, it sells for around $1,500 per bottle. At least I knew my palate was on the ball, even if I wasn't.

The other unforgettable thing about that flight was that there was no 'rubber dress girl' or 'Miss Prissy'. They had been replaced by the most stunning, sultry Argentinean girl in her 20s.

After a couple of hours' sleep we landed in Miami at dawn. Julio's convertible Rolls Royce was waiting on the tarmac to whisk him and 'Miss Argentina' away. The crew and I headed to our hotel to grab a few more hours' sleep, then later on set out for Julio's mansion. Naturally it was right on the water in a full-security estate. When we arrived, Julio was eating, but not with 'Miss Argentina'. He introduced us to a beautiful American blonde southern belle called Candy. So in the space of about 14 hours we had seen Julio with four women. I'm still not sure whether they were all genuine lovers or there just for effect.

After filming a tour of the house we sat down for our interview. Julio surprised us with his openness, most of all his minders. They almost stopped the interview when I mentioned 'a woman in every room', but Julio was enjoying it. The minders went into palpitations at the mention of monogrammed undies but Julio jokingly offered to take his trousers off for the camera, to show he had no monogram. He took it all very well and was a good sport about it. And after the interview, true to his word, he took me down to the cellar and handed me a 1975 Lafite Rothschild – only this one was a magnum! I told him I couldn't accept it but he said he'd be offended if I didn't. So I took it in both hands and cradled it like a baby all the way home.

We only had one more story to do, in Los Angeles, with Bob Hope. I made the mistake of trying to tell of all people, Bob Hope, a joke. I completely screwed up the punch line. Sadly, at the end of July 2003, we also lost this legendary comedian and entertainer just two months after he turned 100.

In July of that year I covered a story I had dreamt about doing since I was a kid – running with the bulls in Pamplona, Spain. I had always been fascinated by the complex, cruel and misguided author Ernest Hemingway and had loved his book *The Sun Also Rises*, set in Pamplona in the mid-1920s during the Festival of San Fermin. Folklore has it that hundreds of years ago a priest was tied to the horns of a raging bull that was then released into the streets. The young men of Pamplona ran into the streets to hit the bull, driving it into a frenzy so that it would kill the priest. Today the idea is less brutal but just as dangerous.

At 8.00 every morning during the second week of July, six bulls, each weighing about a half a tonne, and six giant steers, are released from a corral at the bottom of an 800-metre-long uphill course full of thin and zigzagging cobblestone streets. They lead into an even thinner tunnel, which opens on to a bullring, where the run ends. The bulls follow the steers, which plod along unconcerned about the thousands of young men running in front of them. It's when the bulls get separated from the steers that things go wrong. They get completely confused and have no idea where to go, so they start trying to gore anything that moves. At the end of the run the bulls enter the bullring to confront the picadors and matadors. So 42 bulls run and die every year during the

San Fermin Festival. The powerful beasts are raised just for the event – seven days of running, food and drink, all wrapped up in an eerie feeling of danger and death.

Because the course is only 800 metres long most people think it would be easy, but even the best young Basque runners testing their manhood don't run more than 200 metres on any day. For them there's only one place to try and run and that's at the *encirio* – right in front of the bull, at the tip of his horns. And as if that's not enough they're also supposed to whack the bull with a newspaper. There's an old Spanish saying that: 'Running with the bulls is like banging your head against a brick wall . . . because when it's over, it's wonderful.' In the 1970s there was a 10,000-metre Olympic runner who thought he could easily run in front of the bulls for the entire course, no worries. He was killed at around the 300-metre mark – gored and then crushed.

I linked up with a wealthy New York restaurateur who each year for 20 years had run on all seven days of the festival. On one run a bull had broken his arm and he had still run the next day. He was featured in several tourist postcards because he was regarded as one of the best foreign runners.

He insisted that I make a practice run before I was actually filmed doing it. He always ran the last 150 metres of the course, which are considered the most dangerous because they include the narrow tunnel that opens into the bullring. This is where many people who fall in the panic are hurt. This is where, in the mid-70s, two people were crushed to death under a human mountain 10 people deep. It didn't stop the bulls though – they just climbed over the bodies. After that tragedy the township built doors on both sides of the tunnel that could be opened in an emergency so people could be pulled clear before the mountain of humanity started to rise. And this was where I was to run. The thought of it put me into a cold sweat. It didn't help that one morning, as I nursed a massive hangover, I saw a cruel Spanish policeman bashing a runner back onto the course when he lost his nerve after the race had started – once the race has begun no runner is allowed to climb out over the barricades.

My one consolation was that when a bull gored or crushed me at least Lea was with me in Pamplona. She had come along on this trip, as she did two or three times during my stint at *60 Minutes* when I was going on a particularly exotic trip. It was heartening to see her sitting on top of one of the barricades watching me as I waited on the course to commence this practice run.

Because around 5,000 people run each day it's virtually impossible to see the bulls until they're almost on top of you. So that he knew when to begin running, every day the restaurateur paid a local to sit on top of the barricade next to him and tap him on the shoulder when the bulls were 20 metres away. His advice to me was: always run in the middle of the street, never at the sides where there are too many people; run with one arm out in front of you and one out behind you to try and fend off the crowds; and if you fall with the bulls right behind you don't move an inch, even if it means being trampled. The slightest movement may cause the bull to gore you.

I was to get a head start and get my tap on the shoulder when the bulls were 30 metres away. The restaurateur was going off at his normal 20 metres. I got the tap. So out I went, and at first I couldn't see either the bulls or steers. Hundreds of terrified men ran past me, which naturally made me even more scared. Then I saw those huge black heads, the horns and the angry eyes 10 metres behind me . . . and gaining. I was about halfway through the run and could see the restaurateur running right alongside the biggest bull of all, hitting him over the head with a newspaper. Then I realised the killer tunnel was straight ahead and the bulls were now only seven metres behind me – about two seconds. I took off like a scared rabbit and almost wet myself. I ran into the ring and turned left as the bulls and steers were intercepted by matadors who enticed them over to the other side of the ring and out into the corrals where they would spend their last day alive. All six bulls would be fought and slaughtered that afternoon in the packed bullring.

The next day we were all set up to film my run. We had flown in my old sailing mate, Vernon Moore, who was now a freelance cameraman working out of London. The *60 Minutes* cameraman, Dennis Nicholson, was to shoot the first 70 or 80 metres of my run while Vernon would pick me up for the last 50 or 60 metres, including the risky run through the tunnel. I was very nervy as I stood on the course waiting to begin my run. I knew that to make the story exciting enough I had to run close to the bulls. I could tell when the bulls got closer to me because the panic in the run-ners passing me became more urgent. Then came the tap on my shoulder and out I went into the mayhem, 30 metres ahead of six bulls and six steers. Again I had to spend what seemed like an eternity until I could see the bulls looking towards me out of the human wall. Again the bulls seemed to suddenly and unexpectedly gain on me. They were only a few metres behind me when I really stepped on the gas and ran into the dark tunnel. As I entered there was a distinct smell of faeces from those poor runners who had completely lost control.

Without doubt running with the bulls in Pamplona is the best adrenaline buzz I've ever had. The danger, the panic, the spectacle and the crowds – it has everything that any loopy thrill seeker could want. I have since done three tandem skydives from about 4,000 metres and they didn't produce anywhere near the level of excitement that running with the bulls generated. Nor did doing 600 kilometres per hour in a jet fighter pulling five Gs, that is, with my body taking five times the normal force of gravity.

And to top it all off, I ran again the next day . . . just for fun.

The next month we went way up into the Top End to do a story on Australia's Norforce reservists who were conducting war games with Torres Strait islanders in order to be prepared to protect our northern borders. It was not so much a great story but one of the three times in which I really thought I would die in a plane crash. The three crew and I were flying with a very experienced and cool army pilot in a single-engine plane. I have never flown in a single-engine aeroplane since and nor will I ever again – though that's not to say that the army pilot wasn't fantastic and the plane reliable.

We took off from Weipa on the eastern side of the Gulf of Carpentaria at 4.00am and flew out over the Torres Strait, which is full of tiger sharks. At a given time the residents of a particular island were to turn on the airstrip lights so we could land. Then we were to film an RAAF Hercules land at the same airstrip to drop off Australian reservists who would be conducting war games with the islanders. The problem was that at 5.30 in the morning we couldn't raise the islanders and get them to turn on the lights at the airstrip, and we were running out of fuel. It was pitch black, we were over shark-infested waters, and our altitude was getting lower and lower as our fuel supply dwindled. The pilot was seriously worried that if he had to go much lower we'd hit a mountain.

With only five minutes' worth of fuel remaining, if they didn't turn the lights on very soon we would have to ditch the plane in the sea. The sound recordist, Mark Brewer, and cameraman, Phil Donaghue, were sound asleep in the back. Ben Hawke, the producer, was with me up the front of the plane. Ben and I were absolutely convinced that this was it – we had minutes to live. We decided not to even wake Mark and Phil. They had no idea about our predicament and there was no need for them to. The pilot was great – didn't lose his cool and handled it all beautifully. Then, with only two minutes' worth of fuel left this little airstrip lit up in the middle of the black abyss below us. It was a glorious sight and I've never been so relieved in my life.

One good local investigative story we did not long after that was an exposé on Alby Mangels, the supposed world adventurer. For years Mangels had been making feature films depicting him crossing raging rivers in South America, facing off against dangerous animals in Africa, or being bitten by poisonous snakes. But many of the sequences were concocted and had been set up to make it appear like he was doing something dangerous. He sold his films to TV stations, which aired them as documentaries. His wildlife series was running on Channel Nine at the time we were doing our exposé on him – a clear indication of the independence that *60 Minutes* enjoyed at the network.

We knew he owed money to people he had employed in the past, and even former friends who helped get him started, but we couldn't find anyone willing to be critical and spill the beans on camera. Our last film shoot for the story was in Murray Bridge, South Australia, where we filmed Alby Mangels landing his helicopter at his old primary school. When we had finished I jumped in a taxi and headed to Adelaide airport. As luck would have it, the taxi driver turned out to be a former mate of Mangels and had been owed a great deal of money for years. I explained who I was and what we were doing, and asked him if he would be interviewed on the subject.

'Would I?' he enthused. 'Just point the camera at me and I'll tell everyone what he's really like.'

We later sprung this footage from the interview on Mangels, who was naturally furious. He has not made another 'adventure wildlife' special since.

One of the great things about *60 Minutes* is its independence. It stands alone within the network. The program established its stature and fierce independence early on, when it aired an investigation that its first major sponsor, BHP, was unhappy about. BHP suddenly dropped its millions of dollars a year in advertising. Years later, I would do a 'walk-in' on the headquarters of Toyota, *60 Minutes'* present sponsor. My investigations had nothing to do with the Toyota company itself, rather one of their employees, who had a dubious past at another company. The story's producer and I deliberately made *60 Minutes'* executive producer, Peter Meakin, aware of the walk-in on Toyota only one hour before we were about to do it, but we needn't have been concerned as he didn't object whatsoever. On being told about the walk-in after the event, the then Managing Director, David Leckie, was anything but pleased – yet understood that the very foundation of *60 Minutes'* credibility and success is its complete objectivity, even when it comes to the program's major sponsors.

* * *

Around this time the Australian cricket team was touring Pakistan and there was a huge uproar because some of the Aussie players and management had publicly questioned whether Pakistani umpires were cheating and making more decisions favourable to Pakistan than the visiting team. There was even a subtle suggestion that if decisions didn't improve the Aussies might take their bat and ball and go home.

I rang the Australian captain, Allan Border, and asked him if he would talk to me about it. He begrudgingly agreed and we spent 36 hours travelling to Faisalabad, out in the boondocks of Pakistan. When we arrived, Border gave me the clear impression that the coach, Bob Simpson, wasn't allowing anyone to talk about the growing controversy. Simpson wouldn't even entertain the thought of deigning to talk to us. I believe they were all by now a little embarrassed about the whole thing.

However, we snared an interview with one of the accused umpires and the Pakistani captain, Javed Miandad, who said that Australians had always suffered from 'sour grapes' and their recent behaviour was nothing new. At this point I discovered that despite Simpson putting a blanket ban on all players and officials talking to *60 Minutes*, he and Border were still holding court every day in a hotel restaurant, giving full press conferences to all the cricket writers. It was all right to talk to journalists from every major newspaper in the country but it wasn't okay to go near *60 Minutes*. So one morning we waited until the press conference had got under way and marched in with our camera rolling. I tackled Simpson not only on the question of suspect umpires but also on why he was happy to speak to 'all these newspapers but not *60 Minutes*'. There wasn't much he could say, but Allan Border at least opened up a little bit. Mike Coward, one of the most respected cricket writers in the country, was extremely supportive of our position, as were a couple of other writers.

The crew and I had probably only been on the ground for 48 hours when we faced another 36-hour marathon trip home. We scripted the story on the plane and it aired that weekend.

By the end of 1988 I was exhausted. I'd been away from our marital bed for over 200 nights – more than seven months away, either overseas or around Australia, doing 27 stories – and never looked more forward to holidays at any other time in my career.

11

In 1989 Gerald Stone stepped down as executive producer after beautifully guiding *60 Minutes* for the past decade. And no one blamed him for wanting a change, particularly at a time when we were often being thumped in the ratings by Channel Ten's *The Comedy Company*. The entire unit was relieved to be told that Peter Meakin was temporarily taking over until a more permanent executive producer could be found. With the program fighting against *The Comedy Company*, Meakin was by far the best choice.

One of his first decisions was to commission a court trial – but not just any trial. The ordinary, everyday domestic cat would go on trial. Companion and pet, or feral murderer of native wildlife responsible for the increasing number of extinct species in Australia? Guilty or not guilty of murder? The story was little more than a gimmick but it certainly got everyone talking. If Meakin wanted to get the animal liberationists biting he couldn't have baited them better. And in the lead-up to the airing of the 'trial' tens of thousands of posters were put up all over the country asking whether the cat was guilty or not guilty.

A magnificent old courtroom full of walnut and mahogany was hired, as were two barristers to argue the opposing cases. A former Supreme Court judge was employed to preside over the trial, behaving as if it were a real one. The witnesses called by the defence included little old dears who told how their moggies lit up their lives and provided wonderful friendship in the lone-liness of old age.

'And she wouldn't hurt a fly,' one elderly cat owner told the court.

A factory owner also spoke on behalf of the accused, saying how well the animal kept his premises free of vermin like rats and mice.

The prosecution produced witnesses from the National Parks and Wildlife Service who said a domestic cat that even had two bells around its neck was killing off native birds and other wildlife in huge numbers because it wasn't locked up at night, and that once any cat became wild and then feral it was a master of cunning and created havoc in the bush. For two days the trial raged in front of the six-man, six-woman jury. I thought the evidence leaned towards a guilty verdict but in the end the cat prevailed. It was a not guilty verdict.

Later that month I interviewed a young actress who was launching her first major international feature film. Although she had been acting since her teens and had won acclaim for her role in the television mini-series *Vietnam*, she still had a long way to go. Her name was Nicole Kidman and her profile on *60 Minutes* was to be a major boost to her career in Australia. Through the profile she not only proved herself to be intelligent and dedicated to her craft but someone who had a great sense of humour and didn't take herself seriously – just her job. I asked her, at this stage of her career, what she would like to do most.

'A leading role in a major Shakespearean production,' was her answer.

I realised then how serious she was about making it – and that she also had the brains and beauty to get there.

I've had a fair bit to do with Nicole since and have come to realise that her true strength lies in the close ties that her mum and dad, Janelle and Antony, have forged for the family. Our profile of her included the first family video footage ever shot of a very cute 18-month-old Kidman sliding down the slippery dip in the back yard of the family's Sydney home. But one of the best sequences in the whole profile remains the one in which Janelle and Antony Kidman, Grandma Kidman, Nicole and I are all singing 'Sweet Sixteen' around the family pianola. There were no Hollywood barracudas, minders or even personal publicists in Nicole Kidman's life at this early stage of her career. In fact the producer, Ron Sinclair, and I met her at her tiny one-bedroom unit in Mosman to work out the shooting schedule and how much access we could get for the profile. It was very much easier than it has become in later years, when you do well just to get a reply from any member of the phalanx guarding her.

Up until this time the issue of mercury in our dental fillings had been a ticking time bomb. A maverick dentist in Colorado, Al Huggins, had been strongly campaigning against the American Dental Association's continued defence of the use of dental amalgams that are 52 per cent mercury, one of the deadliest metals in the world. For over 150 years dentists all over the world have been putting this toxic cocktail of lead, zinc and mercury in our mouths. Huggins was convinced there was mounting evidence that proved beyond doubt that the amalgams did in fact slowly release mercury into our bodies, most of which would settle in our key organs and impact on our immune systems. Huggins believed that the new-age synthetic clear-coloured fillings were far safer and that people should have their old mercury amalgams removed and replaced with new synthetic ones.

A continuing debate over the possibility of tens of millions of Americans at worst being poisoned, at best having their immune system compromised, was too much for the American Dental Association to contemplate. It, and other dental organisations all over the world, had enthusiastically supported the use of mercury in amalgam fillings ever since it became apparent in the mid-1800s that it was the mercury that bonded the metals together. Huggins was such a thorn in the American Dental Association's side that they made all sorts of legal threats to shut him up.

Huggins accused the American Dental Association of setting him up with supposed patients who requested that he remove their mercury amalgams and replace them with new fillings, and then turned around, complained about the dental work and sued him for malpractice. It got to the stage where it was no longer viable or safe for Huggins to practise at his multi-million-dollar dental rooms in Colorado Springs. He had to employ other dentists to remove and replace mercury amalgams for fear he would spend every waking moment in court being sued.

Huggins was able to prove that during the procedure to remove a mercury amalgam from the mouth the readings of mercury in and around the mouth and in the air greatly increased, until the amalgam was completely gone. To me, what he was saying at least made a lot of sense. And even if he wasn't completely accurate, why should we continue walking around with a mouthful of mercury because of a technique that was over 150 years old? I had eight mercury amalgams and told Huggins that the first thing I was going to do when I returned to Australia was make an appointment with my local dentist to have them all replaced with synthetic fillings.

Huggins suggested that I have my fillings replaced while I was in Colorado. He wouldn't do it himself, for fear I was an agent for the American Dental Association, but arranged for his senior dentist to come to the surgery one night after midnight to replace all my fillings. The producer, John Penlington, and I decided to film the whole operation and make it a sequence in our story. Not exactly a balanced and objective report, but it was something I believed in strongly.

Before the marathon dental session Huggins had taken a blood sample from me to get my white cell count – a measure of the number of cells that attack infection in the body. My count, while not of concern, was in the higher range, around 10,000. Huggins said it could have been up because I was run down or coming down with a cold – or because my immune system was working around the clock combating the continual leaching of mercury into my body. Twelve hours after all my mercury fillings were removed another blood sample was taken. My white cell count had dropped to about 5,500, a dramatic decrease. Once we finished the story we were to move on to another story in Louisiana, where Huggins suggested I have another blood test. I was still a little sceptical so when we arrived in New Orleans I chose a medical centre that Huggins couldn't possibly have known about. In the space of just three days since my last blood test my white cell count had dropped to 4,000. There had been no change in my health – it was just that an enormous workload had been taken off my white cells.

Over the years, when I've told doctors this story none have been able to explain the sudden drop in my white cell count – unless it was thanks to the removal of a mouthful of mercury. Since then Lea has had all her mercury fillings replaced, and neither Sean nor Amy have ever had one in the first place.

Once the story went to air in Australia it caused a lot of concern and dentists all over the nation were inundated with inquiries from worried patients. At first the Australian Dental Association completely denied that mercury leached from fillings but after several years of mounting and irrefutable evidence it had to admit that leaching does occur and mercury does build up in certain key organs. The Australian dentist who led the fight in this country is Dr Noel Campbell from Victoria, a controversial but sincere advocate for synthetic fillings. That story, and several others I did later with Dr Campbell, certainly encouraged the Australian public to think about the alternatives to having fillings that are more than half mercury in their mouths.

From mercury in our fillings we moved on to a completely different story – a face-to-face debate about capital punishment between Clive Stafford-Smith, a young English lawyer who had saved over 100 people from death row and Sam Jones, Louisiana's senior electric chair executioner.

We had interviewed Clive Stafford-Smith the previous year. He drove tens of thousands of kilometres across the American south from one prison to another, defending and saving as many men and women on death row as he could manage. Most of his clients were dirt poor and couldn't pay him so he struggled each day just to find enough petrol money to travel from state to state. He argued capital punishment made absolutely no difference to a killer in the heat of the moment, that no one has ever thought: 'Oh, I better not shoot you after all because if I do I could get the death sentence.' As a lawyer, he blamed lawyers and the system for much of the problem. He even reminded us that William Shakespeare had got it very right four centuries ago in *Richard III* when he wrote that to find Utopia we would have to kill every lawyer.

In the other corner was Sam Jones, Angola Prison's official executioner, who proudly boasted he had pulled the lever on 18 inmates after strapping them in to 'Old Sparky'. The chair sat in the middle of a room facing a large window that allowed officials, relatives and the media in a second room to watch the ghoulish and painful death. A death where the person eventually bleeds from every orifice as tens of thousands of volts surge through his or her body.

So these two men with completely different philosophies on capital punishment came face to face in a large hotel room in Baton Rouge, Louisiana. Each man regarded the other as the devil himself, representing everything wrong with the system. During the debate both men made their points strongly. Sam Jones said the 18 inmates he had put to death were nothing but 'trash' and deserved everything they got after their horrific and brutal crimes. Clive Stafford-Smith argued that life was precious, that mistakes were being made all the time and sometimes the wrong people were being put to death. Two men couldn't have been more opposed to each other or more passionate about their beliefs.

I myself don't believe in capital punishment because I could never explain to the children that on the one hand life is the most precious thing we have but on the other it's okay if we put people to death. However, it might be a completely different matter if any member of my family were ever victims of violent crime.

I returned home in early August 1989 and spent the next couple of weeks working around Australia before leaving for a five-day trip to London. Under the captaincy of Allan Border the Australian cricket team had just won back the Ashes from the poms. My story was to be nothing other than a positive profile on our hero captain, but after my story in Pakistan the year before I was the very last reporter in the world most of the Australian cricketers wanted to see in their midst. I had spoken to Border before leaving Australia and he had once again begrudgingly agreed to an interview and to have a profile done on him.

The idea was to follow Allan Border through the last test match at The Oval. When I arrived in London the producer, Stephen Taylor, was already there with the crew filming him playing for his English county cricket side of Essex. On the way to the players' dressing room I walked past David Boon, who was being given a massage.

'Gee, you're going to be popular here,' he said to me with that sly smile of his.

'The whole point of the story is to praise Border,' I told him before asking if he would be willing to be interviewed about what sort of a captain and friend Allan Border is.

'Yeah, I'll talk to you but I'll warn you now, a few of the players are still very pissed off at you over the story in Pakistan.'

Boon was true to his word and spoke about Border, unlike Merv Hughes and Dean Jones, who not only wouldn't be interviewed but also completely ignored me when I asked them. They simply turned their backs on me and walked away. But there was one new young bloke in the Test team who was more than happy to sing Border's praises for giving young hopefuls like him a chance. His name was Mark Taylor. Even in his 20s he was mature enough to rise above any grudges from the year before. It was no surprise that the coach, Bob Simpson, flatly refused to take part in the profile on Border.

While still at Essex Oval I saw Border and asked him if there was any chance of filming for a short period on the team bus on the way back to London. The bus had been fitted out with a sofa and a bar and it would have been a great sequence for the story.

'I'll have to speak to the other boys, many of whom are not happy about you being here,' he told me.

He mentioned that Simpson was leaving the ground early and not returning in the team bus. I suggested that rather than further strain the relationship, we wait until he was gone and then film on the bus without him. Border said he'd discuss the proposition with the other players. He came back a short time later saying some of the other players didn't want me or the crew on the team bus.

'You're still very unpopular after Pakistan and a few of the players don't trust you.'

So no filming on the bus. We still needed some pictures other than of him playing cricket. Somehow Stephen convinced Border to allow us to film half a dozen of the team members playing golf at Herefordshire's magnificent golf course the next morning. We arranged to meet in a beautiful, centuries-old sandstone castle that had been turned into a clubhouse.

When I arrived the next morning Bob Simpson walked up to me and pulled me aside. I thought: this is going to be good, wonder what it's all about?

'I just wanted you to know how despicable I think it was how you suggested to Allan Border yesterday that he wait until I had left the ground before you tried to film on board the team bus,' he growled at me.

'Would you have allowed us on the bus?' I asked him.

'Are you kidding? No chance!' he said.

I told him that that's why I had asked Border – to avoid increasing the tension. But I was more concerned about Border telling Simpson about our conversation when we were there primarily to sing Border's praises, so on the way up to the first tee I tackled Border about why he had told Simpson when he didn't have to.

'Why would you tell Simpson about our request in a way that it's now made things so much worse?' I asked Border.

'Mate, I've got to work and travel with these people and have to let them know what's going on.'

I was disappointed in Border running to Simpson

when he didn't have to. And it didn't help that final and main interview with him, which I think was flat and humourless. Nevertheless, we finished the profile and had it to air the very next Sunday after Border had led the team to victory in the sixth and final Test.

After that story I was at home for only a couple of weeks before leaving for a three-week journey, this time to Africa for one of the most memorable trips I ever experienced while at *60 Minutes*. One of the reasons the trip was so memorable was that Lea came along with me. It was the first time to Africa for each of us and we were going to share this experience together. It seemed such a long time ago that I was waiting outside her school gate ready to drive her home in the old Holden. Now, 17 years later we were off on this great adventure to Africa.

The month before, George Adamson, the famous English lion expert featured in the book and film *Born Free*, had been shot dead by Somalian guerrillas near his remote Kora Lion Reserve, 300 kilometres north-east of Nairobi in Kenya. Adamson's campsite was right on the Kenya–Somalia border where Somalian farmers, who once carried staffs to herd goats, were now carrying Russian-made AK-47 assault rifles. The civil war in Somalia was just starting to really heat up and would explode into battles between warlords in the next couple of years. Adamson had just farewelled a guest who was on his way to the dirt airstrip about two kilometres from his campsite when he heard gunfire. He grabbed his gun, jumped into his four-wheel-drive and took off for the airstrip. What he didn't know was that his guest had been ambushed but had made it through to the airstrip unharmed. George Adamson wouldn't be so lucky. As he sped along the dirt road a Somalian guerrilla fired several rounds into the engine and cabin of his vehicle. Adamson lost control of the four-wheel-drive and was killed.

Apart from a mountain of research into the behaviour of lions he also left behind three adolescent lion cubs which had grown up around his campsite at Kora. Our story centred around a young English protégé of George Adamson's, an English vet called Gareth Patterson who had been working with the great naturalist for several years. Now that Adamson was dead someone needed to care for the three lions so they were to be shipped to a reserve in Botswana. Our plan was to fly up to Kora for three days to film the camp and the lions and interview Patterson. At the end of those three days two planes, both Twin Otters, would return to pick up us and the three lions, which would be drugged and crated for the return trip. At the reserve we would have no radio so there would be no way for us to contact anyone or get the planes to return early in case of an emergency, but I had double- and triple-checked with the Kenyan authorities that there was a full platoon of Kenyan soldiers guarding the Kora Lion Reserve campsite from Somalian guerrillas. I was as confident as I could be that Lea would be safe.

Imagine the cold fear and the knot in my stomach when we landed at the airstrip, in the middle of nowhere, to be met by five men only: Gareth Patterson and a former British colonel, who were carrying two modern rifles and a shotgun, and three Kenyan policemen who had spread out around the perimeter of the airstrip. The plane would have been heard from kilometres away so they were on guard in case of an ambush. Even more alarming was the fact that they were armed only with World War I Lee Enfield rifles. And then my heart completely sunk when I saw the look on the faces of the two white men as Lea stepped out of the plane. They were horrified, and subtly called me aside as we unloaded the plane. I explained that I had been assured by the authorities that there was more than enough protection in the area. The two men said that in fact the Kenyan Army had pulled out two weeks before.

We drove to the lion reserve, which turned out to be more of a defensive fort than a campsite. There were several thatched sleeping huts and a main kitchen–dining hut looking out onto a large enclosure holding the three lions – but the entire compound was surrounded by an electrified fence and lit up like a stalag. There were bunkers dug out at the foot of the fence and filled with mattresses, onto which we were told to dive if we were attacked. No one was allowed to leave the compound without permission, and never at night.

And here I am having brought my own wife into such an alarming situation. I was painfully aware that she was probably the only woman within a 100-kilometre radius. Absolutely filled with dread, I knew that if we got through the next three days alive it would be through luck rather than good sense on my part. The producer, cameraman and sound recordist never let on to Lea just how concerned they were for their safety, let alone hers. And I stayed mum, too.

That night after dinner the three policemen told the retired colonel that there had been a lot of guerrilla activity on the border, about five kilometres away, and that they wanted to return to their village and families. They were terrified. Naturally the colonel wanted them to stay and an argument erupted. This was great. Now we had the Kenyan cops almost mutinying and guerrilla activity building up on the border. After much negotiating it was agreed that one policeman could leave, taking one of our two vehicles with him. Apart from going off with the Kenyan policeman back to his village there was nothing to do except finish filming the story and pray we got out okay. For the next three days and nights I never slept a wink wondering what I would do with Lea if we were overrun by a horde of Somalian guerrillas. Strange things go through your mind at a time like this. I kept telling myself that if we did get out of this it would be one of the most remarkable stories and experiences that Lea and I would ever have together – and it remains so today.

The adolescent lions were much bigger than I expected them to be. Part of the story was me getting deep and meaningful with the lions, walking right up to them in their cage and patting them – a walk in the park compared to dealing with the Somalian guerrillas I was convinced were about to attack and take Lea. Each day we filmed early in the morning and then rested after lunch, as the temperature soared into the 40s. Everyone managed to sleep – except me. We continued filming when the heat began to subside in the afternoon. The lions got to know me a little better with each passing day, but still I was told never to make any sudden moves or show fear. I certainly didn't move much, but I reckon the lions must have smelt the fear all over me.

The camp's latrine was still just as George Adamson had built it. There were several trenches in a line and each would be used then covered over before moving on to the next trench. But it was what we sat on that blew us all away – the toilet seats were huge elephant jaws that allowed us to sit about 30 centimetres off the ground.

At night we'd sit inside the compound eating smoked crocodile, or barbecued eland or impala, while sipping on gin and tonics. Above us was the most brilliant blanket of stars you could imagine. It was so clear one night that we could see not one but two satellites orbiting earth. All the time, jackals paced up and down outside the electrified fence hoping that one of us might wander out for a midnight walk. Not likely.

The sound of the two planes circling above us after three days at the lion reserve still ranks as one of the greatest moments of relief in my life. The lions were drugged, which had made them groggy and manageable, and we filmed them as they were carefully placed in their wooden crates. The crates were loaded into the two Otters and tied down, and the crew, Lea and I, and the retired British colonel and Gareth Patterson took off for Nairobi. The two Kenyan policemen left in the Land Rover and headed back to their villages.

The three lions were eventually shipped to the Botswana National Park, where just 18 months later they were killed and skinned by poachers. The Kora campsite has been transplanted to Kenya's Natural Museum in Nairobi as a tribute to George Adamson and his life's work with lions.

We scripted our harrowing story on life inside the Kora Lion Reserve and shipped the film, script and editing instructions back to Australia from Harare in Zimbabwe before moving on to our next story, about whether or not Zimbabwe should be collecting and selling ivory to the world's markets, particularly those in Asia. Under the Zimbabwe Government's culling program villagers killed old elephants and used the meat as an important food source and sold the ivory to the government, increasing the village's finances. The problem for Zimbabwean authorities was trying to convince villagers not to kill young rogue bulls that trampled and ate their crops. The government's argument was that the money the villagers made from the ivory taken from the old elephants would more than make up for the loss of their crops. Despite Lea's and my distaste for the ivory trade, the program *was* proving to be very successful.

For three days we followed the spoor of several herds of elephants so we could film them. I'll never forget one particular African sunset. We were sitting quietly by a large waterhole waiting for the elephants to turn up. Slowly and quietly four massive bulls emerged from the scrub to suss out whether or not it was safe for the rest of the herd to follow. The bulls act as scouts while the cows care for and lead the juveniles. As the four bulls approached the waterhole the rest of the herd began making their way out of the scrub. Eventually there were about 35 elephants, a spectacular sunset behind them as a backdrop. I remember once again pinching myself with one hand, while I held Lea's hand with the other.

My last overseas trip for the year was a four-weeker, culminating in a trip to Canada's wild north-west territories in the Arctic Circle. The movement against fashion houses that used fur, whether wild or farmed, and against fur traders had gathered a lot of support around the world. Animal liberationists were becoming extremely aggressive to fur wearers. In cities like New York, London and Paris it wasn't unusual to see a beautifully groomed woman walking down the street completely unaware that her full-length mink coat had been vandalised, a giant X spray-painted on it. In late November every year animal lovers held 'Fur Free Friday', which included a demonstration march through the streets of Manhattan. We were to start off by filming the march and doing interviews with protestors and the march's organisers.

From there we were to fly to Winnipeg in Canada and then on to the far north-west. We had an enormous distance to cover, and flew first to Toronto then Winnipeg, where we stayed overnight. The next day we headed further north, to Yellowknife, on the edge of one of the biggest lakes in the territories, the Great Slave Lake. Yellowknife brought back childhood memories of reading about the Canadian Mounties in the Yukon with their huskies. It was a tough-talkin' and hard-drinkin' town covered in snow for 11 months of the year.

We had flown here to balance the report by showing the point of view of the Eskimos, a people who had been decimated and had their land and much of their livelihood taken from them in the name of progress. One of their fledgling industries was the trapping of muskrat, beaver, mink, lynx and rabbit for their fur. They had done it for thousands of years and needed to continue doing it now more than ever. They sold high-quality skins to fur traders, and used the meat to feed their families and the lesser-grade skins to clothe them.

Our filming schedule involved going out every day for three days on the Great Slave Lake with a delightful family of Eskimos who lived on the north arm of the huge lake. This husband, wife, son and daughter were so gentle, hospitable and generous with everything they had – and wanted to get their message across to animal liberationists that their people needed to trap to survive. We used skidoos and sleds to move our equipment and ourselves around this magnificent frozen lake. The skidoos were fun enough, but they also enabled us to scoot from the family's back yard, down a bank and straight onto the hard-packed ice of the lake. And from there we could just take off across it. Imagine driving past dozens of tiny islands surrounded by ice. It was a bizarre feeling to be able to walk on and off islands, collecting traps. Apart from what I saw when I flew in a helicopter through the Himalayan Mountains near Kathmandu, this was the most stunning scenery I had ever seen.

One of the downsides was that it took us about 35 minutes every morning just to put all our layers of clothes on – mittens, covered by ski gloves, which were covered by gloves designed for the Arctic Circle, thermal underwear, two pairs of trousers, and special walking boots we had bought in New York that were made to withstand temperatures as low as −45° Celsius. It was just as well because one day a blizzard set in and the temperature dropped to −38°. The gloves were so thick I couldn't even pinch myself this time.

After arriving back in Australia in December producer Ron Sinclair and I scripted our four stories from the trip, which would all go to air the next year. While the experiences, places and people of that year had been remarkable I was starting to become obsessive about getting home and not wasting a minute of the time that I could spend with Lea and the kids.

Wherever I was in the world, depending on what the telecommunications system was like, I'd ring Lea and the kids, and lately I had been ringing them twice a day. I tried to speak to Sean and Amy each night before they went to bed, which was normally just before I was to go out filming for the day on the other side of the world. After we'd finished shooting and before dinner that night I'd ring them again, when they were getting ready for school the next day. Sean was eight and wanted his Dad to be at his soccer or footy games – he was starting to take my long absences from home badly. Amy, who was five, was just starting first class, and was as cute as a button. She has always been fair-skinned and dark-haired while Sean has an olive complexion and fairer hair. They are both very different in many ways – except in their love and loyalty for each other. Amy would often see her big brother upset after talking to me on the phone and become affected herself. After I had consistently rung home twice a day for a while Lea had to tell me not to ring home so much.

'I know how important it is to you to speak with us as often as possible but it's not good for the kids,' she said. 'I hate to say this but I think it would be better if you didn't ring as often.'

I could tell she was heartbroken about having to tell me this. My spirits sank as I realised I had been selfish by ringing as much as I had been. It had got to the stage where sometimes if I couldn't reach them before I went to bed at night I couldn't sleep. I would stay awake until I had spoken to them – even if that meant waiting most of the night. It was becoming a psychological crutch. I couldn't stop thinking about how much of the children's childhood I was missing. That, coupled with my own tough childhood, played on my mind. I had always promised myself that because of all the family values I missed out on as a child I would make up for it through sharing every available second of my time with my own kids during their childhoods. That whole philosophy seemed to be at risk of falling apart and I would sometimes panic about it. It was a difficult time for all of us but Lea held it together beautifully. She was the glue binding us together, always reassuring the children and me that everything was fine.

Lots of the other crew members' families saw them off at the airport for big overseas trips or met them when they returned. But we never did. We always said goodbye at the front door, but eventually even that became heart-wrenching. It was just terrible. Every time I got into a taxi to go to the airport tears were rolling down our cheeks as we waved goodbye to each other. The years I spent away from home are years I will never get back. No one lying on their deathbed ever says they spent too much time with their family. No one ever says that.

But once I arrived back home for six glorious weeks off over December and January, all that was forgotten. Cameraman Nick Lee used to say: 'The best thing of all about going away is coming home.' And he was so right!

Some of the best times Sean, Ames and I had together were when I told them bedtime stories about King Arthur, Lady Guinevere, Sir Lancelot, Sir Galahad and of course Merlin, the magician. What made our bedtime stories different was that I made them up as I went along. I also acted out (very badly) battles, festivals and dragon-wrestling all over the bedroom. And throughout the tales of kidnapping, courage and good overcoming evil there were two new, key characters in the court of King Arthur – the brave knight, Sir Sean, and his beautiful and kind sister, Lady Amy. These two heroes figured prominently in most storylines. And of course the kids always loved it when their names were mentioned – Ames sucking her thumb, Sean twirling his hair, both of them missing nothing. A lot of fun. Recently Sean bought me Sir Thomas Mallory's *Tales of King Arthur* and inscribed it beautifully with: 'Dearest Dad, hope that this book fills you with as many great memories as it does for me. Yet was unable to find any references to Lady Amy or Sir Sean?! Love always, your son, Sean.' When I read that I cried like a baby for the first time in many, many years.

Naturally after not seeing each other as a family for most of the year going away on holidays was always important to us. Lea and I encouraged Sean and Amy to want to explore Australia first, and we were fortunate enough to have wonderful holidays on the Great Barrier Reef, Tasmania, the Northern Territory, including Kakadu, and skiing at Perisher in New South Wales. We also holidayed for many years at Byron Bay until it became too crowded and trendy, then started spending the bulk of our annual break in Mollymook on the south coast of New South Wales. Just the four of us lapping up all that sun, surf, fishing, and barbecue breakfasts and dinners. It could not have got any better. Then, in January 1990, our wonderful holiday destination almost became a place of tragedy.

Sean and I had driven to the shops to get the morning papers and some food to cook up for brunch while Lea and Amy went for a swim at the southern end of Mollymook Beach, around the corner and out of sight of the surf-lifesaving club. They weren't there long when an elderly woman got into trouble about 25 metres from the shore. She was waving her arm above her head. A man in his 70s, a friend of the woman, ran down to the water's edge, screaming that she was in trouble and heading into the water to try and rescue her. Lea knew immediately there was no way he could cope and looked around to see who else was around – there were a couple of blokes on the beach but they didn't budge. She asked a young mother with a toddler if she could leave Amy with her while she tried to do what she could for the woman.

Lea, who's a strong swimmer, plunged into the surf and swam towards the woman, who by now had been swept out 50 metres. Her elderly friend had reached her, but had been forced to let go of her – neither of them were good swimmers. He was slowly floating out to sea when Lea reached the woman, who was now unconscious and floating face down. Lea yelled at her to try and turn over onto her back. She didn't respond, and as hard as Lea tried she couldn't turn her over onto her back. Lea was weakening quickly and was struggling to keep her head above the water. When they had been swept out about 150 metres Lea started going under herself. It was obvious there was nothing more she could do for the woman and Lea was forced to let her go so she could save herself.

A surfer plucked Lea out of the water and pulled her onto his surfboard. She was so exhausted from the physical and mental stress that she could barely make it onto his board. He paddled to nearby rocks, where fortunately there were people standing watching the drama unfold who could help Lea get a foothold and reach safety. Meanwhile the surf club's rubber ducky had picked up the elderly gentleman – but there was no sign of the woman. It took lifesavers another half hour or so to locate her body. They believed that after the woman was swept out she had had a heart attack. By the time Lea reached her there was very little she could have done.

Lea collected Amy and in a daze walked back to the beach house we were renting. Sean and I arrived home a few minutes later to find Lea shaking and in tears. It had been such a traumatic experience. Lea took the woman's death very badly, and on and off over the next few weeks she would wake in the morning having relived the experience overnight. Each time she had dug her long fingernails deep into the palms of her hands, as if she had hold of something and couldn't let it go.

For years Lea has regretted that she never got the chance to thank the surfer who saved her. He had rejoined the search and rescue straight after depositing Lea on the rocks, and she never saw him again. Shortly afterwards, the local police came to take a statement about the incident from Lea. Typical of Lea, she played down her role in the rescue, saying that she did very little. However, the surfer gave the police a full account of how Lea had almost sacrificed her own life to try and save the woman. About a month later we received a letter from the police saying they were recommending Lea to the New South Wales Governor for a bravery award. We were already very proud of what Lea had done, and were even more so now that the police had recognised her heroic efforts.

We didn't give it much more thought after that; we wanted Lea to try and forget, and not have more night-mares about it. Then out of the blue, later that year, we were sent a notification that Lea would receive a bravery award from the New South Wales Governor, His Excellency Rear Admiral Peter Sinclair for her actions at Mollymook Beach. Sean, Amy and I also attended the governor's annual garden party where bravery and community awards are presented. It was particularly special because it took the attention away from me and well and truly focused it on our heroic Mum. I was the one always on television or in magazines and getting the accolades but not this time – it was all Lea. It's so hard to put into words just how proud we all were of her. A truly humble heroine.

12

By February 1990 I was back in harness and off for a quick – and I mean quick – visit to Los Angeles to interview Bette Midler. The crew and I were to arrive in Los Angeles about 10.30 in the morning, check into our hotel to clean up, do the interview with Bette Midler mid-afternoon, stay overnight, and fly home the next day.

As with most major profiles, I'd done hours of reading on Bette Midler, going back as far as I could into her life. We were half expecting her to be difficult and perhaps uncooperative, but couldn't have been more wrong. She was one tiny ball of energy and humour, and she was charming. It was a very funny interview and she was very generous with what she spoke about. She had recently given birth to her first child and at one stage I asked her if she and her husband planned on having any more children.

She laughed and shot back: 'Why do you want to

know that – you'd like to watch us trying wouldn't you?'

Being a little prudish I was horrified she might think that of me and said: 'I'm not someone who sits in the corner and watches!'

After that I went to Melbourne for my first introduction to a neurological disease that had exploded – Alzheimer's disease, also known by families of sufferers as 'the endless funeral'. It is a slow and cruel affliction during which brain cells are destroyed and memory is lost, until the patient has reverted to infancy and then dies. Between the ages of 60 and 65 we have a one in 20 chance of getting it but over 80 years of age the likelihood jumps dramatically to one in four.

Don Hewitt, the founder of the American *60 Minutes* on CBS, had always said never to do a boring monologue on world poverty but to go and interview the world's poorest family. That way your message would be far more powerful. So for our story, which was one of the first in-depth looks at Alzheimer's in Australia, we looked at Alzheimer's through the eyes of Melbourne journalist and broadcaster Claudia Wright. Claudia was only in her late 40s when she contracted the disease, very early by most standards. At 53 she and her family agreed to allow *60 Minutes* to spend a week with her in an attempt to shed more light on this tragic, heartbreaking illness which now affects hundreds of thousands of Australians.

Claudia grew up in Bendigo, the daughter of a Caucasian mother and an Asian dad. Because of her slightly Asian appearance she was constantly ridiculed at school and called a 'ching chong'. That only made her more determined. Throughout her journalistic career, from the 1960s to the 1980s, Claudia had a fearsome reputation of taking on the establishment over any issue. She sent fear and loathing into the hearts of the Catholic Church when she took priests to task on radio over controversial issues like homosexuality, abortion and celibacy. It was no surprise she earned the nickname 'Claws'. She was a journalist who said what she thought and damn the consequences. On more than one occasion she had to employ bodyguards after a public outburst.

In 1990 this once eloquent woman had difficulty speaking – she had to agonisingly search for the words that once came to her so easily and fluently – and she could no longer read or write. Brian White, the great broadcaster and journalist who had worked with Claudia in radio for years, told us at the time that: 'A journalist like Claudia getting Alzheimer's disease is just like an artist going blind.' To enable her to use her home telephone her family had to colour code her friends' and family members' numbers on the automatic dial – she still knew her colours. But once on the phone she might then forget who she was speaking to. For Claudia it was no longer a matter of remembering where she'd left her car keys, it was not even knowing she had a car or how to operate it. Claudia was given regular concentration tests by Dr John Currie who at the time was practising at Melbourne's Mental Health Research Institute, and we went along to film her during one. She was asked to follow a small, slow-moving red light on a wall with her eyes but after only a few seconds she lost concentration and found it too difficult to keep up. The saddest moment came during a simple test for five year olds where Claudia had to arrange a set of blocks in the same pattern as another set. She just couldn't add that last block to make the set.

During one of our interviews I asked Claudia how she coped with simple things like getting dressed.

'Pants are easy to put on but dresses like the one I'm wearing are difficult because I've got about 15 of these . . . 15 things on the back . . . what are they called again?' she asked.

'You mean buttons,' I replied.

'Yes, that's them, buttons can make dressing very hard for me.'

When we paid her mum and dad a visit in Bendigo she couldn't even remember her father's name – Claude. As a parent myself I can only imagine how hard it was for her elderly mother and father to see their once vibrant firebrand of a daughter reduced to what she had become.

At the other end of the family scale, Claudia had two young sons, one of whom was only 11 years of age. They were watching their strong, outspoken mum slowly creep back to infancy.

'It's terrifying', Claudia said. 'I've got this horrible thing dragging me around all the time and all my family can do is watch.'

'Why Packer, Mr Polo?'
'Do they pay you much to do this, son?'

Mark Day and I celebrating our black tie dinner with Julio Iglesias' 1975 Lafite Rothchild.

Africa – one of my most memorable trips especially because Lea was with me.

Lea, our brave heroine, after being presented her bravery award by the then New South Wales Governor, Peter Sinclair. (Photo: Ross Warr)

Minus 38°C and fur trapping with Arctic Circle Eskimos.

Producer, Ron Sinclair, and me in the Arctic Circle – it took 30 minutes every day just to get dressed.

Louisiana's infamous 'Old Sparky' responsible for the deaths of dozens of death row prisoners.

It was the desperate poverty of children all over the world which always broke your heart.

Bette Midler – a very funny but natural woman.

Claudia Wright, a journalist breaking down barriers and relating her most important
story – her Alzheimer's disease.

Bianca Bailey – one of the most special, resilient and positive people I've ever met. (Photo: Stephen Taylor)

Not long after Margaret Bailey became Queensland Mother of the Year, Lea, Amy and I surprised her with a *This is Your Life* tribute. *From left:* Lea, Lucy, Margaret and Bianca Bailey, me and Amy. (Photo: Peter Freestone)

Red-faced embarrassment? No, just sunburnt after swimming with Madonna.

Only 14 hours on the ground staying at the world's most expensive hotel in the south of France near Cannes – and then straight back to Australia.

Inside an IRA training camp – life imprisonment just for being caught with them.
(Photo: Nick Lee)

She was determined to go ahead with the story despite how exhausting it was for her.

'I think what we're doing is great and so crucial to so many Australians,' she said.

Claudia may have been a reporter who had lost the abilities to fully communicate but the *60 Minutes* report was probably one of the most personal and important stories she ever did. In fact, CBS's *60 Minutes* ran an Australian edition one night across America and included Claudia Wright's courageous story.

You could count on one hand the number of people I've interviewed who I've continued to have any type of lasting or personal relationship with after completing a story. But in August 1990 we were lucky enough to do a story on two of the most extraordinary people I have ever met in my career, and they became lifelong friends of our family. Bianca Bailey was born in January 1986 with Congenital Quadrilateral Amputations, a rare birth defect that strikes one newborn in every 100,000. She had no legs and no left arm, but had part of her right upper arm. She was immediately put up for adoption by her parents, who felt that they could not cope. Shortly after, she was adopted by a woman named Margaret Bailey.

When *60 Minutes* producer Stephen Taylor, the crew and I first went to Ipswich in Queensland to meet Bianca she was four and was about to enter hospital for her seventh bone graft operation. She was able to hop along using her partial right arm as a crutch. She wore a hard plastic cover to protect the limb but her bone would constantly wear through her skin and protrude, hence her constant need for bone grafts. In addition, because Bianca had no real extremities her body heated up very quickly, which was not only uncomfortable but also caused medical complications. Just when you think what a miserable place the world can be you meet people like Bianca and Margaret who are truly inspirational.

'Bianca's already lived a lifetime of experience,' said Margaret during the *60 Minutes* interview. 'She's very mature for her age and extremely intelligent.'

For Margaret, just taking Bianca to the bathroom was a major effort. Then there were the costs of an electric wheelchair and modifications to the family home. To purchase a simple but special plastic bowl for the disabled cost Margaret $20. She was forced to send back the special dessertspoon when she saw the bill for $90. A teaspoon was $32. It was little wonder that Margaret Bailey and her local church group formed the Bianca Bailey Trust Fund to raise money to enable Bianca to lead as normal a life as possible.

Apart from having two of her own children, Margaret adopted a beautiful little boy named Jonathan. As if Margaret didn't have enough on her plate, in 1988 she then adopted six-year-old Lucy, who had been born with Down syndrome. Margaret wanted Bianca to grow up with a sibling, and in the back of her mind was the thought that one day Lucy might be able to assist Bianca physically. And that's just the way it panned out.

Ever since they started growing up together Bianca has been the 'brains' while Lucy has happily been the 'brawn'. The two of them fight like any other sisters but are very close.

Their interview with *60 Minutes* was an emotional one for all of us. Margaret had spoken about how Bianca, even at a very early age, used to ask if she would ever be able to hold a baby or even have children of her own.

'The thing in the world she'd like most is an elbow which would mean a world of difference with what she can do.'

All Bianca wished for was that she had been born with an elbow, which would have allowed her to have a prosthetic forearm so that she could hold things. At that point Margaret and I both started to get very teary and I was barely able to continue. After the interview I walked outside the Baileys' house with tears rolling down my cheeks and called the *60 Minutes* executive producer, Peter Meakin. I asked him if we could donate a modest sum to the Bianca Bailey Trust Fund because this unsung hero of a mother was doing it very tough indeed. Meakin gave his approval and so began a relationship between the Baileys and the Munro family and also with the Channel Nine Network over the next decade.

A few years after adopting Lucy, Margaret's husband walked out. She has battled on alone since then.

I've done several stories with Bianca and her family over the years, culminating in a tribute to Margaret on

This is Your Life in 1997. The year before, she had been rightly honoured as Queensland's Mother of the Year. After we plugged the Bianca Bailey Trust Fund at the end of *This is Your Life*, generous Aussies donated well over $100,000. That money enabled Margaret to finish off most of the disabled modifications to the house, buy Bianca a new electric wheelchair and even a van with an electric lift for her constant trips to and from hospital. Australians took Margaret, Bianca, Lucy and the rest of the family to their hearts.

Bianca, Lucy, Sean and Amy have grown up seeing each other regularly and remain good mates today. Ames and Bianca, being close in age, often write to each other. Fortunately God has given Bianca extreme intelligence. Despite missing huge slabs of her schooling throughout primary and high school she remains near the top of the class in most of her subjects. She is becoming more and more involved in public speaking on behalf of the disabled. She's nobody's fool and can be a real tough little nut if she wants to be, which will ensure she has a bright and successful future.

In November I flew to Greece and straight into an insane asylum from the dark ages. On Leros, a tiny island just off the coast of Turkey in the Aegean Sea, an insane asylum had been set up in the 1930s and virtually forgotten. An absolute hellhole, it housed around 500 inmates, both men and women, and was designed for epileptics and people with mild mental illnesses. If some of them had arrived mildly mentally disabled, by 1990 they were completely and utterly insane with no hope for the future. Many of the women were clothed in little more than hessian potato sacks, with no underwear and nothing personal, nothing they could call their own. The scene made *One Flew Over the Cuckoo's Nest* look like a five-star hotel. It shocked all of us and we planned to expose this forgotten island to the world.

During our second day on Leros one of the psychiatric nurses took exception to us filming in a particularly horrific women's ward, even though we had been given permission to be there. Through a series of misunderstandings brought about by language difficulties we found ourselves surrounded by an angry mob of staff and patients. They demanded we hand back the undeveloped film we had shot. The producer, Ron Sinclair, and I told the cameraman and sound recordist to lock themselves in the car, but at one stage things became so heated the crowd threatened to roll the car. Once the local island police arrived things settled down. They put us under house arrest for our protection, and to placate the locals, ordered us to leave the island on the first flight back to Athens the next morning.

We were already at the airport the next day when the plane arrived. When the pilot emerged from the 20-seater commuter aircraft he was white with fear. He had just flown the one-hour flight across the Aegean Sea in a force eight gale. The plane had been thrown about so much that a couple of passengers had been injured falling out of their seats or by loose carry-on luggage that had turned into missiles. He said there was no way he was returning until the wind had abated. Police explained that the aircraft had to depart otherwise the islanders, who depended on the asylum for their livelihood, might riot and overrun the airport. Talk about being caught between a rock and a hard place. Stay and risk being torn apart, or leave and risk dying in a plane crash.

The authorities convinced the pilot to risk the flight back to Athens – and so began the second of three flights during which I actually prayed because I believed I was about to die. Continually the plane would abruptly plummet 50 metres before being swept up again like an empty can, back to where we had been only seconds before. There were several doctors on board who broke open their whisky flasks to settle their nerves and stop other passengers from panicking and screaming out. I kept a watch out for any islands we passed over because if we were lucky enough to survive the crash we'd have to swim for it.

I'll never know how, but we made it back to Athens. From there we flew straight to Rome to script the exposé on Leros Island and send it back to Australia to go to air. We then moved on to Rio de Janeiro and São Paulo. The world was just learning about the so-called 'Brazilian Death Squads' specifically targeting street children. Tourism was being severely curtailed by the thousands of street children begging outside the five-star hotels along Copacabana and Ipanema Beaches and the hotels, resorts and tour companies hired death squads to rid the streets of them. But we didn't realise until we arrived and started digging that many of the death squads consisted of off-duty Brazilian policemen.

It was the final report in what had been a pretty depressing year of stories. I was so upset by all these morbid stories that the senior producers at *60 Minutes* steered me clear of such assignments, particularly those involving children, for the next year or so. As a reporter you generally try to make yourself as immune as humanly possible to the tragic lives you briefly pass through. But as brief as three or four days of filming might be, the research is certainly intense enough to plunge you deep inside their daily lives and you can't help but be affected. Often you might continue to help out in some small way for a time after completing the story. Occasionally you might keep in contact for a little while with the people you interviewed. Very rarely can you afford yourself the luxury of maintaining long-term relationships with people because otherwise you'd have no life with your own family. You always find yourself thinking how fortunate life can be and how lucky you are.

My annual return to *60 Minutes* was becoming harder and harder – as much for Lea and the kids as it was for me. I wasn't handling the travel any better, and if there was ever a way I could leave a day later or fly home a day earlier I would. One unkind producer suggested I even checked on wind speeds and tailwinds. One of my old mates from newspaper days who had moved on to become a producer at *60 Minutes*, Ben Hawke, had by now nicknamed me 'psycho boy' because of my continual urge to get home as soon as we'd finished the last story on a world trip. Lea continued to carry most of the load at home, coping with the loneliness.

'The nights were always the hardest,' she said years later. 'Family and friends would always be so generous with their invitations but it was all about missing your partner.'

Lea and I had been together for almost 20 years and more than ever before we were realising that the job wasn't worth the heartache of missing each other and the kids. So we agreed that I would try and do more stories in Australia, and quietly let it be known that as soon as a replacement reporter could be found I'd like to leave and perhaps join *A Current Affair*. This was regarded as, at the very least, a sideways career move, but the die was cast – Lea and I had made up our minds.

13

Nineteen ninety-one started well because I got to spend the first couple of months doing stories around the country. Then, in late March I had a three-week trip to San Francisco, Denver, New York, London, and then Dublin for the one story I had been longing to do, and had chipped away at, since the first day I walked into the *60 Minutes* office. I was to go inside the IRA, the Irish Republican Army. Producer Stephen Taylor had for years maintained contact with senior officials in the political arm of the IRA, Sinn Fein. After countless midnight phone calls from his home in Sydney to designated telephone booths in Dublin, Taylor was able to organise for a full *60 Minutes* crew to go out on an armed training exercise with an active service unit. It was going to be dangerous, but we were told that it would take place in the Republic of Ireland, in the south, not in Northern Ireland, which was crawling with 40,000 British troops. This was a time when if you were even found with a balaclava in your possession in Northern Ireland you could be locked up, no questions asked, under harsh British legislation.

Up until Osama Bin Laden launched his frightening airliner attacks on New York and Washington DC in 2001, the IRA was the most lethal and sophisticated terrorist organisation in the world. It was comprised of separate operational cells of volunteers to make sure very few knew anyone else's identity. Behind the balaclavas they could have been relatives and not even know it. One cell handled intelligence gathering and identified targets. Another was in charge of weapons. There was a cell that took care of the logistics of an operation and worked out escape routes. A further cell organised cars and safe houses. And then there were the active service units, who pulled the triggers and detonated the bombs. When joining up, volunteers are told the IRA can only offer them two things: prison or an early grave.

We were going into Ireland only two months after the IRA had launched one of its most daring raids in years. In February 1991 it had launched a mortar attack against number 10 Downing Street. The British Prime Minister, John Major, and his entire cabinet, were meeting there at the time. Most of the mortars fell five metres short of their target, but one did manage to get through.

The British Government had outlawed anyone, particularly the media, from even talking to the IRA – anyone who did risked a five-year gaol sentence. The UK media were banned from running anything about the IRA. The story we were about to do would be banned in the UK and we could be arrested and locked up.

We arrived in Dublin a couple of days before the 75th anniversary of the Easter uprising by Catholics against British rule in 1916. The uprising resulted in the partitioning of the island into the Republic of Ireland and Northern Ireland, the latter of which is governed by the UK. The uprising also led to the formation of the IRA. Today Britain shells out almost $2 billion dollars a year to protect her subjects against the IRA in Northern Ireland.

It was a pretty emotional and explosive period in history to be flagrantly breaking British law by filming an IRA unit. It crossed my mind more than once that if the British Special Branch, the crack intelligence group responsible for putting so many IRA and loyalist terrorists behind bars in the infamous Maze Prison, got wind of our plans they could follow us to the rendezvous point and either capture or kill a couple of very senior men in the terrorist army. The four media people from Australia who got in the way and were also taken out by the helicopter gunships would just be unfortunate casualties.

It was all about to play out like a le Carré novel. We were staying at the Shelbourne Hotel, one of Dublin's grand old ladies, when the co-producer, Andrea Keir, was told by our major contact in Dublin, 'John', that we were in fact being watched by the British Special Branch. Fearing that we might have been loose-mouthed or might lead the Special Branch to the operation, IRA intelligence would now watch the Special Branch, while Special Branch watched us. We were ordered not to make any calls to anyone until John contacted us again. My very first thought was that this would be the first time that I wouldn't be able to speak to Lea or the kids. I dare not sneak off and make some clandestine call from a phone booth for fear of putting the story at risk. I was concerned too that Lea would become worried that something was wrong when she failed to hear from 'the sook'.

For five days we sat around the hotel waiting for a call. Early on the sixth day it came. John told us the Special Branch had stopped following us two days before and it was now deemed safe to allow us into the operation. We were told to move immediately and meet John at a pre-designated spot where we had already parked our white station wagon. He told us he would sit in the left rear passenger seat, where his army mates expected him to sit. If he wasn't sitting there it meant there was trouble and to call it all off.

We did as he instructed and set out for a destination one hour's drive north-west of Dublin. I was driving and on two occasions, about 20 minutes apart, John leaned forward and said to me: 'Pull the car over a wee bit and let the boys go past.' Each time, a different car rolled on past, the three men inside giving us a slight smirk as they went by. John explained that the IRA had followed us out of Dublin to make sure the Special Branch wasn't following us. We arrived in a small, typical Irish town where John told me to park the car while he went and bought the *Irish Times* newspaper. We then entered a nearby pub. Four tough-looking faces turned to look the five of us up and down. We walked through to a back room where we had to wait for our second but unknown escort to make contact. We didn't know it until later but John's *Irish Times* would identify to the second contact who we were. After about 20 minutes the second man arrived. He and John, who also had never set eyes on each other before, went outside to speak in private. When they came back in John handed us over to this new man – a complete and utter stranger with no name – who was going to get into our car and direct us to an armed training exercise with the IRA.

We had been driving for about 30 minutes when I asked him where the operation was taking place.

'In the north,' he said.

'You mean Northern Ireland?' I asked.

'Right in North Armagh,' he proudly said with a smile.

Not only was the IRA going to open its operational training to an Australian television crew but they were going to do it right under the noses of the British, in one of the most violent and bloody towns in the north.

This second man managed to get us into the north without us seeing one British soldier. We had used a maze of back roads without passing through one checkpoint – something the crew and I never believed possible on any of our previous trips to Ireland.

We arrived at a tiny farmhouse and got out of the car.

There were two British Sphinx helicopter gunships patrolling almost directly above us and three balaclava-clad terrorists, hiding in bushes around us, were acting as the perimeter guards. While I was fearful that we might be spotted by the helicopters above, I felt confident that the IRA had things covered on the ground. They assured us they had secured the area for up to a radius of two kilometres.

'If a British soldier dare to walk in on his own on foot, he won't be walkin' out,' our second contact told us.

All four of us were carefully given full body searches before we entered the farmhouse. Getting inside, out of the view of the gunships, was such a relief. The air wing of the British Army had every right to be on alert. The week before we arrived the IRA had shot down one of their $20-million Sphinx choppers with an anti-aircraft machine gun. We waited for over an hour as IRA members from different cells arrived, all donning balaclavas before they got out of their cars. We were to see only one face all day – that of the man who had brought us into the north. The other dozen or so army volunteers never once took their balaclavas off.

Someone brought the pistols and rifles; someone else the firing pins; someone else again arrived with the ammunition; and another brought a much larger piece of equipment wrapped up in a hessian bag. A five-person unit consisting of three men and two women, all new recruits aged in their early 20s, were to take part in the training exercise. They gathered inside the farmhouse, where the armaments master instructed them in how to pull apart the pistols and rifles, and put them back together. Then he lifted the large hessian bag onto a table, the one piece of furniture in the farmhouse. He pulled out a 12mm anti-aircraft gun, the very same one that had recently been used to bring down the British helicopter. The four of us from *60 Minutes* all looked at each other, the enormity of the situation we were now fully committed to sinking in. Five years' gaol just for talking to the IRA and 20 years for being caught with a single weapon – and here we were surrounded by an entire arsenal, including the hottest weapon in Northern Ireland, which the British and the Royal Ulster constabulary were scouring the countryside for. I expected those gunships to come thundering over the undulating hillsides and blow us all away at any moment. The armaments teacher proceeded to pull apart the machine gun and show the volunteers how to assemble it. Meanwhile, we could hear the helicopter gunships patrolling in the distance. It was certainly difficult for me to maintain full concentration for what I was there to do.

The only condition the IRA had put on *60 Minutes* when they agreed to such extraordinary and risky access was that we brought with us from London a voice scrambler. The main interview for the story was to be with 'Patrick', a high-ranking member of the General Senior Headquarters Staff of the IRA, also known as the Army Council. Patrick was one of only seven council members who controlled tens of millions of dollars in cash and weapons, and organised crime that bankrolled their terrorist operations. This man was very high on the UK's most-wanted list and insisted that we use the scrambler so he could not be identified by his voice. He of course wore a balaclava, and even white gloves in case any distinguishing marks, such as tattoos, moles or scars were later picked up by the Special Branch when they watched our story go to air. My Irish past played on my mind as I considered how hard I should go with my questions for Patrick, when all an IRA volunteer would have to do is put a bullet in my head.

'How many people in the world know what you do?' I asked this large and obviously fit IRA commander.

'Including the seven in the Army Council, only 12 people know my position within the IRA,' he said. 'And until the unfinished business of 1916 is completed and every British soldier is out of a united Ireland our war will continue. Every British soldier will either march out of Ireland or be carried out in a coffin.

'If the Irish people were black and not white I believe the rest of the world would understand more easily how we have been treated like slaves by the English for centuries,' he added, his scrambled voice taking on an almost demonic tone.

'But does that mean you have to murder innocent men, women and children as they do their shopping?' I asked.

'One of the great tragedies of war are the civilian casualties,' he answered.

And that sums up what the IRA hides behind – the absolute belief that it's at war with the British. That way they can justify in their own minds the deliberate slaughter of innocent people.

And sometimes the IRA gets it horribly wrong. A year before our interview, two young men were shot dead outside a cafe in Holland by IRA gunmen. They had been targeted by the intelligence cell as crack British Special Forces on leave from active service in Belfast. The IRA was making the point that even on holidays British soldiers were not safe. But the IRA killed the wrong men. Stephen Melrose and Nick Spanos were two Australian lawyers out for the night with friends, who watched as the IRA pumped 20 rounds into the young men.

'How can you possibly justify that?' I asked Patrick.

'We had expected the two soldiers at the same bar the lawyers were drinking at, they were driving a similar car and had short hair like British soldiers,' he answered.

'If that's all you based their identities on, can you understand the families of the two Australians saying you're nothing but scum of the earth, murderers and thugs?' I said, pushing him.

'We are remorseful, but we don't expect the families of those young men to understand our cause,' he said, almost as if reciting it.

Once our filming and interviews had been completed inside the farmhouse Patrick surprised us by announcing that we were all to walk down to the field next door. Word had come through that the gunships had moved to another area and there was enough time for some target practice before they returned. This particular field was chosen because it was below the line of sight of any British snipers, who scoured the horizon with their deadly telescopic scopes. After about 45 minutes of filming their target practice we all returned to the farm-house. Within an hour of completing filming, all the weapons and ammunition had been carted off in differ-ent directions by various people. The four of us were left completely alone, almost as if the whole thing had been a dream. I pinched myself as hard as I could. It hurt.

Cameraman Nick Lee had shot five rolls – 50 minutes' worth – of film. It was enough to convict all of us and send us to gaol. If we were arrested, the pommie authorities could imprison us for up to two weeks – no questions asked and no charges laid – under the British *Terrorist Act*. Our Australian lawyers had given us the name of a law firm in England who would defend us if necessary. We drove back to Dublin holding our breath through several checkpoints. That night I flew straight to Amsterdam, carrying the five precious rolls of film. I hid them in the ceiling of the house of an old friend who was also willing to take the risk – while the British had no jurisdction to arrest us in Amsterdam, they no doubt would have done everything they could to prevent the footage from being shown in other parts of the world. With the film well out of British reach I returned to Dublin, where we filmed a re-enactment of the saga of how our contacts got us to the training exercise. We all then flew to Amsterdam and overnighted there before flying home via Frankfurt, giving a very wide berth to anywhere British.

Four months later, after our story had been aired in Australia and had been covered by the media in the UK, I flew into London's Heathrow Airport with the same crew. We were sure we'd be pulled aside and questioned, and were almost disappointed when we just sailed through immigration and customs.

Only four weeks after returning to Australia with our IRA story I flew out again, this time for the Cannes Film Festival, in the south of France. Cannes during festival time is a bit like Las Vegas, an ugly, gauche and shallow city which is fascinating to see . . . once. I went to Cannes for one night only for an interview with Madonna, who was releasing the film of her world tour, *In Bed With Madonna*, and immediately returned to Australia. The round trip took 72 hours and I was only on the ground for 14 hours.

We stayed where Madonna was, one of the most luxurious and expensive hotels in the world – the Hotel Cap d'Antibes, situated right on the Point of Antibes, a 10-minute drive from Cannes. My tiny, very average, room without a view cost US$1,400 for the night. Because the hotel is so popular, patrons must pay the cost of their room for their entire stay before they can check in. Madonna later told us quietly that she had had to pay US$250,000 deposit before she could move her entourage in. It was nothing to pass Eddie Murphy walking through the hotel's magnificent gardens or sit next to Billy Crystal in the Eden Roc restaurant on the edge of the Mediterranean Sea. In fact, on the morning before the interview, I went for a swim in the hotel pool, which also looks out over the Mediterranean, and found myself swimming alongside Madonna herself. I introduced myself as one of the four million reporters about to interview her that day. She didn't look the least bit interested, and who could blame her, until I mentioned that Molly Meldrum said to say 'gidday'. Her face lit up and she asked, with genuine interest, how Molly was. Just mentioning Australia's musical guru by name had broken the ice with Madonna and helped make the interview more friendly.

The downside was that Madonna Inc controlled everything. The interviews were set up like a cattle call, and all the videotaping was completely controlled by Madonna – we had to use Madonna's cameras, crews, audio assistants, the lot. It was the first time I hadn't used one of our own Australian *60 Minutes* crews. If she didn't like a question or an interviewer she had total veto over whether the question and answer was erased from the tape, or the interviewer left with no tape whatsoever. It certainly compromised the questions a reporter might ask. The interview time was strictly limited to 20 minutes, after which time the camera operators would simply stop filming.

Madonna was doing 16 television interviews that afternoon. Our producer, Stephen Taylor, and I badgered her minders and got ourselves bumped up from interview number 12 to interview number four – a real bonus as she would be fresher and more accommodating in her fourth interview than in her twelfth. We all waited on a patio area outside the interview room, and the cattle call began. 'Interview number one – the United Kingdom.' Up stepped Terry Wogan, a well-known pommie interviewer. France was followed by Germany, then 'Australia'. In we went.

Madonna's skin and figure are unbelievable. Folklore has it that to be a bodyguard for Madonna you virtually have to be a mini-marathoner. At the time I interviewed her she was running up to 20 kilometres a day. And while she came across as a little hard, she has a quick brain and a fine mind for business. Except for me being lobster red with sunburn from my morning swim, the interview went well. I closed it by asking her when she might find time to come to Australia. 'Oh I've been asked so many times,' she said before turning to look straight down the lens of the camera and saying: 'I'm coming, I'm coming!' To which I replied: 'I bet you say that to all the boys.' She had a good laugh at that before the profile ended with the 'tick, tick, tick' of the *60 Minutes* stopwatch.

One of the great loves I have for journalism is the variety of people you meet and places you go. One moment you're in the middle of an IRA training operation, the next you're swimming next to Madonna in France. One week you're in a war zone, the next you're hiking out of Kathmandu for the Himalayas. Then you might be sitting down with Jennifer Lopez, Ricky Martin or Britney Spears. It's almost surreal, but swinging from one subject to a very different subject is half the excitement. To be confident about doing it week in and week out depends entirely on how good your research and preparation are. If that's in place then there's no real difficulty in mentally switching from one story to the next. I have always taken a lot of pride in remembering the names of all the subjects in a story because it's important and courteous. People would often remark: 'Aren't you good remembering all these names.' But when I have completely immersed myself in the next story, I often can't remember one name from the previous week.

Just four weeks after the Madonna interview we flew to Las Vegas for the five days leading up to boxer Jeff Fenech's first attempt to take the super-featherweight world championship belt from Ghana's Azuma Nelson. Fenech was the red-hot favourite. He had already won three world crowns in other weight divisions, and was now poised to take his fourth. Fenech had signed a contract with promoter Don King, who had secured him US$5 million for the fight. I got the impression that Fenech hadn't liked King from the start, nor any of us in the *60 Minutes* crew. Nevertheless we still filmed him having dinner one night with King and his body-guards.

Loud and annoying, King yelled to the whole restaurant as Fenech arrived: 'Here he comes, the thunder from down under.'

Anyone who deals with King comes away checking that they still have all their fingers – as a young man he served time for manslaughter after he beat a man to death.

Despite Fenech being all over Nelson on the night, at the end of the final round Nelson retained his world super-featherweight title. The fight ended in a bitter and controversial draw, with many ringsiders having no doubt the decision should have gone to Fenech. The result is still being debated today and will go down as one of the most unfair decisions in Australian Boxing history.

Jeff Fenech has always been a close friend of Mike Tyson, who was also in Las Vegas and in full training at the same gym Fenech was using. Tyson agreed to allow us to film him during one of his training sessions as a favour to Fenech. It was a real bonus to get Tyson in the story talking about the upcoming Fenech–Nelson bout. As we filmed Tyson training I was mesmerised by how animal-like he was. His moves and power were so awesome they sent shivers down my back – when you look at him you know immediately that, physically, this man is easily capable of killing. At the end of the session Fenech introduced us all – including Andrea Keir, the producer and only woman in the group – to Tyson. He gave Andrea a hug. It was only later when we saw that she was upset that she told us Tyson had thrust his crotch into her as they hugged. None of us had noticed it at the time – and what the hell could any of us have done up against Mike Tyson for God's sake? I was furious to think this bastard could take such liberties with a woman. Of course Tyson got his just deserts because within a year he was charged with rape and was on his way to gaol.

Jeff Fenech just wasn't the same boxer after his bout

against Azuma Nelson in Vegas. They had a rematch in Melbourne the next year, and Azuma took that one fair and square.

By the end of the year I had done 29 stories and although most of those had been done in Australia I was now at the point where I didn't think I could face being away from Lea and the kids for extended periods. There was nothing wrong with the workload; in fact, I revelled in it because while I was working it took my mind off my homesickness. What I hated was at the end of the day having to go back to those endless hotel corridors and the loneliness of a hotel room.

At the beginning of 1992 the Nine Network's CEO, David Leckie, and Peter Meakin, the director of news and current affairs, were now well aware that they had to find a replacement for me, and had assured me that this would be my last year at *60 Minutes*. John Westacott, whom I had known for 25 years, from my newspaper days, was to take over as executive producer from Meakin, who had been filling in for two years while they found a permanent replacement for Gerald Stone. Westacott knew what a crybaby I was about wanting to be home, and was pretty good about keeping me in the country for most of 1992. Instead of being overseas for up to 16 weeks of the year I was to spend only seven weeks out of the country. It was to make the year so much easier. The Network had been very good to our family but I had to get out. I was uncertain about whether they could find another post for me, but if it meant resigning altogether so be it. I was fully prepared to leave, though I had no idea where I might go.

Ironically I would do more stories in my final year at *60 Minutes* than any other year – 32 of them. I started off with profiles with Sean Connery and Burt Reynolds, then spent the rest of the year working on a variety of investigations, including a report on understanding and being more tolerant towards people with Down syndrome, the problem of asbestos in Australian homes, and the ever-climbing divorce rate and how marriage counselling is an answer for many couples.

But the standout story for me that year came in October. It was about one of the most notorious and feared criminals in New South Wales history, who was writing his life story. He was known as Arthur Stanley 'Neddy' Smith, but once told me that even he wasn't sure what his real name was or the correct date of his birth. A bull of a man with enormous strength who was never shy about using it. In the late 1970s and then 1980s, Neddy set up a perfect corrupt relationship with detectives in the New South Wales Armed Hold-up Squad and other senior police officers. He eventually became so cosy with the police that they knew which banks, payroll vans and offices Neddy's gang was targeting before the robberies were even committed.

During my years at *Willesee* I convinced Neddy Smith to give his first ever on-camera interview to me after a car ran him down during Sydney's heroin wars in the mid-1980s. I think he trusted me because I never bulled to him and told him straight out what I thought. I also got on well with his wife, Debra, and their kids. It's reputed he's killed up to a dozen people. Our crim–reporter relationship had continued for almost a decade, till now, when he was planning on publishing his first book.

Neddy had agreed to give *60 Minutes* the first glimpse of his book, which exposed all sorts of illegal deals he had going on with corrupt cops. Perhaps the most chilling arrangement he had was called 'The Green Light' and it gave Neddy and his gang the green light to rob and kill anyone, just as long as they got their fair share of all that was stolen. The only thing the green light did not allow for was killing a policeman. On several occasions Neddy and his gang would be driving out of a factory having robbed the payroll office, while the armed hold-up detectives would be driving into the factory supposedly to 'investigate'. Both groups would actually wave as they passed each other. Several hours later the crims and the cops would meet to divvy up the money. It was a perfect scam and went on for years. This volatile allegation was contained in his book and *60 Minutes* wanted to expose it first.

There were two problems in getting the story: Neddy was in a maximum-security prison, where we weren't allowed to film, and he wanted to be paid $10,000 for his interview. We solved the first problem by arranging to interview Neddy from his wife's home over the phone. The money became the stumbling block. There was pressure on me from within *60 Minutes* that we could pay the money to him through his publisher or into his children's bank accounts, or even by buying the family a van to get around in, but I said right from the start that there was no way I would be involved in a story where we paid a known criminal for an interview. I couldn't and wouldn't do it. I also told Neddy and his wife this. In the end he begrudgingly decided to forego payment and stick with me for the interview because he had dealt with me in the past and trusted me. When the story went to air it sent shockwaves through the New South Wales Police Force and set off a series of arrests. Neddy Smith is still in prison and is suffering from Parkinson's disease.

I had never made a secret of my distaste for cheque-book journalism among senior Channel Nine executives. Often I was quoted in newspaper, magazine and radio interviews about the dangers of it. If people are being paid to say things, particularly to criticise others, then you have to question their motives. It leaves the way open to pay people to say anything to suit the story. Having started out in newspapers, where paying for stories was unheard of, I always found it very difficult to accept. Yes, many times I have reluctantly gone along with it to make sure a story didn't go somewhere else, but I just lose most of the enthusiasm for the story if I know it's been 'purchased'. All the excitement of the challenge in getting it and executing it disappears for me.

Once *60 Minutes* and the *Australian Women's Weekly* paid $250,000 to Lindy Chamberlain for her first interview after her release from prison in the mid-1980s, it became more and more accepted. People knew they could demand money, and if they didn't get it from one news outlet there would be someone else willing to offer it. A real ugly side to journalism, it has grown even more in recent years. Today even newspapers sometimes pay for their stories. At one stage two of the networks, including Channel Nine, tried to come to an agreement that they would no longer pay for stories but the plan never really got off the ground.

At the end of 1992 the Nine Network decided to replace me with Charles Wooley and move me into the role of senior reporter on *A Current Affair*. This was a great relief; I had been at *60 Minutes* for six-and-a-half years and could not have possibly done another year. Then David Leckie called me into his office to tell me that Mike Willesee would be taking over the hosting role of *A Current Affair* from Jana Wendt, and ask me if I would fill in for Willesee when he was away on holidays or on assignment, and to host the eight-week summer edition of the program during December and January. I was pleased with this arrangement – I had always been willing to take a backwards step into daily current affairs reporting for the sake of my family life, but now I would also be the part-time host.

Because I was almost obsessed about making up for lost time with Lea and the kids I really didn't think about the professional repercussions of leaving the incredibly dedicated and professional team at *60 Minutes*. Without doubt they are among the best camera operators, the best sound recordists, the best editors and the best producers in the world. And that's not to say that cameramen like Drew Benjamin and Mark Munro (no relation) at *A Current Affair* aren't at the top of their field, because they are. What I immediately missed when I moved to *A Current Affair* was the luxury of the much longer reports that *60 Minutes* can afford to present in its one-hour format. During my period at *60 Minutes* the average length of a story was probably around 13 to 15 minutes, while when I joined *A Current Affair*, the average length of a story was about five minutes. The executive producer of *A Current Affair* at the time, Stephen Rice, was confident enough to allow me to go ahead and organise any story in the country after briefly bouncing the idea off him. If Willesee couldn't do a leading story, it fell to me.

All that really mattered, though, was that I was now home full-time with Lea, 11-year-old Sean and eight-year-old Amy. I would occasionally have to work weekends but generally I worked Monday to Friday. A working day could be eight hours or eighteen hours, but most nights Lea, Sean, Amy and I would all sit down to a family dinner together. No television, no radio – just conversations about our days. Lea found the initial adjustment difficult, until I got out of most of my bad habits from living in four-star hotels around the world – wet towels on beds, clothes on floors, toiletries spilled out over the bathroom sink. However, the children adjusted pretty quickly to my homecoming and were delighted to see so much more of me. I couldn't wait for each Saturday so I could go and watch their various sports. Life was so much better.

14

My first year of working once again with Michael Willesee started with a controversial and damaging bang.

In late March 1993 three male drifters stabbed and shot dead a 14-year-old girl, Deborah Gale. Her boyfriend, Robert Steele, 22, shot her to death after Raymond Bassett, 25, and Leonard Leadbeater, 41, had both stabbed her. Leadbeater, the leader of the men, was getting over various failed businesses and romances.

After setting Deborah Gale's body alight, the three men drove to Dalby Caravan Park, just west of Toowoomba, and abducted four children to use as human shields should the police come after them in relation to Deborah's murder. They released two of the children but kept 11-year-old Trevor and his nine-year-old sister, Tonia, as hostages and drove towards the Queensland–New South Wales border. When they realised that the police had a full description of the car they were driving and that the media were broadcasting it they dumped their car and stole another. In the process of stealing it they shot and killed three miners. The murders were committed in full view of the two children. The men had an arsenal of guns, including a shotgun, a .303, two .22 rifles, another rifle, several knives and well over 500 rounds of ammunition.

On the morning of the 31st of March the three gunmen, with their two young hostages, entered an isolated farmhouse at Cangai, between Grafton and Glen Innes in north-eastern New South Wales. Fortunately the farmer was out on the property mustering and his wife was on her way into town to do the weekly shopping. Inside, the men found four more guns, including two shotguns. They barricaded themselves in with the hostages.

Large numbers of police and negotiators were on the scene very soon. The police negotiators used the farmhouse's phone line to speak to the gunmen, but each time the police got off the line, the gunmen would receive a call from the media. Michael Willesee was driving across the Sydney Harbour Bridge on his way to work when he received a call from our boss, Stephen Rice, who told him that *A Current Affair* had Leadbeater on the phone, waiting for an interview. Not only did Willesee not have the time to change or have make-up put on, but more importantly no time for much research. He went straight to the studio, where he was connected to Leadbeater, who made it frighteningly clear to Willesee that there was no way he was walking out of that farmhouse alive. He would never give himself up or go back to gaol.

'Well, if you don't want to go to prison why have you behaved like this?' Willesee asked him.

'We had to kill the 14-year-old girl because she said she was going to the cops about us. We shot her through the head and burned her body to give us time to get out of the state,' he said in a relaxed, almost flippant way. He confirmed that he and his gang had also killed the three miners. 'I'd much rather be in South Australia killing cops. I've had homicidal urges all my life,' he told Willesee on national television, 'but consider myself a controlled psychopath.' Leadbeater then began to rant and rave about suicide being a crime 'so the only way I can go is to have the cops take me out'.

It was at this stage that Willesee was able to get an undertaking from him that they wouldn't hurt the children and would soon release them. Willesee asked if he could speak to young Trevor.

'We're safe,' Trevor lied as soon as he got on the phone. 'Leonard told me he'd let us go and I believe him. He said he'd let us go when the female police officer arrives here.'

His nine-year-old sister, Tonia, was next on the phone. 'Are you OK?' Willesee asked her.

'Yes,' came the almost inaudible reply.

'Are you scared?' Willesee asked.

'No,' she said.

Willesee then spoke to Robert Steele. 'Are you afraid?' he asked Steele.

'Ever known a psychopath to be afraid, mate?'

'Have you enjoyed the killing spree so far?'

'Do psychopaths usually enjoy killing?' Steele asked Willesee.

'I don't know, do they?'

'Course they do,' came Steele's chilling reply. Steele also made it clear on national television later that night that he too wanted to die at the scene.

By the time Willesee had finished talking to the gunmen and their hostages I had made my way to Grafton in a light aircraft with cameraman Drew Benjamin. At Grafton Airport we got into a chopper and flew 20 minutes or so west to Cangai. Our plan was to film some aerial shots of the property and land nearby so that our pilot, a nice young Scottish bloke called Graham Davidson, could drop Drew and I off to film some more footage. Graham would return to Grafton, then fly back to collect us in an hour so that we could then get our story beamed out around the country. We did our aerial shots then landed half a kilometre from the centre of the siege. Just as we did, a police helicopter dropped out of nowhere, particularly close to our helicopter. Drew and I got out and and started walking towards the farmhouse, which was surrounded by 50 or so police and ambulance officers, as Graham took off back to Grafton. We were met by local uniformed police and members of the SWAT team and told it was not only a restricted area but that there was also a no-fly zone over the farmhouse. We filmed very little before being bundled into a police four-wheel-drive vehicle and driven about four kilometres to the police command post, where most of the media contingent was corralled. It was a dead mobile phone area so we couldn't reach Graham to tell him not to come back to pick us up. We hitched a ride back into town to send our footage back to Channel Nine.

Not long after police negotiators and Michael Willesee had spoken to the gunmen they released the children unharmed. Their parents, Rita and Greg, were grateful to Willesee, giving him much of the credit for getting the gunmen to agree not to harm Trevor and Tonia. The siege dragged on though. Finally, Raymond Bassett gave himself up but Leadbeater and Steele continued the standoff overnight. At 6.00am Robert Steele surrendered, walking calmly out of the house smoking a cigarette. He told police that they would never take Leadbeater alive . . . and they didn't. At 11.30am police rushed the farmhouse and found Leadbeater's body lying on a mattress in the kitchen. He had blown his head off with one of the shotguns. After 26 hours, the Cangai siege was over.

In the aftermath, Willesee's interview with the children was widely discussed in the media. Some commentators believed he'd saved the kids; most thought he should have left it to the police. I was roundly criticised for breaking a supposed no-fly zone when there was none. You would have thought we'd landed our helicopter on the roof of the farmhouse for all the jumping up and down the authorities did. At Leonard Leadbeater's coronial inquest, 10 days after the siege, the New South Wales deputy state coroner,

Peter Gould, strongly criticised both Willesee and myself. 'They weren't reporting news,' he said. 'It was a media event targeted to titillate their audience.' He said that Willesee's interview with the children was 'a commercial marketing exercise to grab the ratings at any cost' and that landing the helicopter near the farmhouse showed 'a complete disregard for the safety of anyone'.

Willesee was away on assignment when Peter Gould made his claims from the bench and as I was hosting *A Current Affair* in his absence I gave the program's reply. I told our audience that Mr Gould was wrong on every count. 'Willesee talked to the children and found them to be safe. He also extracted an undertaking from the gunman to release the children. And in less than one hour Leadbeater did just that,' I said.

The police wanted a scalp and tried hard to lay charges against me, but couldn't find any grounds. Instead they went after Graham Davidson, who, not realising that we had been moved on by the police, had returned to the farmhouse to pick us up. He had been intercepted by a police helicopter and later charged with flying dangerously – a charge that if proven would probably mean the end of his flying career and liquidation of his fledgling business. Channel Nine returned his loyalty and agreed to defend him because we knew that aviation authorities had never instigated a no-fly zone. Police on the ground also knew we had landed a safe distance from the farmhouse. The lawyer-fest rolled in and out of court for the next 21 months, finally ending up in the New South Wales District Court before a full jury, presided over by Judge Gallen.

Throughout the legal wrangling, every criticism levelled at the 'Channel Nine pilot' was deliciously reported and dissected by the media. The reporting indicated to me more than ever the lack of objectivity and balance in some quarters of the media to whom anything commercial, popular or tabloid is the devil incarnate. Too much of the reporting of the trial was one-sided at best. In the final week in court, one paper ran a report on Monday, but just three days later, when the jury returned a 'not guilty' verdict, they were suddenly no longer interested in reporting on it. The public was largely denied the final verdict as very few media bothered to cover it, perhaps because Judge Gallen's summing up stuck in their throats.

The police helicopter pilots had accused Davidson of making a dangerous turn, bringing our chopper perilously close to a police helicopter, and of doing so in a restricted no-fly zone. But Judge Gallen openly questioned their evidence, pointing out that they had been 'evasive' and 'ill at ease'. Regarding the supposed no-fly zone he said: 'Although it was apparently thought at one time that the area had been restricted for flying it turned out that it had not been and there is no suggestion that Mr Davidson entered an area which he was not lawfully entitled to enter while flying his aircraft.'

Our case had been helped by a Channel Ten crew who had been hiding on the other side of a nearby river and actually filmed our helicopter landing. The film proved that there was certainly no dangerous flying whatsoever on Davidson's part.

Around the middle of 1993 I received a call from Ron Hicks, a journalist I had worked with as a kid in the radio room at the *Daily Mirror*. For a long time Ron had been extremely concerned about child sexual abuse in the community. He said he had access to a man who had been involved in a police–paedophile protection racket in New South Wales that had flourished for a staggering 17 years. It had been led by a detective sergeant in the New South Wales police force and Phillip Harold Bell, a paedophile and a multi-millionaire merchant banker. Ron's contact was a man named Colin Fisk, who had been Bell's offsider.

Ron brought Fisk to our office at *A Current Affair*. With me was a young producer also new to the program, John McAvoy, who would work on the investigation with me. We had already checked Fisk with our police contacts, who had confirmed he was a known paedophile. However, Fisk objected to being called a paedophile, preferring the term 'pederast'. 'A pederast is attracted to boys in their mid-teens not younger,' he said, as if he was ordering an ice-cream.

His story was shocking, and believable, enough to warrant further investigating. Fisk claimed that between 1972 and 1989 up to 300 boys had passed through his and Phillip Bell's lives. 'We called them "Bell's Boys",' said Fisk. In mid-1989 Fisk and Bell had a major falling out, and Fisk went to the cops. After being granted immunity from prosecution he confessed all. More than a year went by before approval was given to launch a major task force, 'Operation Speedo', in January 1991 – 18 months after the police–paedophile protection racket had broken up. By then more than half of the nine policemen who had been involved had already left the police service, including the ringleader.

The task force discovered that the paedophiles, largely bankrolled by Bell, had preyed mostly on 10- to 14-year-old boys. Once the boys hit adolescence they were usually discarded. The ring had operated in Sydney's eastern suburbs, northern beaches and near Kempsey on the mid-north coast of New South Wales.

'If one of them was caught and arrested inquiries would be made as to who charged him, and the police protecting us would either try and take the case over and it would never make it to court, or they would offer a bribe to the arresting police to drop the charges,' Fisk told the task force. He said $10,000 was the 'going rate'. Bell held dinners, barbecues and harbour cruises on his boat for the corrupt detectives, and Bell and Fisk even attended police functions.

Most of the boys were from working-class families, battlers who'd gratefully accept any financial help. Bell would endear himself to a boy and then his unwitting family. Sometimes he'd offer to pay for the boy's education or take him on an overseas trip. He would shower him with gifts and cash.

'The problem was that the boys were living in luxury

far beyond their means. In the end some of them were totally confused with their whole lives,' said Fisk, who also claimed he saw one 15 year old commit suicide. 'I put that down to Bell's wealth and non-caring attitude, real non-caring attitude. I've also seen various boys go to heroin.'

The mother of one of the boys lodged a complaint with police and a member of the paedophile ring was taken into custody. Two of the corrupt detectives were called, immediately took over the case, marched the busted paedophile to his bank and got him to withdraw $8,000 in cash on the spot. The mother of the boy heard nothing from the police until the task force came knocking six years later. But if she thought she would at last get some justice she was wrong.

The task force's investigations took another year and were finally all pulled together and completed in February 1992. The official findings revealed that: 'Corrupt practices did exist between serving officers of the New South Wales Police Service and paedophiles up until the 31st of March 1989.' However, when our investigation went to air on *A Current Affair* in November 1993, 21 months after the task force had released its findings, only two paedophiles – and no police officers – had gone to gaol as a result of the task force.

In more recent years, though, authorities have had a little more success. After our investigation went to air we were asked to hand over every piece of paper and videotape to the Royal Commission into Corruption in the New South Wales Police Service. As a result, Phillip

Harold Bell became a prime target and was finally arrested in South Africa at an exclusive beach resort where he owned a house. He was extradited to Australia where he faced trial and is now serving a very long and very necessary sentence. It's frightening to think just how many young lives and families he ruined.

One of the darkest and most disturbing things McAvoy and I uncovered during our research came from New South Wales Parliament Hansard in October 1990, not long before approval was given for the task force. Labor MP Deirdre Grusovin asked the then Attorney-General, John Dowd: 'When did the Attorney-General first become aware that a police officer involved in the "Mr Bubbles" investigation was linked with a police–paedophile protection racket?' Mister Dowd's reply was: 'I will not interfere with the matters which are the subject of police investigation.'

Deirdre Grusovin was complaining that no one had been convicted of Australia's most notorious child sexual abuse case because one of the investigating officers was a senior member of Bell's police–paedophile protection racket. Five little girls aged between three and four who attended Seabeach Kindergarten, near Mona Vale on Sydney's northern beaches, were found to have con-clusive signs of vaginal or anal penetration. Many of the children spoke of being taken from the kindergarten to a house where they had bubble baths with 'Mr Bubbles'. Tony Deren, whose wife was licensed to run the kinder-garten, was charged. He maintained his innocence and his wife stuck by him. In the end the magistrate dismissed the charges against Deren. He said that the children's evidence had become contaminated because the parents and children had been allowed to swap information and allegations among themselves; most of the evidence had now become second-hand and confused. Another major complaint about the case was that a probationary constable had been put in charge of taking some of the police statements from the children. Tony Deren was released and later awarded $250,000 in compensation.

I had worked on a story about the 'Mr Bubbles' case at *60 Minutes* so I knew it well. Imagine then my horror at the end of 1993 when I realised that a corrupt cop inside the police-paedophile protection racket may have put insurmountable objects in the way to make sure the 'Mr Bubbles' child abuse case was never solved.

While working on the police–paedophile racket story I came to realise how fortunate I was to be working with an enthusiastic and dedicated young journalist like John McAvoy. He had started doing his degree in journalism at the University of Queensland, then pestered first Jana Wendt and later Ray Martin, who sometimes filled in for Jana, for a chance to work on *A Current Affair*. He made it very clear he would drop everything and move from Brisbane to Sydney to start as a researcher. Like most journalism students in Australia he felt he wasn't being taught the basics of research, scripting, structure and production values. He felt he could learn much more as a working journalist than if he was just learning theory in a classroom. And like me, he had dreamed about doing journalism years before leaving school. He eventually got his wish of working as a researcher, but on the *Today* show. After a brief stint there he moved to *A Current Affair* as a researcher. Not long after that he had the misfortune of being appointed to work with me, first as a researcher, then as an associate producer and later as a full producer. Today he is one of *60 Minutes'* most respected producers. McAvoy and I began a wonderful eight-year working relationship, which turned into something much deeper – he became a surrogate son to me. He was so keen to learn and listen, and not make the same mistake twice.

John McAvoy deserves a beatification for putting up with me for so long because it's no secret that I can be too hands-on with stories. People often ask me if I prepare my own interviews, do my own research and script my own stories. Answer: yes, yes and yes! There is a blurred line between newsreaders and journalists who present news and current affairs; some viewers still think that we're all told where to stand, what to say and what to ask. Not me. I really enjoy 'producing' a story, deciding on what pictures and sequences will help make it. I also love preparing my interviews and then later scripting the story. McAvoy also deserves a bravery medal – for questioning or probing me on the decisions I made. He wasn't afraid to disagree or to speak his mind. I admired this in him greatly and it helped seal our lifelong friendship. I was now 40 years of age and needed something or someone to help me maintain my enthusiasm – and for the next eight years John McAvoy became that someone.

*   *   *

At the end of 1993 the ratings for *A Current Affair* were not what the network had hoped they would be. The Nine Network and Michael Willesee jointly decided to go different ways. Ray Martin, who had been working at the *Midday* show for almost a decade, was asked to replace Willesee as host. I would continue to fill in when he was away on assignment, on holidays and during December and January for the summer edition. It was a perfect setup for me; I hadn't been as happy as I was for many years. I had never worked with Ray Martin before. We didn't have a great deal to do with each other because I was out on the road most of the time or I was buried in my office researching or scripting – but he proved himself to be a real team player and someone who genuinely cared about the wellbeing of staff.

Early in 1994 McAvoy and I profiled movie director Steven Spielberg, one of the greatest creative geniuses of the last century. Our interview took place during a lightning visit to Los Angeles. The nominations for the 1994 Academy Awards had been announced the night before and two of his movies had received a total of 15 nominations – 12 for *Schindler's List* and three for *Jurassic Park*. I shook hands with this rather unassuming and gentle man and congratulated him on his 15 nominations.

'Fifteen? It's 12,' he corrected me.

'That's right' I said, '12 for *Schindler's List* and three for *Jurassic Park*.'

'Oh yeah, *Jurassic Park*, I forgot about that movie,' he said, referring to one of the greatest box-office success stories in history.

In fact, at that time Spielberg was responsible for half of the top nine grossing films in history, including movies like *Jaws*, *ET* and *Indiana Jones*. But he had still not been rewarded with the ultimate prize for any director – an Academy Award. It was almost as if voting members of the academy had deliberately ignored him.

'I have never felt stung by the academy,' he told me in our interview. 'If I wasn't nominated, I wasn't nominated. I might have been disappointed but it wasn't going to ruin my life.'

This time Spielberg had his best chance yet, with those 15 nominations, including a best director nomination for *Schindler's List*. Oskar Schindler was a Nazi and black marketeer who ran a pots and pans factory in Kraków, Poland. He was also a Christian who secretly protected, and saved the lives of, over 1,000 Polish Jews during World War II. Their ancestors now number 6,000 around the world, including over 30 in Australia. Oskar Schindler's story was one of heroism and conscience.

His remarkable story had been told to the world by Australia's own internationally renowned author, Thomas Keneally, who wrote *Schindler's Ark* in the early 1980s. Spielberg read the book, fell in love with it and decided that one day he would make a movie about Oskar Schindler. Spielberg himself had an ancestral holocaust background.

'My family had lost 10 relatives to the concentration

camps,' he told us. 'Growing up I always remember our home was full of conversation about the holocaust and Nazi brutality.' He explained how as a five year old his uncle started to teach him to count. 'He taught me by counting the numbers the Nazis had tattooed on his forearm: "There's a four and a five and if you turn the six upside down it becomes a nine."'

With a budget of $50 million, Spielberg explained that it normally wouldn't have been easy to get a movie like *Schindler's List* past Hollywood's bean counters. Only someone with Steven Spielberg's clout could ever have gotten the finance to make a three-hour movie about the holocaust in black and white with no major film stars.

'I told producers that my contract with Universal allows me to make any movie I want,' he said. 'Even if I wanted to do a movie on the contents of a telephone book I could. So I told producers that *Schindler's List* was going to be my telephone book.'

Spielberg didn't realise, though, how much making the movie would emotionally affect him. He admitted that at one stage during production he had become so depressed about Nazi depravity and cruelty that he phoned his friend, zany comedian and star, Robin Williams, for some comic relief.

'I phoned him twice,' Spielberg told me. 'I said to him, "Robin, I'm having a tough time here in Poland." He said he could hear it in my voice. I didn't have to ask him to make me laugh; I began talking to him and he just started going into those Robin Williams famous riffs.' Spielberg told me that the only times he laughed during the making of *Schindler's List* were during the two conversations he had with Robin Williams.

'I tried hard to stay apart from the story and yet so much of it was reaching me on a level that had never reached me during the production of any other film. I broke down a number of times during shooting,' he admitted.

Spielberg was extremely generous with his time, even taking our four-person crew on a tour of the huge multi-million-dollar two-storey production building Universal Studios had built specifically for him. He had designed and furnished it in native American, south-western Santa Fe style. Once again, the true, gold-plated, triple-A-rated megastar did not disappoint – he was a thorough gentleman. And Spielberg did take out that best director Oscar for *Schindler's List*.

Now that I was at *A Current Affair* I had gone from having to be away from the family for up to eight months a year to only about six weeks a year, but even if I was going overseas for one week I would still get that feeling of dread in the pit of my stomach – that feeling you get when you don't want to do something but know you have to. And it hit me in late 1994 when I travelled to the United States to interview Billy Joel. He and Elton John were in the midst of a two-year world tour in which they performed together, singing each other's songs. McAvoy had made a good contact – Billy Joel's chief of security, an Australian, Noel Rush, who was a martial arts expert and Joel's personal bodyguard. The Piano Man agreed to an interview about the tour and his recent and very public break-up from super-model Christie Brinkley. The couple had a daughter, Alexa, who was eight years old at the time, and whom they were both devoted to. I'd interviewed Elton John numerous times over the years but never Billy Joel, and I was looking forward to it. He didn't disappoint either. He was direct, honest and very funny.

During the interview he revealed that he would never again perform his smash hit *All About Soul* live. He had written the song about Christie Brinkley.

'I don't sing it any more,' he told me.

'Because of your break with Christie?' I asked him.

'Probably,' he answered.

'Just too hard to sing?'

'Probably,' came the reply, indicating he wanted to get off the subject.

It was only after researching Joel for the story that I discovered he had tried to commit suicide when he was 21. He swallowed two dozen pills and washed them down with furniture polish but was found.

'That's why I wrote the song "Second Wind,"' he said. 'The song is all about suicide not being any kind of solution. That it's only the coward's way out.'

Billy Joel agreed to allow me and our cameraman, Mark Munro, on stage with him and the band during one of his concerts in Milwaukee, not far from Chicago. I was tucked away in the shadows near the drummer, having been told not to move; Mark shot from the wings of the stage. Even all the incredible people I'd met and places I'd been in my career did not prepare me for the spectacle of being on stage with Billy Joel as he performed in front of over 60,000 screaming fans. I was mesmerised. Joel was belting out *River of Dreams*, his latest hit single, and I was so consumed by it I didn't hear the roadies screaming at me to get off stage because the lighting was about to change and in a moment I'd be visible to the whole audience.

After his break-up with his wife, Joel made no secret of the fact that he was again single and ready to party.

'They're attracted to the music I make,' he told us.

'Are you sure it's not your face?' I asked him.

'Forget the face,' he answered. 'I look in the mirror and think it's pretty funny that it's the face of a rock star. But now that I'm unmarried again I look down at the girls at the foot of the stage and say "Wait a minute, there's a lot of beautiful young women out here!"' he said.

'So you're having a pretty good time?' I asked him.

'It has its upside,' he answered, laughing.

Following the concert I got another taste of the lifestyle of a rock superstar. We had finished shooting, had packed up and were waiting in our car, which was seventh in a convoy of nine vehicles lined up directly behind the huge stage, ready to make a quick getaway to beat the crowds. Once Elton John and Billy Joel had finished their duet finale they ran straight off the stage into their waiting cars – a limousine for Elton, a Dodge Ram van for Billy. And from there, in this bizarre nine-vehicle convoy, we had a full police escort out of the Milwaukee Braves Baseball Stadium and back into the city. They even had police posted at major intersections so we could sail straight through the traffic lights. That night getting to sleep was a lot more difficult than usual, as I tried to come down from such a high.

15

In early 1995 the network's director of news and current affairs, Peter Meakin, rang me at home and put an idea to me. Channel Nine were going to bring *This is Your Life* – a program centred on surprising and paying tribute to famous and successful Australians – back on to the airwaves, and wanted me to audition for the job of host. The program was originally an American concept, and Channel Seven had bought the rights from the US producers and screened an Australian version of the show from 1975 to 1981. Then Channel Nine bought the rights, sat on them for a number of years, and had now decided to resurrect the program. I was a young journalist working in newspapers when *This is Your Life* first screened on Australian TV, hosted for a year each by Michael Willesee and Digby Wolfe, then for the last five years by one of television's great gentlemen, Roger Climpson. I knew I'd be in good company, but would certainly have some very big shoes to fill if I got, and accepted, the position.

I definitely wanted the chance to host my own program, but I had always thought I would end up hosting a program like *A Current Affair* first. Journalism was still very much my priority. Each year on *A Current Affair* I would do somewhere between 60 and 70 video-taped stories that would take me out on the road. They were the lifeblood that kept me enthused and curious. It was imperative to me that my ability to do stories for *A Current Affair* not be compromised. I told the network I'd love to have a go at doing *This is Your Life*, so long as it had no affect on me still being able to do stories for *A Current Affair*.

We initially did a pilot show for the network exec-utives. Our guest of honour was a woman who worked in the station's music library, Olga Byron. She had worked for Nine all through the *Tonight Show* variety years, the Mike Walsh era and then for the *Midday* show. We produced the pilot as we would a genuine *This is Your Life*, springing the surprise on Olga at the Sydney Opera House, and having her family and friends walk through the doors as on the real show. It turned out to be a very funny program and good enough to run on national television if we ever needed to. I think everyone was happy with my audition and I got the job.

We started with a tentative 10 shows that first year because no one had any idea how *This is Your Life* would rate, let alone that it would become one of the most consistently top-rating programs in Australia. It was approximately a $500,000 investment and the network naturally wanted to gauge what sort of reception the program would get before producing more episodes. That first season ran from late September until late November, and the very first show to air was on Debra Byrne, whom we surprised during a curtain call for a musical she was performing in. The 2,000 or so people in the audience had no idea what was going on either. In that first season we also paid tribute to comedian Garry McDonald, journalist Michael Willesee, athlete Melinda Gainsford-Taylor, author Bryce Courtenay, paralympian Anne Currie, musician John Williamson, music guru Molly Meldrum, comedienne and actress Magda Szubanski, and golfer Greg Norman.

Surprise is absolutely paramount to the success of the show. It has to be fair dinkum. The public isn't stupid – it can pick bad acting or feigned shock very easily. For this reason every program is produced with all the secrecy of an SAS army operation. From the moment our staff have the very first conversation with the spouse, partner, agent or management team of the person we're surprising, it's made clear that the surprise must be genuine – no pretence whatsoever. Staff tell them that if they feel they can't maintain weeks and weeks of clandestine phone calls, whispering and back room meetings then it's better to drop the whole idea immediately rather than go through weeks of research and hard work and have to drop the show. Most partners understand but by the end of the ordeal they're relieved it's over. For many of them it's the first time in their lives together that one has kept a secret from the other. On many occasions a guest of honour has commented that they thought their partner might have been having an extra-marital affair because of unusual goings on, strange messages or phone calls that ended abruptly.

The lengths our staff go to to ensure the surprise and that the show is spontaneous are extraordinary. We have never even used the names of those we're honouring on our work board. Every guest of honour is given an alias by the executive producer, David Mitchell, so that anyone wandering into our office, from the mailboy up, has no idea who we are featuring from week to week. Some of the more clever aliases we have used include 'Washer' for David Atkins, one of the country's most famous 'tap' dancers. Or 'Peas' for the only show in which we've featured two guests of honour at the same time, Steve and Mark Waugh – 'peas' for two peas in a pod. We labelled Gabi Hollows, the selfless wife of eye doctor the late Fred Hollows, who has continued his great work with the Hollows Foundation, 'Wilma', as in the *Flintstones'* Fred and Wilma. Raelene Boyle's alias was 'Simmer'. Ian Kiernan, the man who took clean up Sydney to the nation and then the world was known around the office only as 'Mr Sheen'. One of my all-time favourite shows paid tribute to the modest Pat Farmer, a former ultra-marathon runner. Staff only ever referred to him as 'Dairy'. We called Patti Newton, Bert's tower of strength, 'Beef'. Marcia Hines became 'Beans', as in 'Beans means Heinz'.

Right from the start we promised ourselves that if any

guest of honour discovered that we were planning a show on him or her we would drop the program immediately. There have been two prime examples. Our producers were about two or three weeks into researching a show on the gravelly-voiced, no-nonsense actor Bill Hunter, who was well known by Australian audiences for roles in films like *Gallipoli*, *Muriel's Wedding* and *The Adventures of Priscilla, Queen of the Desert*. One night he and his wife, who had agreed to the producers' plans, were watching television at home when a promo for *This is Your Life* came on. He turned to her and asked her to never coop-erate with us if we approached her about doing a show in his honour. Needless to say, that was the end of that. Another example is musician and comedian Red Symons. He was woken at 3.00 in the morning by his phone ringing. He picked it up, not realising that his wife had already picked it up in another room and was talking to his sister in London. He overheard his wife excitedly telling her: '*This is Your Life* is even going to fly you out from London for the show!' Red carefully put down the phone and quietly went back to bed, saying nothing to anyone for weeks . . . and weeks. In fact, so many weeks went by that he thought we had changed our minds and decided not to do him, even though we had no idea he had overheard the phone call, and every-thing was still on track. Only a couple of weeks before we were to record the program Red announced in his weekly newspaper column that he had overheard that crucial phone call between his wife and sister and that he was sure 'we had forgotten about him'. We had no choice but to drop it. We wouldn't end up surprising him for another 18 months.

One of the great aspects of *This is Your Life* in the 1990s and into the new millennium, as opposed to the first Australian version in the late 1970s, is the inclusion of the unsung hero – the unknown and everyday person who has given so much of their life to others and yet hasn't been recognised publicly. When *This is Your Life* first began in America in the late 1940s – as a radio show – it focused wholly on unsung heroes. The show's creator was Ralph Edwards, a man who had a reputation for being a humanitarian and a great supporter of the battler. The famous US General Omar Bradley asked Ralph Edwards if there was anything Ralph could do to help some of the thousands of soldiers returning from World War II who were shockingly maimed and disabled. Most of them had little hope and few prospects, and were confronted by becoming an enormous burden on their families. In 1948 Edwards launched *This is Your Life* on the NBC radio network, with the aim of doing everything he could to help these returned servicemen get a good start back in society so they had a better chance to find work. In 1952 he switched from radio to the NBC television network, and *This is Your Life* began. Initially, the US television program focused on unsung heroes from the war but then moved more towards celebrities.

When the Nine Network launched its version in 1995 we all agreed to start honouring unsung heroes and Australians who had reached the pinnacle of their field without receiving the recognition they deserved. Our first such profile was of 33-year-old Anne Currie. She was born with no legs and her right arm malformed. After being put up for adoption she was embraced by the loving Currie family, which included four children who were all strong swimmers. It took nearly three years for them to teach Anne to float, but as soon as she was over that first hurdle she proved to be a magnificent swimmer and went on to win various state and national swimming titles for the disabled. Eventually she captained the Australian Paralympic team in the Barcelona Paralympics in 1992 and came home with three gold medals and three world records for Australia.

Apart from introducing unsung heroes to Australia's *This is Your Life*, we felt that there was no reason to change what had been a successful format – the initial surprise and shock-horror of the guest of honour backed up by an emotional roller-coaster ride through the ups and downs of the guest's life. Once a person walked through those doors they were vulnerable to the rawest of emotions, though always supported by their closest family and friends. The idea was to continually pull on the guest's heartstrings and therefore the viewer's also. I've never actually wept during the filming of a show although I have come close on a couple of occasions. When I'm at home it's a different story. Lea and I will regularly be sitting in the privacy of our own home openly weeping, as a long lost relative or best friend is being wept over and hugged after walking through the sliding doors. Living through the production of the show doesn't make me immune to tears. It's just that sort of show.

It was Australia's top-selling author, Bryce Courtenay, who in that first year set the high mark for unbridled, raw emotion. Four years earlier his youngest son, Damon, had died of AIDS. A haemophiliac, he had contracted HIV through a contaminated blood transfusion and had gone on to develop full-blown AIDS. Damon wanted to write his story but after he became too weak he asked his dad to tell the story for him, and so Bryce wrote his best-seller *April Fool's Day*, so named because Damon died on the 1st of April. For the duration of his illness he had been loved and nursed by his girlfriend, Celeste. Damon had died in her arms and Bryce's whole family regarded her as one of them. During the recording of *This is Your Life* Celeste couldn't actually be at the show because in the four years since Damon's death she had fallen in love and was about to give birth. She had earlier videotaped a message, which we played during the recording of the show. 'I just want to send you all my love,' she said. 'Life goes on and I've met another person and I'm having a baby ... so Bryce, I hope you're going to be the surrogate grandfather of this little baby.'

We knew she had had the baby just hours before we started recording the show, and when I suddenly revealed it to Bryce he completely lost it and wept uncontrollably. It was one of the most emotional moments we've ever had on *This is Your Life*. Half the audience were crying, two of the studio cameramen were also wiping tears away, and I was only just managing to hold myself together. That moment became a benchmark we would often equal, but never surpass, throughout the next decade.

In that first year, because the program hadn't gone to air for 15 years, we were sometimes flying blind when it came to handling some elements. For example, what do you do when Greg Norman, who had just won the 1995 Australian Open Golf Tournament, is clearly not happy that you've surprised him in front of a 400-person fundraiser for Melbourne's Royal Children's Hospital? As it was *This is Your Life*'s first year back on air and Greg lives in the US anyway, I'm sure he had no idea who this bloke was walking up behind him with a red book, while everyone applauded and cheered him. It must really be an awful position to be put in, standing there smiling and pretending to enjoy those first frightening moments. Greg thought he had to be in Sydney first thing the next morning to shoot a television commercial. He flies his own personal jet and just that day had gone out to the airport with his co-pilot to log his flight plan for his flight to Sydney that evening at 8.00pm.

So at 6.30pm out I walked from behind a curtain and confronted him. At first he naturally looked confused. I explained to the audience that we had cameras hidden behind that same curtain and would be ready to start recording the show after a 20-minute break. The audience members got up to stretch or call the babysitter to tell them they'd be late, and Greg turned to me and asked where his wife, Laura, and manager were. He said he needed to speak to them immediately. It was not looking good. Greg, Laura, Greg's manager and I had an urgent stand-up conference.

'But I've got a flight plan logged to fly out of here in the next hour,' he said.

'Your co-pilot cancelled the flight plan,' Laura told him. Not happy Jan!

'But I have to shoot that television commercial first thing tomorrow,' he pleaded.

'No,' said his manager, 'we had that secretly moved to the day after.' The look on Greg's face said it all – he felt he had lost control of his life and that those closest to him had been plotting behind his back.

'Well, can't we at least fly to Sydney after this show is over?'

'No,' I said, 'because by the time we finish recording the show it'll be too late to fly into Sydney Airport because of the 11.00pm curfew.'

I thought he might refuse to do the show. I went into verbal overdrive, explaining to him that this was the culmination of eight weeks of work and planning on the crew's part, not to mention the people who had agreed to come on the program to honour him and were now waiting behind the doors.

'I promise you that five minutes into it you'll love it,' I told him.

He turned to his beautiful wife, Laura, who gave him that look that only a husband and wife understand and, though still not completely sure, he was led away to have his make-up applied. We got away with it – but only just.

Within those first few minutes of his mum and dad, Merv and Janis, and sister Toini, walking out to surprise and honour him, he certainly settled in and started to enjoy an evening that was his alone. Golfers Steve Elkington and Karrie Webb flew in for the night to honour him, as did his first teacher, golf pro Charlie Earp.

'A lot of members [at the Royal Queensland Golf Club] were complaining we had wild pigs on the course,' Charlie told the audience. 'When he first joined me the committee members were on my back to get rid of him. He was practising so much he was tearing up the turf.' I had brought producer John McAvoy across with me from *A Current Affair* for that first year of *This is Your Life* and he did a great job not only of convincing Laura Norman that we do the tribute in the first place, but also scoring videotaped messages from the likes of former president George Bush, comedian and golfer Bob Hope, and Greg Norman's great mate Kerry Packer. Kerry said: 'I'd just like to say on my own behalf, and also on behalf of a great many Australians, how proud we are of you being an Australian, what you've achieved and how you've managed to do it with such dignity and such charm, which reflects great credit on you and on the country. Have a good night.'

Four years later another guest of honour had me extremely worried that he might not do the show. We surprised Pat Farmer, the ultra-marathon runner, in Sydney's Centennial Park, where he was making a television commercial. Pat, being the modest and humble man he is, was not happy 'because there are much better people you should be doing than me'. 'No, I'm not sure about this,' he said, which really worried me. He looked genuinely put out by the whole thing and I just wasn't sure whether he'd go along with it. Again, I did some fast talking, trying to convince him he was more than a worthy Australian and should accept the honour, which he eventually did.

His was an extremely emotional show given that the year before he had lost his soul mate and wife of 14 years, Lisa. At only 31 Lisa had had a heart attack while driving her car, only minutes after dropping their two young children off at day care. She had died instantly. Producers put together a magnificent and emotional tribute to Pat using tape recordings of Lisa reciting a poem she had written for Pat during those long periods when he was running hundreds of kilometres through the Australian desert or across the US. It was called 'I Love You and I Miss You When We're Apart'. Their children, Brooke and Dillon, were sitting on the studio sofa next to their father watching and listening to this heart-tugging declaration of love. Naturally it affected many of us, not least of all Pat.

It's difficult to comprehend just how much work and planning goes into one *This is Your Life* program. Fortunately David Mitchell and I have always been lucky enough to have the most thoughtful and caring producers and researchers you could wish for. So often

I've been told, and received many letters about, how wonderful the producers had been. You can just imagine some of the difficulties they face, especially when it comes to family feuds. In one case, at the last minute, the guest of honour's partner refused to allow the show to go ahead if the guest of honour's parents were invited to take part! Imagine the poor producer having to ring the parents the day before we recorded the show to alert them to the fact we were going to pay tribute to their child but they were not welcome. It was heartbreaking.

All of the research, planning and organisation for a show is done over a period of about six weeks by a staff of up to 10 people. Once the producer and researcher have met with the closest person to our prime target they start trying to find that long lost classmate, or that coach, teacher or mentor who was so instrumental in their career. Over the years staff have had to do everything from scouring London's council records to locating someone living in Canada to tracking down a family who hadn't been seen or heard of for 40 years. They not only tracked the family down but even convinced a couple of family members to walk through the doors on the night. We try to fly at least one person in from overseas for each show, depending on whether there is anyone available and the budget for that show.

Once everyone is in place for the show the producer will spend at least two days writing the script for the usual 30-minute show – longer of course if the show is to be one hour. David Mitchell goes through the finished script and makes his changes and suggestions, then passes the draft of the script to me the week before we are to record the show. During that week I'll do at least three drafts of the script, rewriting different areas and making my own suggestions. When the producer and I have settled on the final script we go to the next stage, which we call 'going to the book'. This is when our production assistant types up everything I am to read out of the red book, including the guest of honour's life story, the names of those who will appear on the show and suggested questions for me to ask them about their relationship with the guest of honour. I have always made a point of trying to read through the entire script in the book at least a dozen times on the day we record a show. Then I can make eye contact with our guest rather than just slavishly read everything. Eye contact always makes people feel far more comfortable.

Another crucial element is rehearsals. Many of the people who come on the show to give tributes to our guests have never set foot in a television station before and are often nervous. At rehearsals they learn where to stand when they come through the doors and get a chance to practise what they want to say and decide how they'll deliver their tribute. It's also important that they know where to walk to and sit once their appearance is completed.

I should point out though that rehearsals are not only imperative for novices but also for the host! You'd think after hosting scores of shows that I might have it down pat. Not so. In Brisbane in 2000 when we paid tribute to probably our greatest-ever Olympic head coach of swimming, Don Talbot, I was also involved in a major investigation for *A Current Affair*. I was working on the story in Brisbane's CBD and couldn't get up to the Channel Nine studios on Mount Coot-tha, where the rehearsal for *This is Your Life* was taking place. It was a 25-minute drive each way and I just couldn't get up there, rehearse and get back down to the city in time to finish taping the story for *A Current Affair*. I stayed in the city, completed the story, then raced up to Mount Coot-tha just in time to host *A Current Affair*; as soon as that was over, I went into another studio at Channel Nine to record *This is Your Life*.

The sting had already been done – I had surprised Don in his dressing gown and jarmies at his home on the Gold Coast at 7.00 that morning. Now, 12 hours later, I walked through the doors with him to record the show. I was supposed to have a brief chat with him then, while Don was still standing with me, introduce our first guest, who would walk through the doors. Because I hadn't made it to rehearsals I forgot about the guest, told Don to take a seat and began to read his life story. That was when floor manager, Mike Moore, stepped in and stopped me in front of the 200 or so people in the audience. I had forgotten to introduce one of Australia's greatest-ever swimmers, dual Olympic gold medallist Kieren Perkins! I nearly died from embarrassment. Not only had I insulted Kieren, but now Don and I had to walk through the doors all over again so we could film it properly. I'll always be grateful to Kieren for being so understanding and such a gentleman about it. There are

An impromptu reunion of some of the old 60 Minutes' team after George Negus' tribute show. *From left:* me, George Negus, Ian Leslie, Jennifer Byrne, Ray Martin and Gerald Stone. (Photo: Peter Freestone)

Being such professionals, our team and the whole restaurant even managed to fool Steve Vizard. (Photo: Barry Bell)

One of our most elaborate stings for car racing icon, Peter Brock. (Photo: Barry Bell)

My great mate, Mike Moore, studio floor manager and my link to the outside world during recordings of *This is Your Life*. (Photo: Peter Freestone)

Hosting an evening with Princess Diana – 10 months before her tragic death.

Ever since our school days, I was always just 'one of the girls'. *From left:* Deirdre Macken, Lea, Helen Dalley, me, Jacqui Fingleton, Trish Butler and Jenny Cregan.

Barbra Streisand – reluctant to pose for a publicity photo until after the interview.
(Photo: John McAvoy)

Crocodile hunting in Arnhem Land with local Aborigines and cameraman, Mark Munro (no relation).

Sean and I with one of the crocodiles about to be skinned and then cut up for food for the local community. (Photo: John McAvoy)

Our crew accompanying General Peter Cosgrove at the emotional farewell tour of his troops in East Timor ... in a Blackhawk helicopter again! *From left:* me, cameraman Mark Munro, General Cosgrove and John McAvoy.

SAS training – my head was only millimetres from the cardboard cut outs that were shot up with live ammunition in the pitch dark. (Photo: Anna Dokoza)

Celebrating 30 years as a journalist with a 'special edition' of the *Daily Telegraph*.
From left: Peter Meakin, me, Col Allan and News Limited CEO, John Hartigan.
(Photo: Gary Penrose)

Vera – much more than a great Aunt, more like a surrogate mother.

The Munro family today: Sean, Lea, Amy and me.
(Photo: Kate McInerney)

many high-profile people in Australia whose egos would never have allowed them to forgive me, but not Kieren Perkins. It was the only rehearsal I've missed in all of the 150 or so episodes we've done, and needless to say, I have never missed one since.

From the moment of the surprise until the moment we record the program we make sure that the guest of honour is accompanied by one of our staff. We call it 'babysitting' the guest of honour and we do it so that he or she can't make a few sneaky phone calls to find out who might, or might not, be appearing on the show. Even if it means trailing behind the guest the entire day we have to do it to ensure every element of the program is a complete surprise.

Each show is pre-recorded but we run it as if it's live to air. For a 30-minute program the script is divided into four segments to allow for commercial breaks, and the only time we stop during the recording is to throw to the commercial breaks. Sometimes we run well over the allotted airtime and have to cut the show down. The audience is mostly made up of the general public who have phoned up wanting to be a part of a *This is Your Life* audience. Some of the family and friends of the guest of honour also sit in the audience, but are only phoned and told of the tribute a day or two before the recording, and on the condition that they promise not to contact the guest of honour before the show.

Many people think the guest of honour gets to keep the red book. They don't – but what they do get is a beautiful, red, leather-bound photo album, with their name and *This is Your Life* gold-embossed on the front, and a tape of the uncut version of the entire program. The album contains all the photographs taken for the show, from the moment of the surprise, to the people walking through the sliding doors, the group shot at the end of the show and the photos taken during the party we hold after every show. Waiters and caterers wheel food and grog onto the studio floor for a two-hour get-together. It's not unheard of that the after-show party will kick on well into the early hours of the morning at another location or at the hotel where we have sent the guest of honour for the night with their partner. I remember Rebecca Gibney's and Paula Duncan's parties going on for what seemed like days. We were all complete wrecks . . . but it was fun.

Paula Duncan's *This is Your Life* surprise was probably the most elaborate we've ever done. On the night, Paula believed she was going to be judging the best costume at a fancy-dress ball at a secret location. Producers had cleared the Channel Nine car park and installed three giant spotlights that could be seen shining up into the night sky from several kilometres away. We had provided a limousine for Paula and her former husband, John Orcsik, who was our undercover agent and had helped to arrange everything. As they turned into the street approaching Channel Nine John gave us a signal on his mobile phone that they were only a minute away. At that point at least 20 *This is Your Life* staff and other Channel Nine employees took their positions at the beginning of the red carpet. It was like a movie set. We lined up another four limousines so that Paula would think she was just one of many hire cars arriving. Staff members emerged from the limos, were offered a cocktail, walked down the red carpet and disappeared behind a huge black curtain which hid the whole *This is Your Life* set and an audience of 200 people who were watching everything on monitors. Entertainment reporter Richard Wilkins even pretended to interview guests as they arrived for the gala evening. As Paula's limousine slowly edged closer to the red carpet she suspected nothing – she could only see waiters with trays full of glasses, spotlights scanning the night sky and Richard Wilkins chatting to people as they emerged from their cars.

I was hiding nearby with the red book. We knew Paula was extremely vulnerable because her mother, Rita, was dangerously ill – so ill she was unable to either come on the show or even tape a video message for her daughter. Paula hopped out of the car, did a quick interview with Richard Wilkins, and then I pounced. It's always a magic moment. I'm watching the guest of honour's eyes closely for any sign that they're expecting me, for any sign that someone close to them has tipped them off. Paula showed absolutely no such sign. All she could do was look at me, look at the red book, look back at me. Until I actually utter the words 'This is your life' the person is trapped and can't really do anything. I can almost suspend time for a crucial two or three seconds to allow the enormity of what's happening to sink in and, more importantly, to have that raw shock visually etched on their face. Paula promptly burst into tears. I asked her if she was okay to continue or if she wanted a few moments alone. She said she was fine and wanted to bat on.

I led her down the red carpet and through the curtain leading to the studio where she was met by the applause of 200 people, many of whom were family, friends and associates from the entertainment industry and the charities she's always supported. Over the years Paula has worked tirelessly for numerous charities, raising well over $1 million. The night was a great success and culminated in the appearance of a final surprise guest – Paula's older sister, Carmen Duncan, whom we had flown in from Los Angeles.

Two days after we recorded the show Paula's mother, Rita Duncan, passed away, so Paula's *This is Your Life* tribute was dedicated to her.

Steve Vizard and Peter Brock's surprises were two other stings in which our resident 'stingster', Andrew Rodgers, certainly came up with some bizarre ideas. The trouble with people like Steve and Peter is that they're so media savvy we really needed to be extra careful so as not to be caught out. Just one glimpse of me anywhere in the area would blow the whole thing. For Steve's sting we organised for one of his business friends to invite him to dinner at a new restaurant in Melbourne, and got the restaurant's owners on side. Andrew then had a false wall built about five metres in front of the table where Steve would be sitting. It was made of two-way mirror so that the cameraman could film Steve through it – while all Steve would see was his own reflection. A tiny microphone was hidden in the flowers at Steve's table to pick up conversation, and the sound recordist hid behind the mirror with the cameraman. If I were to walk into the restaurant holding the red book, Steve would immediately realise what was coming so we decided that I would walk into the restaurant as a patron, 'accidentally' run into him and say gidday.

I walked in, we saw each other, said hello and, being as quick as he is, Steve asked me jokingly where the red book was. At that moment a waiter appeared from nowhere carrying a silver tray with a lid. With great flair he lifted the lid and instead of producing some exotic dish, there was the red book.

'It's right here, Steve,' I said. 'Steve Vizard, this is your life.'

He knew something wasn't quite right – there was no film crew anywhere to be seen. 'Even I know you need a crew to get this on tape,' he said.

'Oh them,' I said smugly. I walked to the false wall and lifted out a panel to reveal the crew who were still recording. Even Steve Vizard was speechless. Then the entire crowd of about 50 people in the restaurant turned to Steve and gave him a standing ovation – they, of course, were all part of the sting.

Surprising Peter Brock was just as difficult and required an even more elaborate ploy. Andrew, who also produced this particular show, pretended to be a director of commercials and had Peter's management team, who were in on the sting, ask Peter to take part in a commercial promoting a particular car engine oil. Andrew hired a number of old racing cars that Peter had raced in 20 years before and provided him with a script about how important the oil had been to him over the decades that he raced in these old cars. He was to say his lines while taking the audience on a tour of these magnificently preserved vintage cars. Then he was to open a door and walk out of shot. But when he opened the door I was standing there with the red book. Once again, there were those crucial silent seconds as Peter's eyes darted everywhere, searching for answers. Another successful sting executed beautifully by Andrew.

Our famous and respected author Thomas Keneally eloquently summed up just how important surprise is to the success of *This is Your Life*. He wrote the foreword for Volume II of *This is Your Life – True Stories of Great Australians*.

> *After I survived the show I was asked by nearly everyone I met, 'Did you know it was on? Is it really a surprise?' It's obvious people hope the experience was a shock, an ambush, however kindly, in which families, friends and the production staff connived. And of which you knew nothing until Mike Munro or whoever the presenter was stepped forward with the mike and said your name and told you that This is Your Life. In a fraudulent world, people seem to want assurance that this at least is unrehearsed, that the apparent amazement of the subjects of the program is real amazement. The truth is that, in*

every case, the waylaying and the benign kidnapping is an utter surprise. The program wouldn't be such compulsive viewing if it were not so.

We had ambushed Tom in the office of his literary agent. He continued:

I was kept under guard till the evening. I had no idea who would be at the studio and appear on the program. I was kept in a room playing Trivial Pursuit with one of the show's minders, and I said to her, 'There's one thing for certain. Steven Spielberg won't be on it because he hates giving interviews!' I was wrong about that as well!

16

I was now working pretty hard. As well as doing around 20 *This is Your Life* programs a year I was still researching, taping and scripting stories for *A Current Affair*. There wasn't a lot of time for holidays. During one four-year period I got only two weeks' holiday a year – but as long as I was busy and was still able to spend most weekends with Lea, Sean and Amy I didn't mind.

In early 1996 I was to cover one of the most controversial and highest-rating stories of my career so far. The Chief-of-Staff of *A Current Affair* at the time, Louise Payne, saw a Melbourne newspaper article about Australia's then high unemployment rate that quoted an 18-year-old unemployed youth from St Albans, a poor, working-class area in the western suburbs. The young man's name was Shane Paxton. The article also touched on the fact that many Australians experienced institutionalised unemployment, that even two or three generations in the same family might never have had long-term employment. Shane Paxton told how he had never had a job, that his mother had been unemployed for most of her life and that her father, Shane's grandfather, had also been unemployed for most of his life – three generations of unemployment. He said that most of the people in their street were also unemployed.

Our Executive Producer, Neil Mooney, and I felt that it was a very important social issue to examine. Our story started out as a sympathetic look at just how difficult it is for our long-term unemployed not only to get back into the workplace, but even to find the incentive to try. Producer John McAvoy and I contacted the Paxtons – Shane Paxton, 18, his mother, Dawn, his younger brother, Mark, 17, and sister, Bindy, 20, and asked if they would like to tell their very personal story to the nation. Dawn asked that we pay them for their time. She suggested a fee of $600 to cover herself, Shane, Mark and Bindy. When it comes to genuine battlers I don't have my usual distaste for chequebook journalism – if we have to pay *anyone*, I'd prefer to help sick or poor families rather than someone who is better off and well known. We agreed to pay the Paxtons $600 for their time.

All the members of the Paxton family were on some form of social security benefits, provided by the old Department of Social Security. They maintained that they regularly went up to the St Albans Commonwealth Employment Service office to try and find work. Staff at the office confirmed this, saying they turned up once or twice a week. There was no real reason to doubt these kids at all. I felt desperately sorry for them.

'It's not what you know but who you know,' Shane told me during our first interview together. 'You need experience but no one's willing to give you that experience to get you started.'

His younger brother Mark told us that he rarely got out of bed before noon each day, so we filmed Mark getting out of bed at that time.

'There's no reason to get out of bed,' Mark said. 'I'll normally wake at about 9.00 and wonder what reason I've got to get out of bed. And I'll think to myself there's no reason and I'll go back to sleep.'

According to figures published by the Australian Bureau of Statistics in 1996 the average duration for unemployment was 14 months. The figures also indicated that one in five unemployed were out of work for at least two years. It was certainly an issue that had many Australians talking, but Dawn told us: 'Society just doesn't care.' If it did, why would her children believe that unemployment had virtually become a way of life in their suburb of St Albans?

Shane took us for a walk down his street, indicating all the houses where either the breadwinner or two or three residents were out of work.

'There are four families in that house,' he said, pointing across the road. 'Each family has a room each and they're all unemployed. In that house the mum, dad, son and daughter are all unemployed. There's a 23 year old in there who's been unemployed for four years.'

The Paxtons all agreed that they had become part of a growing generational underclass of unemployed.

So I asked Dawn Paxton where she thought her children might be in five years' time.

'Here,' she answered immediately. 'I think they will still be here at home.'

'And not for lack of trying?' I asked her.

'Not for lack of trying, just the lack of opportunities,' she said. I then asked her what hope she had for any grandchildren and where they might end up.

'Here,' she said again.

'So that would be another generation, a fourth generation, and you honestly believe that?' I asked.

'I honestly think that,' Mrs Paxton said.

She also told us of one local 14-year-old boy's reaction when she asked him what he wanted to do with his life: 'He said if he is still alive at 21 he'll rob a bank. But not for the money, just so police will shoot him.'

The crew and I travelled to Canberra to interview Professor Bob Gregory, a leading expert on the labour market and long-term unemployment. He made it clear that he believed there was a real danger of Australia developing pockets of underclass communities as had occurred in poor areas of the United States.

'If you start without a job for a long long time it may travel through the family from one generation to another,' he told us in the interview. 'Large numbers of youths who can't find jobs then tend to group together. The behaviour patterns change, dress patterns change and it makes it harder for them to find jobs.'

Shane Paxton backed that up, claiming he'd had

three job interviews the week before we arrived on their doorstep.

'They all asked me how long I'd been on the dole and once I told them they think "No thanks, you're a loser."'

Shane's brother, Mark, said: 'I spend a lot of my days flicking through the Yellow Pages and ringing businesses to see if they need work but that's no use.' Dawn added that: 'Some days they do come home depressed and questioning whether the knock backs are personal or not. It's so bad for their self-esteem.'

For the story we filmed Dawn Paxton preparing dinner one night. It consisted of nothing more than about 10 potatoes. I've seen the contents of many fridges over the years while doing stories but the Paxton's fridge was *the* emptiest and most miserable I've ever seen. All it contained were the potatoes and half a litre of milk – that was it.

'I'm not having potatoes because there aren't enough,' Dawn said. 'I'm just having toast for dinner.' My heart broke for them. So I offered to take $200 of the $600 payment up to their local supermarket and buy a shopping trolley full of groceries, fruit and vegetables.

'No thanks, the kids have decided to divide all the money up individually so we all get $150 each,' she told me after our filming was all completed. McAvoy and I looked at each other, thinking this was pretty unusual for a mother who had just been telling us how little food there was in the house.

'But that'll only leave you $150 for all the food you need,' I said to her.

'I probably won't get to spend my money on food anyway because Shane's dog and my dog had a fight and we have some hefty vet bills we have to pay for first,' she said. There were at least three dogs in the house at the time. It was then I realised what Professor Gregory meant when he talked about behaviour patterns changing among the institutionalised unemployed. McAvoy wasn't quite so sure. As we drove away that day we differed in our opinions about whether the Paxtons *really* wanted to work or not. I still believed they did so the story we put to air focused on society's obligation to understand and help families like the Paxtons a lot more.

The public's reaction was swift and obvious. *A Current Affair* was inundated with callers and letter writers who made it clear they had no sympathy whatsoever for the family. The public also castigated me for supposedly being a supporter of 'dole bludgers'. 'How can you promote bone laziness like that?' one writer asked me. I had already moved on to a different story, believing I had socially and morally done the right thing and portrayed the issue as it should have been portrayed. I also thought it was the end of the Paxton story. But I could not have been more wrong.

Two days after the story went to air *A Current Affair* received a call from the general manager of the South Molle Island resort in the Whitsundays, a tropical paradise on the Great Barrier Reef catering to thousands of Australian and international tourists every year. He offered to interview the three Paxton siblings for jobs on the idyllic island, a world away from St Albans.

'It's a fantastic place to work as you can imagine, particularly for young people,' he told me when I phoned him to make sure the offer was genuine. 'I don't ask much of the staff. Our conditions certainly aren't unreasonable. Staff virtually get free run of the resort outside their work hours. It's a very pleasant place to work and live.'

There had been a backlash against the Paxtons after our story so it was heartening to know that there was an understanding employer out there who cared enough to give three battlers a chance. The resort already had plenty of résumés from young hopefuls who could have filled the positions – it was a simple matter of the general manager wanting to give the Paxton kids a start.

I saw this as a nice follow-up to our story on the sad issue of generational unemployment, and a chance for the Paxtons to well and truly break the cycle. If they were successful in getting the jobs, it would set them on their way in the then booming hospitality industry. The resort manager had earmarked a kitchen hand job for the older boy, Shane. It entailed washing dishes and keeping the kitchen clean and workable. Mark would be interviewed for the job of assistant greenkeeper on the golf course, which involved mowing, weeding, landscaping and raking the bunkers. And Bindy would be going for the job of waitress, serving in the restaurant and bringing room service to the resort's guests. The three would have all food, accommodation and uniforms provided for them and would be paid $245 each a week, double what they were receiving on the dole. As well as a good start in working life it was also a great opportunity to save a lot of money.

I spoke first with Dawn and then with Shane, both of them agreeing that it could be a great opportunity – on a tropical island paradise at that. Mark and Bindy also agreed to give it a go. There was no way they could afford to fly all the way to North Queensland so *A Current Affair* decided to fly them there, while the South Molle resort offered to pay for their accommodation. They would fly from Melbourne to Sydney where they would change for a flight to Hamilton Island, from which they'd take a 30-minute boat trip to South Molle Island. We filmed them as they farewelled their mum at Melbourne Airport.

'Shane is really cool and happy about it,' she said. 'He hopes he gets the job. Bindy is excited but a little sad about leaving home. And Mark is just grumpy because he's up before 2.00pm.'

As Shane, Mark and Bindy Paxton stepped from the ferry onto the South Molle Island jetty they looked around, and liked what they saw. 'This looks pretty good,' Shane said as we were directed to our rooms. Everyone had a good feeling: the three young people who now had a real chance to turn their lives around, the humanitarian manager of the resort giving them that chance, and us at *A Current Affair* who had so far made it all happen.

We filmed the first meeting between the resort manager and the Paxtons. He showed the kids a pile of at least a dozen job applications that had come to him in the last week alone.

'Now I would like the three of you to tell me why I should choose you instead of picking one of these people,' he said.

Shane Paxton went first: 'I'm hard-working and believe I can do any of the work you're wanting me to do. I'm also good at talking to people and not shy.' His younger brother, Mark, then had his say: 'I'm a big boy and can lift lots of things. I have no problem with getting along with people. I'm honest, hard-working and I won't let you down.' Bindy said: 'I'm in a band, so I'm used to working with people and dealing with the public.' So far, so good. It was obvious they had the jobs if they wanted them.

McAvoy, myself and the two-man camera crew had planned that should the kids get the jobs we would stay the next two days to film them working, in their accommodation and during their leisure times, along the way getting their reactions to their new jobs, whether they missed home and what their jobs meant for the future. I was already thinking how some of the more unkind people who wrote to me accusing them of being 'bludgers' would have to eat their words once they saw them hard at work.

The meeting was drawing to a close when Shane asked: 'What about my hair, what happens with that?' Shane's hair, which was extremely long, at least halfway down his back, was tied tightly back into a ponytail for the meeting, but in our previous discussions he had sometimes worn it out. Mark's hair was much shorter, probably shoulder-length, and also tied back in a pony-tail.

The resort manager didn't look the least bit concerned that there might be a problem when he answered: 'Oh, everyone here has grooming standards. There will have to be haircuts for you and Mark but we can do that here for you. But there are no exceptions because our guests expect all our staff to be neat, tidy and well groomed. And so do I.' The mood in the office changed immediately and dramatically. There were no more smiles from the Paxtons and they were no longer looking the resort manager in the eye.

Shane said: 'I don't want the job because I don't want to cut my hair.' Mark agreed: 'This is a really great chance and thanks for the opportunity but I will have to say no too because I don't want to cut my hair either.' McAvoy and I just looked at each.

'But this is such a great chance,' the manager said, just as surprised. 'The ball is in your court but I'm not going to beg you to take the jobs because there are so many others who want them. I just thought you'd do anything to get a start.'

Mark put an end to any further discussion, leaning across the table and putting his hand out to him. 'Well, thanks a lot for the chance,' said Mark. 'I'm sorry I couldn't accept.'

'So am I,' the stunned resort manager said.

Shane leaned forward to shake hands and said: 'I'm sorry too.'

I piped up, asking Shane: 'You don't think you're selling your future out by just not wanting to have your hair cut?'

His younger brother Mark answered for him: 'But Shane Paxton has long hair. He doesn't have short hair. The long hair is a part of him, that's the way he is.'

The boys had been on the island for less than two hours and it was all over. This had suddenly become a much more controversial story. No longer was it a warm 'happy ending' follow-up to the report on unemployment. Their refusal to have their hair cut would enrage many Australians.

Bindy, however, accepted her job as a waitress and was taken on an orientation tour of the resort, while Shane and Mark headed for a swim, biding their time until they could return to Melbourne. Bindy was shown through the restaurants and bars, the pool area and finally the laundry, where she would be fitted out with a uniform – a floral blouse and khaki shorts. Bindy made no secret of her distaste for the outfit and announced she didn't want to wear it.

'Why don't you like it?' I asked.

Her answer, like Shane and Mark declining to cut their hair, was to ring out around the country when the story went to air. 'I like purple,' she said, dressed in her own purple top and purple mini-skirt.

'Will you still give it a chance?' I pressed.

'No,' she said.

'Do you still want the job?'

'Oh, I'd love the job.'

'So wear the uniform,' I said.

'If it was black, maybe,' she answered.

A woman working in the laundry, folding clothes, chimed in: 'There's lots of things grown ups got to do that they don't like doing and uniforms are one of them.'

Bindy made it plain she didn't want the job if she had to wear the resort's uniform. She had resigned within an hour of accepting the job.

The woman folding clothes couldn't contain herself. 'You know you've got everyone giving you a chance and you're going to turn it down because you don't like the uniform. I think this is very unfair and very selfish.'

They glared at each other for a moment then Bindy said: 'I don't think so.' She joined her brothers after donning her swimming costume which was, of course, purple.

The resort manager said he was 'flabbergasted'. 'As far as the two boys are concerned it's just got to be easier not to have a job. And if hair is more important than having a job, then obviously having a job isn't important.' But the Paxtons, right or wrong, stood firmly by their decisions, deeply believing in their stance.

'We didn't ask them for this,' Bindy said. 'They asked us to come here.' I put it to the three of them in our last interview together that here was an island resort offering them a dream start.

'We're not disagreeing with that,' Mark answered. 'It is a beautiful island and a great place to work, but I've had my hair half my life and I'm not getting rid of it just so I can come here and laze about in the sun,' he said.

'But could you be throwing away a fantastic opportunity?' I asked.

'I'm not throwing it away,' Shane said. 'I would take the opportunity but I'm just not cutting my hair for it. It does not affect how I work. It does not change who I am, just for a job.'

'Even though there are rules and standards for everyone?'

'The rules are stupid,' he answered.

The resort manager was still shaking his head. 'Initially I felt sorry for them but, gees, not any more. We all make compromises in our jobs and do things we don't particularly like. I washed pots and pans for two years and didn't like that.'

We brought our return flight forward and left the next day. Everyone at *A Current Affair* knew that this had become a great 'issue' story, a talking point that would make many Australians furious, particularly those who were out of work and would do anything for a job. On the other hand, there was labour market expert Professor Bob Gregory's remarks that long-term generational unemployment can lead to a change in dress and behaviour patterns. It was set to be one hell of a social debate. And we weren't disappointed. I was accused of everything from setting the Paxtons up to being a 'lover of dole bludgers'. In middle Australia there was much discussion about their money being used to pay unemployment benefits to people who clearly did not want to work.

When asked about the Paxtons, Prime Minister John Howard weighed in, promising a much tougher stance on dole payments. 'I am going to see that our system runs in a way that people who are not trying are treated as those people should be treated,' he told *A Current Affair*. Over the next 18 months the unemployment benefits system was overhauled and the Commonwealth Employment Service and Department of Social Security were replaced by Centrelink. Whether or not it's a better system still remains to be seen.

Not surprisingly, South Molle Island Resort received over 750 applications for the jobs that the Paxtons turned down. Trevor Wallace, also from Victoria, scored the kitchen hand's job and shaved his beard and cut his shoulder-length hair in order to get it. He even borrowed $800 for his airfare. Nathan Thurcoff, an 18-year-old who got the assistant greenkeeper's job, cut his hair before he arrived at the resort but agreed to cut it again when management asked him to shorten it even more. Karen Costello, 17, took the position as waitress saying, 'It's not the best uniform ever but it's part of the job . . . and it means a start for me.'

Nineteen ninety-six was certainly a big year for me. Later that year I was asked to host one of the largest gala charity nights ever seen in Sydney, held at the Sydney Entertainment Centre and broadcast on the Nine Network. For many of Australia's social aristocrats it was one of the most sought-after events to be seen at, even if tickets were $1,000 a seat. The reason for this unprecedented interest was the evening's guest of honour – Princess Diana. All the money raised would go to the Victor Chang Cardiac Research Institute, named in honour of pioneering heart transplant genius Dr Victor Chang, who was murdered by triads from Malaysia in 1991 after refusing to cooperate in a body-part-stealing racket.

I had met Princess Diana briefly on a *60 Minutes* assignment in London, but only as one of many in a line, not as a master of ceremonies. Despite the fact that she had been in Australia for less than 24 hours she was utterly charming. Some of the organisers had expected her to be overly demanding but she was the perfect guest of honour. She won the audience's hearts at one point when she went to leave the stage just before a group of children was to present her with a thankyou gift, then realised what she'd done and returned. The audience saw it as an innocent gaff that any of us could make, and applauded her. Diana's friend Sting performed 'Fields of Gold' and 'Fragile'. It was a glittering affair but Diana couldn't stay long. At the end of the speeches, performances and appearances by heart transplant recipients she stayed for only one dance, with Neville Wran, former Premier of New South Wales and a member of the board of the Victor Chang Institute. As Princess Diana left the room that night who would have guessed that in exactly 10 months to the day she would be dead?

The next big social event on my calendar might have been a little less extravagant than a huge charity gala with the world's favourite royal but it was certainly a memorable one. During my early years as a newspaper cadet my first contacts were the kids I'd grown up with, including Lea and five of her friends – Trish Butler, Jenny Cregan, Helen Dalley, Jacqui Fingleton and Deirdre Macken – who were still attending the private Catholic girls school Loreto Kirribilli during our early years of courtship.

The girls have maintained their friendship right up until today, more than 30 years later. And for most of those years they've regarded me as 'one of the girls' too. I had already been in journalism for three or four years by the time they left school, when both Helen Dalley and Deirdre Macken also decided on a career in journalism. Years later, Helen, who works for Channel Nine's *Sunday* program, would actually fill in for me hosting *A Current Affair*. And Deirdre is a well-known newspaper columnist. More importantly, the six women are all great mums and wives who love to get together without their husbands. During 1996 they all turned a very young 40 and organised a dinner at an elegant restaurant with a water view. No men allowed. Or at least that's what they thought. As the practical joker who can't help himself, for weeks I hatched a plan to gatecrash the convent-girls-only dinner.

I rang a close family friend, Sister Elisabeth Keane, a nun at Loreto Kirribilli, and asked her if she could find the very biggest school tunic, white blouse and black stockings – the entire school uniform. The difficulty of course was finding a uniform large enough for me to fit into. While I waited for Sister Elisabeth to locate such an elephantine outfit, I hired a blonde wig and stole one of Lea's bras. Sister Elisabeth came through with the uniform, so on the night of the dinner I kissed Lea farewell, telling her to have a great time with all the girls, then as soon as she'd left I grabbed my disguise and headed straight for Channel Nine. The make-up staff were primed and ready to transform me into a convent schoolgirl, complete with pigtails and a beauty spot. A touch of rouge here, a scrape of mascara there and I became the ugliest schoolgirl, capable of a successful career haunting houses. I passed the first test when the taxi driver didn't look twice at me in the cab. Come to think of it, I don't think he even looked once.

As soon as I entered the cultured atmosphere of the exclusive waterside restaurant the maître d' ran up to me and said: 'Mate, we don't allow transvestite strippers in this type of establishment.' I was horrified. I knew I was not a pretty sight but surely I didn't look like a transvestite stripper? I explained to him that I was there to play a practical joke on my wife, pointing guardedly to Lea and the girls. 'Just make sure you keep your clothes on,' he warned me.

I sat at the bar, not too far from them, and ordered a drink. I thought these barely 40, intelligent women would spot their former school clobber pretty quickly. No reaction. Not even a glimpse my way. I had known each of these women for over 30 years and they didn't notice me five metres away. I didn't know whether to be hurt or pleased with the disguise. I got up and began to circle their table as if I were looking for someone.

I went around twice – nothing from any of them. Helen briefly looked up at me but immediately went back to her conversation. She would later say she did 'half notice this Amazonian-like woman'. Eventually I had to literally prop my face only millimetres from Lea's, at which point she screamed, bringing most conversation in the restaurant to a screeching stop. As the other girls realised, one by one, that it was me behind all the make-up and pigtails the temporary silence around the table turned to hilarity. I certainly didn't want to be standing up on show for much longer so I pleaded with them to allow me to join them. Graciously they all agreed and 'us girls' had a wonderful night together – we even have a photograph to remember it by.

Not long after my night in drag, Denis Hanlin from Sony Music came up with my next big assignment – to interview a legend in the world of entertainment, Barbra Streisand, who was promoting her most recent single and album, *Higher Ground*. Only five interviewers in the world had been chosen to meet this hugely talented and unique woman. And I was one of them. Here is a woman who not only has one of the great voices of modern times, but is the only female to ever write, produce, direct and star in the same feature film, *Yentl*. Here is the only female performer in history who can boast number one hits spanning 34 years. Here also is a woman who is outspoken about politics and social issues and puts her money where her mouth is – through the Barbra Streisand Foundation she has given well over $30 million to charities for AIDS sufferers, women's issues, the environment and children's rights. She even sent 12 world-renowned scientists to the initial Kyoto Environmental Summit in Japan. Sony Music was keen for the interview to go well because Streisand was teetering on the brink of deciding to tour Australia in the future.

The interview was to take place in Malibu, outside Los Angeles, in a mansion that was a two-minute drive from Streisand's own home and would be rented out for the day only. Producer John McAvoy went ahead the day before me to make sure everything was set up and ready to go. Because we were dealing with staff from Sony Australia and Sony's international office, Barbra Streisand's personal staff members, the camera crews, lighting and producers, her security contingent and even people from her charitable foundation, something could easily go wrong if McAvoy wasn't on the ground early to protect our interests.

As excited as I was about interviewing one of the 20th century's most famous entertainers, as the departure date got closer I got the familiar gut-wrenching ball in my stomach at the thought of being away from my family. I decided to go just for the day. The interview was set down for between 2.00 and 3.00pm. I arrived at Los Angeles late that morning, drove to our hotel, showered and changed, and headed out to Malibu for the interview. I was booked to fly out at 10.30 that same night – for me the perfect way to visit Los Angeles.

As we arrived at the $15 million mansion overlooking the Pacific Ocean we thought we might have the wrong place because of the huge number of cars, vans and trucks parked outside. We thought it must have been the venue for a convention because there were close to 40 vehicles. We were to discover that they belonged to a battalion of minders, technicians, decorators, and film and music executives and their assistants. There were probably 50 or 60 people in this one house for this one day for this one woman. In all the interviews I'd done with megastars over the years I'd never seen anything like this.

Barbra Streisand had already done her one interview for the North American market and the interviews at Malibu were for the UK, Australia, France and Italy. Our interview was to be the second one of the afternoon and was to be not one minute longer than 20 minutes. If we went over, a minder would step in and politely stop the interview. I had read mountains of newspaper features about Barbra Streisand, going back to the early 1960s when she had her first number one hit. I had read two books written about her life and had watched numerous films and television interviews. I knew her backwards.

The whisper swept around the mansion that she had arrived. She entered the room and checked the lighting and camera angle. She looked striking in a blood-red velvet pantsuit with a matching choker, but the thing that really struck me was the incredible quality of her skin, and her beautiful fine hands and fingers. Her high cheekbones were pretty impressive too. She immediately put us at ease with her charm and easy-going manner – but at the same time I certainly got the impression that this was a woman not to trifle with. Suddenly the 20-minute clock was ticking away.

I tried to start by asking her whether, as a child, she always wanted to be famous, but she interrupted me and asked: 'How do you say "Barbra" in an Australian accent?'

'Bar-bra?' I said, not hearing a lot of difference really.

'Bar-*bra*, Bar-*bra*,' she repeated, emphasising the second syllable.

'Did you always want to be famous?' I continued on.

'I always wanted to be seen and acknowledged and I guess fame came out of that,' she replied. She spent the first 14 years of her life never leaving the borough of Brooklyn in New York. Extremely poor, she grew up on Polaski Street and did not take the 30-minute subway trip to the glittering island of Manhattan until she was a teenager. Her father died when she was only a toddler but she has still managed to adore him all her life. 'I always felt different because I was the only kid on the block with no father. So, apart from my singing voice, the fact that I had no father was really the basis for my local identity.' Her mother remarried, and although she always loved her mother she didn't have much time for her stepfather: 'My stepfather didn't treat me well and my childhood was tough. His name was Kind but he was anything but kind.'

By the time she was seven she knew she wanted to entertain in some way. 'Then at 14 I went to Manhattan for the first time to see a play on Broadway.' The play was *The Diary of Anne Frank* and the experience was to have a lasting effect on the young Streisand. 'I'll never forget that moment coming out of the subway station on 50th Street off Seventh Avenue. It was a big corner with subway stations, lights everywhere, and theatres. For me, it was like "My God! This is all going on while I'm just over there in Brooklyn."' The play itself had an impact too. 'The play was about this 14-year-old Jewish girl and I thought, that's me. And that's when I decided that I could also do that up on stage,' she said as one of the minders in my eyeline signalled to me that five minutes of the interview had gone already.

I think she sensed pretty early on in the interview that I had done my research, which not only made her comfortable but also generous when it came to the more personal questions about her early life. There had been very little money coming into the household so both her mother and stepfather worked and a lady often babysat her. The lady would spend her time knitting 'Her name was Toby Burracauw and she made my first doll out of a hot-water bottle, which was the only doll I had for years. It was my treasured possession for years until I received a proper doll and realised what I'd missed out on. But I don't think it's bad to be deprived material- istically. It only becomes bad when children miss out emotionally and spiritually.' Today Barbra Streisand has one of the most impressive and valuable antique doll collections in the world.

One thing she did have plenty of as a child was natural, raw talent. 'I never had a formal singing lesson in my life,' she said. 'I sang and hit a note because my willpower said I want to hit that note. So I did hit that difficult F note. But I didn't understand it technically at all. And now it's funny because I meet someone somewhere and they tell me they teach the "Streisand Method" and I ask them "What is that? Tell me what you think it is that I do,"' she said, laughing at herself.

Like so many performers before and after her, Streisand's first major break came on the *Ed Sullivan Show* in the mid-1960s. 'I look at myself at 18 on *Ed Sullivan* and, to me, I can't ever imagine how I got famous,' she said. 'I look at this gawky girl singing kinda phonetically and this ridiculous hairdo, arms flailing. The voice doesn't sound particularly great to me. And I think to myself, who saw that and decided this girl is going to be a star? I cannot figure it out. I can see it now, but not then.'

I was signalled that I had about seven minutes left. She seemed happy with the way the interview was going so I ploughed into some uncharted territory. 'You've always been a non-conformist, is that why even in the early days you refused to change your looks or have a nose job?' I asked apprehensively. But Streisand didn't blink an eyelid.

'That's true. Right from the beginning I fought against them wanting to change my name, capping my teeth and having a nose job. But I was also afraid,' she said, laughing. 'I didn't want someone coming along and chopping my nose off. And I couldn't even imagine someone drilling my teeth down. I couldn't see it, and love being natural anyway,' she said.

We briefly discussed her complete and blissful love for actor James Brolin, to whom she was married in 1998. 'He's a real man,' she boasted. I now had the time-keeper madly winding me up, indicating that the inter-view was well and truly over. I asked her whether she might ever tour Australia. 'If I tour at all, Australia I think would be first. Jim has been there in the past and loved it, always talks about it. And it has a reputation for lovely audiences, great venues and it just feels as if it would be good there,' she said prophetically.

Within 18 months, in March 2000, La Streisand did tour Australia, and blew audiences away with the power of her voice and the splendour of the evening. Lea and I saw her perform and were kindly invited by the promoter of the tour and one of the most genuine men in Australian show business, Kevin Jacobsen, to go back-stage with a dozen or so other guests who'd been invited to mingle with Barbra Streisand after the concert. I had been told she was very happy with the one-hour special that went to air and had asked that 'that Australian inter-viewer' be invited backstage. I was certainly flattered. There had been much talk about her bringing out furn-ishings, curtains, even some of her dolls, to decorate her sumptuous green room for entertaining friends and guests. And naturally Lea was keen to meet her. But the concert started late and our daughter Amy had to be picked up at a certain time no matter what. It was dis-appointing that we had to decline going backstage but not nearly as disappointing as it was to the publicist who came to escort us to the green room after the concert.

She just couldn't fathom that we would turn down an audience with Barbra Streisand, daughter or no daughter.

'But what am I going to tell her?' the publicist begged.

'Send her our apologies and tell her we had to pick up our daughter,' I said. 'She's a parent, she'll understand.'

17

At the end of 1998 Ray Martin announced that after five years of hosting *A Current Affair* he was stepping aside. It's a hard daily slog, particularly if you're heavily involved and hands-on. I was asked to step into the firing line and of course accepted. This was the job that I'd wanted for 15 years, ever since I first walked in the door at Channel Nine and began working at *Willesee*. It was something I had yearned for since I had first clapped eyes on Michael Willesee, not that I could ever pretend to be his equal. This was the pinnacle.

But stepping into the role of host of *A Current Affair* wasn't quite what I had expected. Because *A Current Affair* is live every night, for the first time in my career I found myself having to be at the same place at the same time five days a week. Every day at noon I had to record a radio ad promoting that night's stories. And if there was an issue that called for a studio debate or interview for that evening's show then we would conduct that in the middle of the afternoon. I found myself more and more studio-based, which made it much more difficult to get out on the road to do what I *really* loved – putting together stories.

One of my biggest concerns was that *A Current Affair* and *This is Your Life* might clash on the same night. We were constantly moving the production of *A Current Affair*, which was always live to air, around Australia depending on breaking news. Imagine if a *This is Your Life* show, which has taken weeks to compile, was being recorded in Brisbane on the same night that *A Current Affair* had to cover an important national story in Melbourne – it's the stuff nightmares are made of. Rather than compromise either program we tried, where possible, to record *This is Your Life* on weekends. It was my idea but it backfired completely. I was working at least six days a week and wasn't seeing Lea, Sean and Amy nearly as much. By the end of the year I was completely buggered. After five thoroughly enjoyable years as host of *This is Your Life* I asked if I could step aside and concentrate on *A Current Affair*. David Leckie, Nine's chief executive officer, was pretty good about it and suggested instead that I do *This is Your Life* on weeknights after I had come off the *A Current Affair* set. We could record *This is Your Life* 30 minutes later but would have to hope like hell that the shows never clashed in different cities.

The closest we ever came to a clash was when Australian troops were leaving for East Timor and we did *A Current Affair* from aboard one of the departing ships, HMAS *Sydney*, at the wharf in Darwin. I had to be in Brisbane the next morning for a 10.00am *This is Your Life* sting on women's magazine guru Nene King. We finished *A Current Affair* in the early evening. There were no commercial flights to Brisbane that night so we hired a small jet, but we couldn't take off until well after midnight because it was a five-hour flight and we had to honour the 6.00am curfew at Brisbane Airport. I was about to experience another first in all the years of flying I've done – a nonstop five-hour flight in a small jet that didn't have a toilet. It had been a long, stinking hot day in Darwin and we had drunk gallons of water while we were down on the wharf but I naively hoped that I could hold on until we reached Brisbane. No such luck.

The pilot had brought everything from soft drink to sandwiches to fruit but hadn't catered for an urgent call of nature. If I didn't find something to use soon I was going to burst. The Esky was looking a better and better receptacle with every agonising minute. Then I found a jar with a screw-top lid. It was only 'largish' for what was needed but I'd run out of time. And away I went. I was worried it might not be big enough but it was – just. We landed safely at Brisbane Airport that morning and I discreetly took what was once the aircraft's teabag jar with me until I could dispose of it.

It wasn't long before I was back in the Northern Territory to do a story for *A Current Affair*. It was to be one of the most unusual and exciting stories I'd ever covered, in one of the most remote and dangerous locations in the country. And what made it even more exciting for me was the fact that I was taking Sean and Amy along with me. The story was about an innovative saltwater crocodile hunting project among the Bawinanga Aboriginal Community in Maningrida. About 300 kilometres east of Darwin, Maningrida sits on the edge of the Arafura Sea at the top of Arnhem Land. It is one of the most isolated towns in the country with a population of about 200. The Northern Territory Government had issued a permit for the Aboriginal community to cull 100 mature saltwater crocodiles during the year. Saltwater crocodiles have been a protected species in the top end since 1971. As a result, the rivers and tributaries are overrun with what conservationists now estimate could be up to 80,000 crocodiles. The local Aborigines divide the meat up amongst each other and sell the crocodiles' belly skins, which are then sent overseas for treatment. Whole belly skins, depending on their quality and size, can fetch the community up to $4,000 each. Exclusive fashion houses like Hermés and Cartier turn the treated skins into handbags, shoes and belts. A Hermès handbag made from a faultless crocodile belly skin can cost up to $10,000. A pair of shoes can cost up to $4,000.

Aboriginal leader Otto Bulmynere explained how important this project was for locals: 'It carries so many hopes for us. It enables us to look at ways to ensure our children's future by teaching them how our ancestors have caught crocodiles up here for over 40,000 years. And of course it helps bring income into the community so we don't need to rely on social welfare benefits nearly as much.'

Sean was now 17 and about to enter his final year of high school. Ames was 14 and a little apprehensive about going so far from home into an inhospitable and dangerous environment, but she will always follow her big brother anywhere. The two of them are extremely close and loving with each other, which gives Lea and I great comfort because we know they'll always have and support each other no matter what. The kids and I flew up to Darwin very early one Saturday morning. From there we flew in a six-seater light aircraft over hundreds of kilometres of croc-infested waterways, past the Kakadu escarpment and on to Maningrida.

Our assignment was to go out in the dead of night in a flimsy four-metre aluminium runabout to film some of the Aboriginal men hunting full-grown saltwater crocs. The crocodile catcher was Jackie Jurral, who is not only one of the Bawinanga community's most respected elders but makes Crocodile Dundee look like a wimp. At 60 years of age there was nothing Jackie Jurral didn't know about catching saltwater crocs. He had with him two other men from the community – Otto, who was to use a spotlight to find the crocs and Zachariah, whose job was to steer the boat. Including me, the cameraman and the sound recordist there were six men in the tiny boat. Some 30 metres away was a 10-metre cruiser that acted as the support vessel. Sean, Amy, four Aboriginal men who were there to learn about crocodile catching from Jackie, and Ray Hall, a white guy who was the coordinator for the Bawinanga Aboriginal Corporation, sat in that boat watching the action in our little tinny.

The Bawinanga people had been hunting crocs for tens of thousands of years and while Jackie hunted using the same basic principle, he also made use of some helpful modern-day inventions too. Catching these 200-kilogram reptilian shredding machines is tricky and extremely dangerous but Jackie, whose nickname is 'The Professor', made it look so easy. First the men combed the river until Otto's spotlight picked up the red eyes of a croc. The light was strong enough to pick up a croc 100 metres away. Otto kept the light fixed on the croc's eyes, blinding and mesmerising it, while the little tinny made its way to it. Then Jackie swung into action with a special instrument he had made himself. He had tied a small, three-pronged steel barb on the end of a long nylon rope, which was then attached to a pole. He used the pole as a spear to thrust the barb into the scaly, armour-like skin somewhere behind the crocodile's head. Its skin was so thick that it hardly felt a thing. Jackie now 'played' the croc like any big game fisherman would play a marlin. Let him go, reel in, let him go, reel in. Jackie had a delicate touch and brought the powerful and brutal animal carefully to the surface, right next to our tinny.

Then he looped a noose made of thick rope over the croc's upper jaw. Not over the whole snout, only the upper jaw – that way the rope became hopelessly entangled in the croc's teeth as it death-rolled from side to side, trying to free itself. After 10 or 15 death rolls right next to the tinny the entire jaw of the crocodile was tied up as tight as can be. My job was to anchor the rope while Jackie made sure the rope was evenly spread along the snout. Depending on the size of the croc we either hauled it into the tinny or released it. If it was big enough and its belly skin was in good condition it was shot directly in the brain with a .22 rifle. Death was almost instantaneous. On our first night out we caught four medium-size crocs ranging between two and three metres long.

Our second night was even more eventful. Jackie snagged an enormous full-grown male. It dragged the tinny to shallow water where there were mangroves and small trees. Suddenly, Jackie, who was still 'playing' the croc, became caught up in one of the trees. He was tee-tering, about to fall into the water on top of the huge croc, which was continuing to drag the tinny through the water. I lunged forward and grabbed Jackie's belt. His momentum pulled me down towards the water too, but Otto pulled us both back from the brink. Jackie still had hold of the croc on his line and brought him to the surface so he could tie up his jaw. It was only now that we got our first real glimpse of him. He looked about four metres in length – about the same length as our tinny – and around 200 kilograms in weight. It took Jackie much longer to loop the rope over the big male's jaw than the medium-sized crocs we had caught before, but Jackie eventually managed it. The croc's death rolls against the side of our tinny were deafening. The six of us knew we had absolutely no chance of swimming the 30 metres to the support vessel if the runabout capsized.

The croc kept turning, making that gaping jaw harmless. He was far too big to bring into the runabout so we motored over to the bigger boat. Jackie put the barrel of the .22 to the croc's skull and shot him in the brain. We then dragged this huge prehistoric monster onto the deck of the cruiser. He was bigger than we first thought – just over four metres long and weighing 250 kilograms. Sean and Amy were fascinated, and gingerly touched the croc's rock-hard scales and soft underbelly. The croc would provide a lot of meat and its skin would be worth at least $3,000 to the community.

'I'd like to see more Aboriginal people in these parts up here using more of their natural resources in the traditional ways. They can earn income while staying on their ancestral land and they're happier, healthier and have a lot more self-esteem,' Ray Hall said in our interview.

Otto was just as positive: 'We believe our project will eventually build into a successful business. It will enable us to go forward and help our community to provide a real future for our children.'

The trip was a unique experience for Sean and Amy, and one that I think had an enormous impact on them. Too few city people get to really know even one Aboriginal person. Sean and Amy got to know this gentle and generous community, which was untainted by too much white influence – Maningrida is also a dry town where all alcohol is banned. Sean and Amy played with the local kids, and went swimming and had photographs taken with them. It was all very exciting for our children to meet a completely different community in such a desolate but exotic locale. Throw in a bit of crocodile hunting and you've got yourself one hell of an adventure. It was another one of those times I pinched myself – not only was it a fantastic story to cover but I was doing it with my children.

By February 2000, General Peter Cosgrove, then the Commanding Officer of the international peacekeeping force in East Timor, had been by the side of the Australian and international troops for six long, hot months in East Timor. Now, he was handing over command to the United Nations peacekeeping force. Some of the Australian personnel would stay in East Timor as part of the UN operation while for many, including General Cosgrove, it was time to return to their families in Australia. General Cosgrove agreed to allow me and John McAvoy to travel with him on his whistle-stop farewell tour of the troops, including French Canadians, New Zealanders and Fijians as well as Aussies.

I flew to Darwin one Friday morning, hosted *A Current Affair* from there that evening and flew to Dili at dawn on Saturday morning. General Peter Cosgrove is a passionate supporter of the men and women under his command. He heaped praise on them for their courage and hard work, and for maintaining strict discipline in not firing on militia or Indonesian troops, thereby avoiding what could have been a major conflict.

General Cosgrove described those first weeks of September 1999, when Australian Special Air Services (SAS) troops entered East Timor, as a terrifying prospect because 'the people who did all the damage were still around and had gone too far with their killing, burning and looting, and these sorts of criminals roaming the streets create a very dangerous environment.'

'Particularly being aided and abetted by the Indonesian army?' I put to him.

'In some cases their senior officers would have been very disappointed in the behaviour of some of their soldiers,' he admitted. 'So from my point of view our troops here in East Timor are champions and it would be a great shame if they were left here without knowing what I think they've achieved.'

Well, over the next two hectic days he was determined to let them know just that. If he had his way he would have personally thanked every single one of the 10,000-plus international force. So popular was Cosgrove among his troops that one day he attended no fewer than six barbecues during as many hours.

'By the last barbecue I must say I'd had enough of burnt sausages,' he joked, 'but these men and women I was able to mingle with are marvellous young Australians . . . just ordinary people who've done extraordinary things here.'

Our transport for the tour around East Timor was

two army Blackhawk helicopters. I didn't say anything to General Cosgrove, but only a few years earlier a film crew and I had an emergency landing in a Blackhawk chopper while investigating their mechanical worthiness at the main base in Townsville. It turned out to be a highly embarrassing story for the army. Then not long after that there was the tragic Blackhawk disaster which killed 15 SAS troops and flight crew. I was apprehensive about again flying in a Blackhawk, but I figured that if I had to fly in one with anyone, who better than General Peter Cosgrove, Commander of the Interfet Forces in East Timor.

When we stopped in Baliboa he was greeted, almost adored, like a Hollywood celebrity by his old battalion. At one stage he even signed an autograph. Later, when he spoke to the 200 or so men and women you could have heard a pin drop.

'Some people have said to us that this is the biggest operation we've been involved in since Vietnam,' he told them. 'Well, I've actually done the mathematics on it and it is actually the biggest operation for the Australian Defence Forces since World War II. And you've all done a bloody good job. Good luck, stay safe, keep it up and I'll be there to welcome you home.'

Even a cynical old newsman like me marvelled at his passion and sincerity. But his charming wife, Lynn Cosgrove, has known that for almost 30 years. 'Peter is completely happy and satisfied with his chosen career. He's always been so enthusiastic about the army and very comfortable where he is,' she told us. That's no real surprise when you learn that he followed both his grandfather and his father into the army. Now 55, he has worn an army uniform since he was a 14-year-old cadet, and enjoyed a bit of mischief with the best of them.

'I'm not sure that initially the army thought I'd made the right decision,' he told me.

'Why was that?'

'Oh, I was a bit of a larrikin and got into my share of scrapes when I was a cadet officer at Duntroon's Royal Academy Military College in Canberra. But you've got to grow up sometime and I imagine I must have at one stage.' That burst of maturity probably came during his years fighting in Vietnam, which certainly prepared him for his role in East Timor. 'Vietnam allowed me to experience the sort of pressures and tensions that our young leaders and servicemen and women have been under ever since they got to East Timor,' he said.

General Cosgrove is certainly no armchair general either. He roughed it almost as much as his troops during his six months in the sweltering, humid hotbox of East Timor. His office was no bigger than a tiny one-bedroom unit and very spartan. A desk, an army bunk, a few strategic maps, family photos, a few mementos and a bush shower out on a small balcony – that was it. No air-conditioning, just fans. 'My troops are living in pretty deprived circumstances and I just wouldn't sleep at all if I thought that I couldn't at least do that part,' he said.

At this stage you've got to ask: can General Peter Cosgrove be this perfect? 'Why not?' Lynn Cosgrove answered. 'If he does have any bad habits I've forgotten them during his months in East Timor.' But she did admit that when it came to domestic chores he'd 'need a map to find the kitchen'.

We can look forward to two more Cosgroves in the ranks of the Australian Defence Forces – two of their three sons, Phillip and David, have signed up as fourth-generation servicemen.

Before we returned to Australia I broached another matter with General Cosgrove. For almost 20 years I had been trying to do a story on the clandestine SAS Regiment in Perth. There had only been a couple of minor media reports on them in the past and they had been controlled and heavily edited. I told General Cosgrove I wanted to get out on the water and up in the air with these mysterious soldiers who had been nick-named 'the chook killers'; I wanted unfettered access.

Over the next year or so I kept pestering Peter Cosgrove about it, and in early 2001, I made headway. Producer Anna Dokoza and I met to discuss the parameters of the story with the Commander of Special Forces, General Duncan Lewis, whom I'd met while he was serving in East Timor. He placed only one condition on us: we were not to show the faces of the soldiers we filmed or interviewed, to protect them and their families from possible reprisals.

At the time the SAS was made up of three squadrons, with 100 men – and men only – in each. There are another 200 or so men and women in the regiment who support the front-liners with communications and transport. The three squadrons are 'green on standby', soldiers ready at a moment's notice for any military conflict, whether open or secret; 'green on stand down', the backup squadron to the first group; and 'black', a counterterrorist group on 24-hour standby to intercept terrorists or rescue hostages in a national crisis. Little did any of us know that within six months of completing our story the black group would be fighting the Taliban in freezing conditions in Afghanistan following the catastrophe of September 11. Colonel Gus Gilmour, who led those troops into Afghanistan for the war against terrorism, said during our interview: 'It's those with a high intellect who we want. They need to be equipped with a broad range of skills. They include patrol skills, communication, medical, low- and high-altitude parachuting, skin diving, long-range vehicle operations and languages. They are those quiet professionals who are keen to do the job as a team if they're selected.'

The selection process to join the SAS must be one of the most extreme physical and mental challenges ever devised by an organisation. Each year around 150 servicemen apply and only about 30 of them make it. 'If they are selected to join the SAS they do feel they have climbed Mt Everest,' said General Lewis. In fact, by the end of the process I bet most of them *wished* they'd climbed Mt Everest instead. The eight-week process involves martial arts and precision shooting, but probably the hardest part is that each man must spend between 10 and 14 days in the outback on his own, with no contact, taking with him no food or water. Over the years soldiers, not having eaten for perhaps days, have suddenly had a live chicken released from a passing jeep for them, hence their nickname, 'chook killers'.

'It's all part of the toughening process to make sure that if the troops are operating a long way from home in isolation without their normal supply routes of food and water then we know they'll survive,' said General Lewis, not knowing how prophetic his comments were in relation to Afghanistan.

The SAS's two main training bases, both in Perth, contain over $100 million worth of state-of-the-art equipment. One is an entire mock village which has high towers for specialist snipers to practise from and a variety of buildings that the soldiers can use to simulate myriad hostile scenarios. The other contains, amongst other things, a mock Blackhawk helicopter mounted on 10-storey-high vertical rails so that it can be raised and lowered. This allows the soldiers to train at rappelling out of and climbing into choppers. This activity is responsible for most of the injuries sustained by the soldiers, mainly to ankles and knees when they land on the ground.

But perhaps the most fascinating structure within this SAS base is what is known as 'the killing house', where soldiers train in hostage rescue techniques. A windowless, two-storey building the size of a large city warehouse, it has padded interior walls that bullets won't ricochet off, which means it can be used for 360-degree indoor shooting – and *always* with live ammunition.

For filming purposes I was to take part in a training exercise in the killing house, taking the role of a hostage who had to be rescued by the black, or counter-terrorist, squadron. I donned the very latest Kevlar bullet-proof jacket and was told to take a seat. On either side of me, not more than half a metre away, were two cardboard cut-outs of the 'terrorists' standing guard over me. For safety reasons one soldier stood directly behind me to make sure I didn't move an inch, placing myself in front of the live 9mm machine-gun bullets my rescuers would pump into the terrorists. For me it started out as a bit of a novelty, but when they turned the lights out I started to think about the live ammunition and any enthusiasm rapidly drained away. They made me wait what seemed like an eternal five minutes in the pitch black until three soldiers wearing nightscope goggles burst into the room and started firing all around my head. I felt the cardboard bad guys disintegrate on either side of me and a firm hand on my shoulder from the minder behind me, indicating that I should not move. It was all over within seconds. While it was an unbelievable adrenaline buzz it was harrowing sitting there in the darkness wondering if any of these experts might miss their targets and hit me. The cameraman had captured it all using a special nightscope lens while standing on one side of the room out of the line of fire.

'It has been called the "killing house" in the past,' Colonel Gilmour admitted, 'but the emphasis is very much on saving the lives of hostages, not necessarily killing anyone.

'There's a tremendous spin-off from our counter-terrorist training. It places individuals in a very quick-decision-making, chaotic environment. Those skills they achieve through that type of training then transfer across to our other types of operations that we need to conduct.'

Another 'toy' the SAS has is a 200-seat mock plane complete with cockpit, galley kitchen, toilets, entry doors and wings. It's used for live-fire rehearsals of aeroplane hijackings and the seating can be configured to match wide-bodied, dual- or single-aisle and small aircraft.

Our second day of filming was spent in a Hercules aircraft off the West Australian coast watching one of the green squadrons, which specialised in skin diving and parachuting, go through its paces. The tandem jumps I had done from a plane were from 4,000 metres in the air and these guys were jumping with fully laden backpacks into the water from only 400 metres. They were comfortable jumping from such a low height – and were equally comfortable jumping from as high as 8,000 metres. Those high-altitude jumps allow them to drift undetected onto targets from many kilometres away. And if that's not enough, they are experts in parachuting from any height in the dead of night using only their nightscope goggles for vision.

I put it to one sergeant that the SAS has been accused in the past of having a few 'Rambo' types.

'There's absolutely no room for swaggering cowboys in the SAS,' he replied. 'If you've got someone too wrapped up in his own ego and the tough-guy image he's not going to be a contributing member to the team.'

'In fact, probably dangerous?' I asked him.

'Yes, a liability, definitely,' he said.

Before the end of that year at least 150 of the SAS regiment would be fighting in the desolate mountains of Afghanistan searching for Osama Bin Laden. One of them would not come back alive.

In 2001 the disastrous new national television ratings system, Oztam, was introduced. Disastrous because droves of viewers disappeared off the ratings map, which in turn put enormous pressure on the networks to claw their way back into those missing lounge rooms. More and more consumer-related stories were hitting the mark with viewers. The minute-by-minute ratings figures were as clear as day – most times the number of viewers climbed the minute we aired a consumer story. It might be a product survey comparing the quality and price of different brands of washing powder, for instance. Diet and weight-loss stories were extremely popular too. And of course the higher those stories rated the more of them we produced. Consequently we began to do fewer and fewer investigations and tough reports. Being an old tabloid hack I wanted *A Current Affair* to do more hard-hitting investigative stories. For me it was only ever about the assignment. The yarn. I made my views known but the powers that be always had valid and commercial arguments to continue doing consumer-oriented stories.

But it wasn't all toothbrush surveys and vacuum cleaner tests. Senior management was still prepared to spend a fortune sending staff from several programs to New York in 2002 for the anniversary of September 11. *A Current Affair* went live from various points around Manhattan, producer Danny Keens, a cameraman, a sound recordist and I working our butts off for 10 days to cover various aspects of the anniversary and developments since the attacks in 2001. We had to get up at 2.00am each day to be ready for a live cross at 4.30am New York time, which was 6.30pm eastern Australian time. After the program the crew and I grabbed breakfast and went out filming all day for the next morning's stories. Once we had shot our footage and interviews we would hightail it back to our hotel and watch it all before starting the long process of scripting at least two stories a day. Our allocated time to send the footage to Channel Nine in Australia via satellite was 8.00pm New York time. The producer would feed the footage back while I faxed through our scripts. We finished that at around 10.00pm, if all went smoothly. That left us just enough time to grab dinner before bedding down for about three hours and doing it all over again.

By far the story with the greatest emotional impact on whole families was that of widows and widowers who had lost their partners, and children who had lost a parent, on September 11. Thousands and thousands of them. Just from one little hamlet called Middletown in New Jersey, 132 people who were office workers in the World Trade Center or were firemen and policemen who rushed to the site, died that day. No less that 60 children from Middletown lost at least one parent – some kids lost both their parents. Their heartbreaking tragedy brought home to me all the more how significant family is, and just how far I have come in trying to understand and accept the difficulties, intricacies – and above all joys – of family life.

Neither my Mum or I ever had any real understanding about what it might be like growing up in a family. Because Mum had never come from a loving environment herself she naturally found showing any form of affection too awkward and alien. She was certainly equipped with plenty of true grit but wasn't exactly overflowing with affection. And growing up I was the same. When I first met Lea I felt too uncomfortable to hold her hand in public, let alone actually embrace! Lea would often tease me about it saying, 'Oh no! Don't let anyone see you being affectionate.' It's taken a long time, but I've definitely improved. When I first met Lea's extended family – cousins, aunts, uncles and grandparents – I couldn't understand why they all kissed each other, not only when they met but also when they farewelled each other. As a young man, I thought it was all an act, and extremely shallow. Surely they didn't really mean it – it must have been just for show. 'You don't need to kiss everyone, every time when arriving and leaving,' I remember always moaning to Lea. In her quiet wisdom, she said nothing, hoping that one day I would understand. And she was right – these days, I too embrace and kiss everyone in our family. I'm particularly proud that

Sean, now a man himself, is still happy to kiss his father without any hint of embarrassment.

That complete turnaround would never have occurred for me had it not been for the love, patience and understanding that my beautiful childhood-sweet-heart wife has shown me for those three decades. I honestly don't know how Lea has done it. Nor do many of our friends, who always refer to her as Saint Lea. One thing's for sure – I could never have gone as far as I have or found such happiness had it not been for my Lea. It's little wonder I worship the ground she walks on.

EPILOGUE

In early 2003, a little over three months after I finished writing this book, I was removed as host of *A Current Affair*. While it was initially difficult for all our family, I remain full of confidence and eager to face the challenges of this new stage in my life – whatever they may be. I've always believed many of us go through three stages in life and believe I'm now just entering my third stage. As long as I know I have Lea, Sean and Amy by my side, and that we all have our health, what more in life could I want?